The Philip Hofer Bequest

A CATALOGUE OF AN EXHIBITION

OF

The Philip Hofer Bequest

IN THE DEPARTMENT OF

PRINTING AND GRAPHIC ARTS

HARVARD COLLEGE LIBRARY

CAMBRIDGE, MASSACHUSETTS

1988

Copyright ©1988 The President and Fellows of Harvard College

Library of Congress Catalog Card Number 88–71917

ISBN 0–914630–03–2

Printed by Meriden-Stinehour Press
Designed by Stephen Harvard

COVER: Adapted from a bookplate designed by Stephen Harvard for the Philip Hofer bequest, 1984

Introduction

Introduction

THE SCHOLARS AND CONNOISSEURS of the future are the heirs of the bequest of Philip Hofer, just as much as his beloved college that received it. He collected within the context of the university that shaped his interests, and for it he labored to gather a study collection of original material in the graphic arts that would reflect his dual interest in books and prints. The unique character of this collection reflects the man who formed it: wide-ranging, specialized, and complex, yet approachable on many levels and full of surprises.

Graduating from Harvard in 1921, Philip Hofer belonged to a generation expected to honor parental wishes, so he returned to Ohio and family business responsibilities before coming back to Cambridge for an M.A. in Fine Arts in 1929. (For his biography, the reader is referred to William Bentinck-Smith's essay in the *Harvard Library Bulletin*, vol. XXXII, Fall 1984.) In 1927 the new Fogg Art Museum had recently opened its doors on Quincy Street under the direction of Edward W. Forbes and Paul J. Sachs. In addition to its fine collection, it housed a lively group of graduate students, many of whom went on to curatorial positions in major museums. In this atmosphere, Philip Hofer's collecting began to focus on a subject little regarded at that time: the arts of the book. He continued, however, all his life to collect drawings, prints, paintings, small pieces of sculpture, and minor arts. His close friends and colleagues cherish the memory of the annual Christmas summons to his basement study in The Houghton Library, where he would reach into a brass-studded black leather trunk and retrieve a special present—a book, a print, a silk or cashmere scarf, a Japanese bowl, a Swiss alarm clock, a Vermont marble egg. He took delight in finding and sharing these little treasures, but his major collecting never swerved from the arts of the book—illustration and fine printing in particular. He defined the book in its broadest terms and collected both manuscript and printed examples. Many parts of the world were explored, including Islamic and Far Eastern books and scrolls, which were given or bequeathed to the Fogg Art Museum.

As Hofer pursued his graduate studies, his connoisseurship intensified, along with his awareness that within the covers of books were preserved examples of the graphic art of major and minor masters—work that was little known but of potential interest to art historians, artists, printers, and students in many disciplines. At the same time, he explored the development of graphic techniques as seen in books. His collecting was always concerned with original graphic media—woodcut, engraving, etching, lithography or photography—rather than reproductive photo-mechanical illustration, though he began to explore that area as modern technology inevitably influenced the aesthetics of the book. For experience in printing and publishing he established the Cygnet Press with George Parker Winship in the late twenties, and a few books appeared with this Cambridge imprint. At the same time, Hofer's print and drawing collecting continued to refine his taste and to place the graphic arts of the book in their historic and stylistic framework. Although he possessed an eye that instantly recognized quality, even in unfamiliar areas, methodical study prepared the ground and reinforced his choices. This professionalism was developed in his first two curatorial positions, in the Spencer Collection of the New York Public Library from 1930 to 1934, and in the Pierpont Morgan Library from 1934 to 1937.

In 1938 Hofer made his final move back to Cambridge, where he remained until his death in 1984, founding and developing the Department of Printing and Graphic Arts, the first of its kind in a university library. Originally housed in the old Treasure Room of the Widener Library, it moved to its own quarters in the new Houghton Library in 1942. Hofer shouldered the full burden of financing and developing the Department. His custom was to purchase books and manuscripts in this country and Europe, often in large numbers during a trip abroad, but not in bulk lots. He did not buy ready-made collections, but made individual choices. Most of the new acquisitions made their immediate way to the Harvard shelves, but some he retained for his own personal collection in anticipation of a later gift. This situation was often a source of confusion to those innocent of a distinction between his collection and Harvard's. He would sometimes keep books that had a special meaning for him, perhaps by an artist he particularly admired and was beginning to collect. On those shelves might be association copies, a rare binding or provenance, a variant or a large paper copy. Added to some of his early pre-Harvard purchases, these items comprise the 1984 bequest—over 5000 books and manuscripts.

To the end of his life, Hofer was buying and trading, and he had a knack for discovery, abetted by his bookseller friends. To share the collection was his ultimate goal in forming it at Harvard, for this was the context that gave it meaning. To the private collector's personal taste he added the curator's and teacher's purpose of instruction, and with this combination he established the formidable resource whose scope we can but attempt to outline in this catalogue. He insisted that the collection not bear his own name, but be known as the Department of Printing and Graphic Arts, and from it his identity was inseparable.

As a teaching collection, this one may be seen as beginning with the early manuscripts, a field that always interested Hofer. During half a century he managed to acquire over 600 early manuscripts, ranging from the ninth to the sixteenth century and displaying the work of both scribe and illuminator. There are also manuscripts, sketchbooks and drawing books from later periods.

The significance and beauty of letter forms, whether on the manuscript or printed page, were of paramount concern to Hofer. He collected writing manuals in both manuscript and printed form, beginning with the great Italians of the sixteenth century. Not unrelated to these manuals are the type specimens, the products of the great European and American foundries. These publications serve to identify printers and determine dates and issues of variant copies, of importance to both the literary and typographic historian. Hofer carefully watched the modern revival of lettering and calligraphy and not only acquired work by Eric Gill and Graily Hewitt, but commissioned it from Marie Angel, Alfred Fairbank, and Hermann Zapf. This patronage extended to inscriptions on wood and stone from John Howard Benson, Will Carter, David Kindersley and Reynolds Stone. In like manner, Hofer's admiration for the great contemporary printers and typographers led him to collect and commission work from W. A. Dwiggins, Bruce Rogers, Rudolph Ruzicka, Jan van Krimpen, and Giovanni Mardersteig.

The Hofer incunabula section is not a large one. Harvard already had some 3500 titles, so he judiciously selected about a hundred examples, along with the Holford copy of a German blockbook Apocalypse. With this respectable foundation in the history of printing, Hofer concentrated on the sixteenth century. Italy and France have the largest numerical representation, shown in Ruth Mortimer's two catalogues of 1964 and 1974, with 557 French entries and 559 Italian, respectively. The Spanish and Portuguese books of this period, described in Anne Anninger's 1985 exhibition catalogue with checklist, are the exception to the Hofer rule of acquisition, for they include the only group he bought en bloc—fifty-seven titles from the collector H. D. Lyell in 1933. Northern Europe is represented with particular strength in major German and Swiss artists, such as Dürer, Cranach, Baldung Grien, Urs Graf, Hans Schäufelein, and Hans Holbein. Building on the latter's Dance of Death series, Hofer added many other representations of the theme. This section was one of the most significant and personal to him, and his affinity to Holbein was further strengthened in the artist's little watercolor of Tantalus, at one time owned by Hofer. He had Rudolph Ruzicka make a four-color woodcut of this image for the favorite Hofer bookplate, for it is the quintessential emblem of the collector.

Through his publication of *Baroque Book Illustration* in 1951, Hofer raised a neglected area to prominence. That once unfashionable period has since been rehabilitated, and when scholars come to Houghton looking for source material, they find books with engravings designed by Rubens, Poussin, and Rembrandt waiting on the shelves. Hofer's interest in eighteenth-century prints led him to search out the presence in books of the work of artists like Tiepolo and Piranesi, and he built up a large Italian collection of this period, embracing illustrated literature, history, archaeology, and architecture.

He formed significant collections of William Blake and Edward Lear, and also of the great colorplate books of the late eighteenth and early nineteenth century. In this period of such diversity, Hofer represented all the trends, including the little masters, now beginning to receive attention. He also forged ahead in recognizing the great masters in the new medium of lithography, acquiring volumes with illustrations by Delacroix, Daumier, and Toulouse-Lautrec. The revival of etching is represented in books illustrated by Chassériau, Corot, Courbet, and Manet—the prototypes of the *livre de peintre* that dominated the first half of the twentieth century. Collecting work by artists of the School of Paris and by German Expressionists, Hofer organized the 1961 exhibition *The Artist & the Book* at the Boston Museum of Fine Arts, jointly sponsored by the Department of Printing and Graphic Arts and the Museum.

Cutting across countries and centuries are special areas of concentration, like the books on measurement and perspective, exemplified in the Renaissance by Jean Cousin, Jean Pèlerin, and Luca Pacioli. Books on architecture were a major interest, demonstrated in the many editions of Vitruvius, Palladio, Serlio, the Bibienas, Humphrey Repton, and Frank Lloyd Wright. To this group belong the great records of ephemeral architecture and decoration seen in festival books. Fables and bestiaries, with particular emphasis on Aesop, are present in abundance, and books illustrating travel, from the early woodcut records of voyages to Jerusalem to the nineteenth-century colorplate books reproducing both the familiar and the exotic. Scientific books of flora and fauna, herbals, and medical books of anatomy, along with artists' manuals of anatomy and landscape, are well represented in a collection that demonstrates how other generations were taught. Part of this record are the many volumes on technique and process and the examples of master printers through the centuries.

Drawings for book illustration combine Hofer's love of drawings with his scholarly concern for explaining and documenting the process of making illustrated books. His collection of some thousand examples was for his wife, Frances L. Hofer, and it came to the Library in 1978 as her bequest. It is documented in David Becker's 1980 catalogue.

It is impossible to do justice to this vast collection in a single exhibition. Restricted to the bequest, this catalogue is offered as an introduction and guide to the collection, as well as the record of a particular exhibition. Many such exhibitions will be required through the years, and this is but a small beginning. We have tried to represent major areas and to indicate the depth of the collection in related items. We can do no more than point the way and hope that viewers and readers will find some information and a little of the pleasure that Philip Hofer took in the original selection. We see this as a preliminary visit, a short tour such as the collector himself delighted in giving to visitors.

Eleanor M. Garvey
Philip Hofer Curator of
Printing and Graphic Arts

ONLY WITH THE ASSISTANCE of Houghton colleagues, past and present, has the task of organizing the collection and preparing the catalogue been possible. Dennis C. Marnon and Peter Accardo, under the direction of Mollie Della Terza, have been responsible for accessioning the bequest and making the records available. Mastery of the word processor by Brenda Breed and Regina Winters has simplified our task, and the careful copy-reading by Maureen Walsh has eased the path of editors Nancy Finlay and Eleanor M. Garvey.

William H. Bond, Director Emeritus of The Houghton Library, opens our text with an apt and vivid recollection. Present colleagues William Bentinck-Smith, Rodney G. Dennis, Nancy Finlay, Eleanor M. Garvey, Katharine F. Pantzer, Roger E. Stoddard and James E. Walsh are contributors, as are past colleagues Anne Anninger, David P. Becker, Ruth Mortimer, Peter A. Wick, and Roger S. Wieck, the latter five all former members of the Department of Printing and Graphic Arts. Particular thanks go to the Fogg Photographic Services. It has been a special pleasure and reassurance that production has been in the hands of our old friends, The Meriden-Stinehour Company, to whom Philip Hofer for so many years entrusted Library publications.

Initials identify the authors of the catalogue entries. They are

A.A.	Anne Anninger		R.M.	Ruth Mortimer
D.P.B.	David P. Becker		K.F.P.	Katharine F. Pantzer
W.B-S.	William Bentinck-Smith		R.E.S.	Roger E. Stoddard
R.G.D.	Rodney G. Dennis		J.E.W.	James E. Walsh
N.F.	Nancy Finlay		P.A.W.	Peter A. Wick
E.M.G.	Eleanor M. Garvey		R.S.W.	Roger S. Wieck

Philip Hofer, 1898–1984

I FIRST ENCOUNTERED PHILIP HOFER as a powerful force, even, perhaps, a force of nature, in the autumn of 1939. I was a third year graduate student in the English department, and my thesis director was the late Professor Hyder Edward Rollins. I was doing my work in the Elizabethan period, and Rollins advised me that I should take (and for credit, though I needed no more courses for my degree) the seminar in Bibliography offered by a relative newcomer to Harvard, Professor William A. Jackson, who was also in charge of the collection of rare books in Widener Library. I had frequently consulted books in the Treasure Room, then located on the main floor of Widener where the cataloguers of printed books now have their desks, but I did not know Jackson and was unaware of his office, classroom, and workroom in the Lower Treasure Room, immediately below. Nor had I seen or heard of another newcomer, Philip Hofer, Curator of Printing and Graphic Arts, whose office was next to Jackson's and whose personal collection occupied space on the same floor that now houses computers and related electronic equipment. The possibility that such a facility as the Houghton Library might soon be built was still privileged information, not revealed to the public for nearly a year.

I was interviewed by Jackson, was admitted to the course, and quickly discovered that it was precisely the subject on which I wanted to concentrate my future career, as I am sure Hyder Rollins had suspected. That is perhaps a long introduction to a scene in the Lower Treasure Room later that autumn. Jackson's seminar lasted two hours, with a break at the mid-point when he would go out on the threshold of the then unused west door of Widener (he had a key) to enjoy a cigarette; smoking was prohibited anywhere within the building.

During one of those breaks I was wandering about in the area outside the seminar room, a place equipped as a supplementary reading room, and I found the most magnificent illuminated manuscript I had ever seen open on one of the tables. It was a late fourteenth-century French translation of St. Augustine's *City of God*, with superb miniatures and splendid decorations throughout. I beckoned a classmate over to see it, and was just about to turn a leaf to see more when I became mysteriously but unmistakably aware that it would be better not to touch it. Not a word had been spoken, not a sound had been made. I turned and saw for the first time the Roman face and eagle eye of Philip Hofer. He did not introduce himself or utter a syllable. He did not need to. He merely walked to the table, carefully closed the book and carried it off to his private stack, which I then noticed had a steel-barred gate much like those seen in safety deposit vaults. I did not actually meet him until much later and then I sensed that he had not forgotten the episode any more than I had, for there was a certain reserve in his manner: natural enough in one who has seen one of his dearest treasures about to be handled by a stranger, one whom he rightly judged not to know how to treat such a manuscript.

It was the first lesson I learned from Philip Hofer, and an unlikely beginning for a lifetime friendship, but so it eventually proved to be, though not until after World War II, when I returned to Cambridge to join the Houghton staff as Jackson's assistant. There remained a suspicion of reserve in Hofer's manner until I had established at least some degree of professionalism in his eyes; then there was none. And if I had cut my teeth on Jackson's bibliography seminar, and continued my education as his assistant, it was Philip Hofer who taught me, by example and precept, what connoisseurship meant and how the private collector works his magic. Once one was accepted as a friend and colleague, Hofer's warmth and generosity knew no bounds.

Boundless, too, were Philip's kindness and friendship towards younger persons, undergraduates in particular. Those who showed interest and talent in the fields that attracted him found the latchstring always out, and, if they needed it, material aid was unobtrusively available in addition to encouraging words. For many students his friendship was the greatest benefit they carried away from Harvard. And he was the most engaging and delightful of companions for those of all ages. Overlying a profound streak of melancholy and loneliness were an ebullient sense of the ridiculous and a love of congenial company. It was not by chance that Edward Lear was one of his favorite poets and artists; Lear combined many of the same traits.

Philip's range of knowledge, enthusiasm, and sureness of taste were extraordinary. In all this he was ideally matched by his wife, Bunnie, who shared his interests and literally followed him to the ends of the earth in his travels as well as in his collecting. It was never my good fortune to be with the Hofers abroad, but I have been told by other friends that they were the best and most resourceful of traveling companions. When Bunnie's tragic death ended this fruitful partnership, Philip's feeling of loneliness and melancholy could only increase.

Throughout his career he was able to approach artifacts of which he had no previous experience, sometimes exhibited to him in a language that he did not understand, and unerringly decide whether they were worth collecting, which of them he ought to acquire and how much he should pay. This was a part of the secret of his success: he was often able to collect outside the paths worn bare by others, and to establish whole new fields. When the rest of the world woke up to possibilities, often through one of his articles or books, there was Philip Hofer with a core collection already in place, possibly not to be matched by far greater efforts and expenditures.

His instincts extended far beyond books and manuscripts, and made his private quarters in the Houghton stacks an Aladdin's cave that was the wonder and despair of all who visited it. The tip of this iceberg was visible in his curatorial offices during his active career, but when he retired he merely descended into the stack rooms below, where his pursuit of treasures continued unabated.

There the outer room was shelved and full of extraordinary books; the inner room contained more books but mostly other objects. A large table was heaped with correspondence, dozens of pencils and ball-point pens, address books, stationery and stamps (though no calligrapher, he invariably wrote longhand in a distinctive and legible script), and whatever books or manuscripts he happened to be working on. It also held a considerable number of pieces of polished varicolored marble, some in the form of bookends, some plain globes; these he liked to give as gifts on various occasions, or no occasions at all, pure impulse. The floor was cluttered with filing cases, cabinets for medals and coins, trunks of many vintages filled with all kinds of things (one once contained an alarming amount of currency, kept there during some threatened financial crisis in case the banks closed), a very hard cot for naps, two or three chairs, and a coat rack containing academic gowns for sundry honorary degrees that had come his way. Shelves on all four walls held an incredible variety of objects: ancient Chinese pottery horses, Greek and Roman glass and ceramics, Georgian silver and pewter, a large collection of Austra-

Philip Hofer's office in the basement of the Houghton Library.

lian opals bottled in mineral oil for their better display . . . an inventory is impossible. Deep shelves at the far end of the room contained drawings and paintings, framed and unframed; the drawings were later bequeathed to the Fogg Art Museum.

The collections in the inner room had expanded to the point where the aisles in the outer room necessarily silted up with the overflow, making access to the books difficult and sometimes impossible. There, too, were alphabets incised in slate, limestone, and wood, commissioned especially from such eminences as Eric Gill, Reynolds Stone, and John Howard Benson, along with a small collection of early American gravestones salvaged from a dump; brass temple bells from sundry Eastern countries; exotic writing equipment and a hoard of handmade paper laid by for some emergent occasion. That does not begin to exhaust the categories, but must suffice. And, since Philip closely controlled access to his rooms, there was usually an undergrowth of discarded wrappings a foot or two deep, only cleared away when colleagues plaintively warned of their incendiary possibilities.

Although 'retired', Philip was to be found every working day and most weekends securely ensconced in this fabulous lair, always ready to appreciate some remarkable book or manuscript one might have to show him, always willing to listen to a tale of woe or joy, always ready with friendship and advice unless he was currently harassed out of his wits by someone's thoughtless importunities. Of course the visitor did well to gauge his mood before intruding too far or too long.

Philip's capacity for friendship was only equalled by the zest he brought to his vocation. That was the key to his extraordinary abilities as a collector. For what is a collection unless the collector loves it and has deeply enjoyed the pursuit, acquisition, and possession of the objects it contains? Philip Hofer possessed to an unusual degree the love and enjoyment that underlie every great collection, and one of his great gifts was the ability to transmit this sense to others. Teaching can aspire to nothing higher. His collection remains to encapsulate his enthusiasms and to continue his teachings.

William H. Bond
Librarian of the
Houghton Library, Emeritus

The Catalogue

1   BEDE, 673–735
Commentary on Luke
Germany (Gladbach?), mid-12th century

Manuscript on vellum; 182 leaves, with 2 vellum flyleaves at the front and 1 at the back from another manuscript (11th-century). Carolingian minuscule; pen drawing of Bede presenting his work to Bishop Acca, f. 1ʳ; 7 inhabited or vine-leaf initials.

30 x 21 cm. 15th-century brown calf, blind-tooled. 15th-century inscription from the monastery of St. Vitus in Gladbach; subsequently in the library of Charles Yarnold of Great St. Helens; Sir Thomas Phillipps (no. 1092); A. Chester Beatty (Western MS.31); presented by Philip Hofer on 1 August 1983 in honor of James E. Walsh. MS Typ 202.

THIS MANUSCRIPT was acquired by Philip Hofer close to the beginning of his career as a collector. Another example of Northern European Romanesque book production, fMS Typ 703, Augustine's *Ennarationes in psalmos*, may have been the last important early manuscript that he acquired. Between these two acquisitions, the twelfth-century manuscript book remained a subject of constant interest to him. The monastic products of the Romanesque period formed one of the greatest and most consistent periods of bookmaking in the West, and this copy of a popular text by the Venerable Bede provides a good example.

The late Carolingian minuscule script has the legibility of the age and the precision of the Northern scriptoria without the rigid and mechanical quality sometimes associated with twelfth-century German hands. An interesting feature of the writing is the use of a smaller script for the Biblical citations, or *lemmata*, instead of the more customary practice of touching such passages with color. Single curved lines in the margins (ancestors of our quotation marks) also accompany these passages and make clear the structure of the narrative. Throughout the manuscript, a variety of capital scripts in red and black are used for book and chapter headings. The pen-work initials are particularly fine, especially the first (f. 1ᵛ) in which the foot of the "R" is a dragon seen devouring a white vine growing out of the letter's main ascender. The pen drawing depicting the author presenting his works to the dedicatee is accompanied by a poem in three internally rhyming distichs written by the manuscript's main scribe and beginning:

> Ad laudem Christi. Nonnula pater voluisti
> Per me conscribi. Gratia digna tibi . . .

F. 182ᵛ contains a figure drawing made with a dry point.

The three vellum flyleaves, written in an earlier hand, contain passages from the book of Judith and are of importance for the study and establishment of the text of the *Vetus Latina*, the text of the Latin Bible that was in use before (and after) the accepted version known as the Vulgate.

R.G.D.

REF   De Ricci *Census*, 1696, no. 19; Faye and Bond, 270; Light, no. 26; *Illuminated and Calligraphic Manuscripts*, no. 11; A. N. L. Munby, *Phillipps Studies* (Cambridge, 1951–1960) III, 147; E. G. Millar, *The Library of A. Chester Beatty: A Descriptive Catalogue of Western Manuscripts* (Oxford, 1927) I, 107–109; appendix II (text of the Bible fragment) and plate LXXXII; Sotheby and Co., *Catalogue of the Renowned Collections of Western Manuscripts, the Property of A. Chester Beatty, Esq.; The First Portion* (London, 1932) Lot 7, plate 8; M. Bogaert, "Une témoin liturgique de la vieille version latine du livre de Judith," *Revue bénédictine* LXXVII (1967) 14, note 1 and "La version latine du livre de Judith dans la première bible d'Alcala," *Revue bénédictine* LXXVIII (1968) 13, 191–192.

No. 1. Pen drawing of Bede presenting his work to Bishop Acca, from Bede, *Commentary on Luke*.

2 ❧ OFFICE LECTIONARY
Italy (Morimondo), mid-12th century (before 1174/75)

Manuscript on vellum; 233 leaves. Large, angular late Carolingian minuscule script; numerous initials in red and in various colors; large capitals following initials touched with yellow.

37 x 24 cm. 18th-century brown calf over wood boards. Abbey of Morimondo (Diocese of Milan); formerly in the collection of Ulrico Hoepli, ca. 1880; purchased by Philip Hofer from Giuseppe Martini, 1930. MS Typ 223.

IN HIS MEMOIR of Philip Hofer (*Harvard Library Bulletin* XXXII), William Bentinck-Smith tells an extremely pleasant story of a daytrip to Lugano that Philip Hofer took with Frances L. Heckscher to visit the antiquarian bookman Giuseppe Martini. It was apparently the day they decided to become engaged. The day was also marked by the acquisition of this fascinating and important manuscript. On the front paper flyleaf the new owner later wrote the source, price and date of acquisition and added "P.H. had F.L.H. with him!" This office book contains the lessons for Matins (the earliest of the eight daily prayer services), for the yearly feasts of the Sanctorale (individual saints' days), and the Common (days for groups or classes of saints). It was written at the Cistercian Abbey of St. Mary of Morimondo in Italy, near Milan, a house that had an administrative relationship with the French Abbey of Morimond in France in the diocese of Langres with which its manuscripts are sometimes confused. This confusion is added to by the fact that many of the manuscripts from the Italian house are written in an angular hand that bears, at least at first glance, a greater resemblance to French writing than to the more rounded Italian writing style. Whether French scribes were actually at work in Morimondo is a question that still needs to be dealt with. The Houghton Library has in all five manuscripts from this abbey (four surely and one probably) which exhibit both the "French" and a clearly Italian form of letter.

The last page of our manuscript was originally blank, and sometime, probably fairly soon after the lectionary was completed, three new hands wrote in that which gives this book its particular distinction, an inventory of the books kept in the Abbey's library. There is evidence to suggest that this inventory was not complete and that a second leaf containing entries is missing, but the sixty-three entries that we have tell us much: a Bible (in several volumes), service books (including the Lectionary to which the list is attached), Patristic authors, the backbone of most twelfth-century libraries, including Gregory, Jerome, Ambrose, Augustine, and Origen, Biblical commentaries by more recent authors such as Remigius, "monastic" texts by Cassian and Hugh of St. Victor, finally, Priscian's Grammar. Witnesses such as this to the holdings of monastic libraries are precious, and although this catalogue has been published twice (once rather simply in a bookseller's catalogue), it is only now being addressed as carefully as it deserves. Laura Light of the Houghton Library staff (to whom I am indebted for most of this information) has recently read a preliminary report about this catalogue at a convention of medievalists, and her work promises interesting and useful results.

R.G.D.

REF De Ricci *Census*, 1693, no. 5; Faye and Bond, 272; *Illuminated and Calligraphic Manuscripts*, no. 13 and pl. 6; Light, no. 1 and 10, pl. 1 and 6; J. Martini, *A Catalogue of Manuscripts, Early Printed and Other Rare Books* XXII (Lugano, 1931), no. 12, p. 12–13; Jean Leclerq, O.S.B., "Textes et manuscrits cisterciens dans les bibliothèques des Etats-Unis," *Traditio* XVII (1961), 173–181; Laura Light, "The Scriptorium of Morimondo in the Twelfth Century: a Preliminary Investigation," paper read at the 23rd International Congress on Medieval Studies at Western Michigan University, Kalamazoo, 1988.

fundens menti illius lumen gratie spiritualis. quia intelligeret. quia qui a temporalibus aduocabat in tris? incorruptibiles dare ualeret thesauros in celis; Secundum
Scm̄ e; secm̄ mathm.

In illo tempore; cum transiret ihs uidit hominem sedentem in theloneo matheum nomine; & ait illi. Sequere me. Et surgens; secutus est eum. Et factum est discumbentē eo in domo; ecce multi publicani & peccatores uenientes discumbebant cum ihu. & discipulis eius. Et uidentes pharisei; dicebāt discipulis eius. Quare cum publicanis & peccatoribus manducat magister uester? At ihs audiens; ait. Non est opus ualentibus medicus; sed male habentibus; Euntes autē discite quid est misericor-

diam uolo & non sacrificium. Non ueni uocare iustos sed peccatores; Ced. sect. l.
Ecclesiam tuam dn̄e benignus illustra; ut beati mathei euangeliste illuminata doctrinis; ad dona perueniat sempiterna; P
Mauricii cū soc̄r is. VII. le. q sec̄r merita. & exp. eius uidi tha. ih. q inac̄ plur̄ mar. In Sc̄i michahelis le. i. Lectionem
ex omelia beati gregorii pape;

Nove m
angelorum ordines esse testante sacro eloquio scimus; angelos; archangelos; uirtutes; potestates; principatus; dominationes; thronos; cherubin; atq; seraphin.
Esse namq; angelos; & archangelos; pene omnes sacri eloquii pagine testantur. Cherubin uero

No. 2. Office Lectionary from St. Mary of Morimondo.

3 ❧ PSALTER (EARLY SLAVONIC)
Southwestern Russia, second half of the 12th century

Manuscript on vellum; 282 leaves. Cyrillic majuscule script; numerous initials in gold and colors; initial letters of each verse in gold over cinnabar.

20.5 x 16.5 cm. 19th-century dark green leather with silver corners and two silver clasps, possibly English. Purchased by Philip Hofer from H.P. Kraus, 1954. MS Typ 221.

ONE of a very small group of surviving early decorated Russian Psalters, this manuscript sheds important light on the relationship between Russian and Byzantine schools of illumination in the Middle Ages. It contains the simple Psalter text from Psalm 23:6 to the heading of Psalm 143 with lacunae caused by the removal of about twenty-five leaves. Adding in the leaves missing at the beginning, the manuscript must have originally had about 400 leaves. It has been severely cropped in binding and, judging from the care and luxuriousness with which the manuscript was written and decorated, it must have had wide margins and been an imposing book. A number of leaves were cut at the inner margin and repasted on paper stubs, and all were pasted so tightly into the modern binding that one cannot determine the original structure, although it seems likely that the manuscript was composed of eight-leaf gatherings.

Nevertheless, what remains is opulent and fascinating. The whole manuscript was written by a single scribe, sometimes careless about the details of his text but meticulous in the execution of the letters. The largest decoration that survives is a headpiece on f. 129^r at the opening of Psalm 77, the beginning of the second half of the Psalter in the traditional Greek arrangement. Folio 150^r contains a fairly large drawing of two bears walking upright and carrying an object suspended from a pole. Neither the object nor the meaning of this drawing has been explained, but the bears are naturalistic and possess charm. The numerous large initials (there are 106) are mostly zoomorphic, subtle and intricate, predominately Byzantine in style, and reflect designs and techniques commonly used in the better workshops of Constantinople in the twelfth century. The nature of these initials bears witness to a fresh wave of Byzantine artistic influence in western Russia around the middle of the twelfth century.

This description is based on information kindly supplied by Professor Horace Lunt, to whom we offer our thanks.

R.G.D.

REF Faye and Bond, 271; *Illuminated and Calligraphic Manuscripts*, no. 109 and pl. 76; André Grabar, *L'art du Moyen Age en Europe oriental* (Paris, 1968), p. 149; André Grabar, *L'art de la fin de l'antiquité et du Moyen Age* (Paris, 1968) III, pl. 76; David H. Wright, "A Luxuriously Decorated Russian Psalter of the Twelfth Century," *Actes du XVe Congrès Internationale d'Etudes Byzantines* II, part B (Athens, 1981), 919–932.

ноупасетлавъневлобѣсь
лдыцаскоиго∵
и въдлоушвъроуксоу
своіеюнастакнлыа
иесть∵ сла∵
псалмъ двдвъ он∵
е придоша языцн
въдостоанниетвое∵
осквърниша цьркв
въстоуютвою∵
положнша иерслмъ іако
овоцьно ехранилище∵
положиша троупиа рабъ

No. 3. Slavonic Psalter with zoomorphic initial.

4 THE EVANGELIST MARK
Nicaea? late 12th century

Drawing in gouache and gold on vellum.

27 x 20.5 cm. MS Typ 215.

UNTIL RECENTLY, this portrait of the Evangelist Mark, together with similar miniatures of the Evangelists Matthew and John, was tipped into an eleventh-century Gospel Book. The miniature of John is now at Dumbarton Oaks; the manuscript itself and the miniatures of Mark and Matthew are part of the Philip Hofer bequest.

The relationship between the miniatures and the manuscript is far from straightforward. Comparisons with manuscripts in Turin and Florence suggest a date in the early eleventh century for the Gospel Book. The miniatures, on the other hand, have been convincingly dated by Gary Vikan to the late twelfth century. To further complicate matters, eulogistic poems on the leaves facing the headpieces to the Gospels have been scraped away and replaced with sketches of the four Evangelists in light brown ink. Vikan believes that these sketched-in portraits probably date from the early thirteenth century, when, according to a non-scribal colophon, the Gospel Book was given to a monastery of the Eleousa by the uncle of Theodore Lascares I, Emperor of Nicaea (1204–1222). The sketches, which correspond to the completed miniatures both in pose and iconography, would thus be copies of them. Presumably the gouache and gold "models" were tipped into the manuscript when plans to provide new illuminations were abandoned.

One feature of the miniature of Mark will appear unusual to those acquainted with the symbols of the Evangelists in Western iconography. In the Western tradition, following the system of Jerome, Mark is associated with the lion, Matthew with the man, Luke with the ox and John with the eagle. Although the association of Evangelist and symbol is much less consistent in the Greek East, the Hofer manuscript, like several others of its period, follows the order of Irenaeus, in which Mark is linked with the eagle, and John with the lion. The two other Evangelist symbols are the same in both traditions.

Other Byzantine manuscripts in the Hofer bequest include a Synaxarion of ca. 1200 with six miniatures (fMS Typ 243) and two leaves from an eleventh/twelfth-century manuscript with forged paintings of the Evangelists. Previous gifts include a tenth- or eleventh-century roll with the Liturgy of St. Basil (MS Typ 416) and a twelfth-century Gospel Book with the Eusebian Tables and the Revelation of St. John, possibly from Anatolia (MS Typ 294). Hofer also contributed towards the purchase of a tenth-century Greek manuscript of Nemesius, *De natura hominis* (MS Typ 46).

N.F.

REF *Illuminated and Calligraphic Manuscripts*, no. 6, pl. 2; Gary Vikan, *Illuminated Greek Manuscripts from American Collections* (Princeton, 1976), no. 38.

No. 4. Byzantine miniature of the Evangelist Mark.

5 ❧ PROCESSIONAL
France (Paris?), early 13th century

Manuscript on vellum. 8 leaves plus integral pastedowns. Early Gothic script with North French choral notation (last 2½ pages in a later hand).

24 x 8.5 cm. Contemporary blind-stamped whittawed leather with pink leather clasp. Formerly in the collection of Nathan Rosenthal of Munich, 1909; H.P. Kraus; purchased by Philip Hofer, 1954. MS Typ 209.

THIS small monastic manuscript in agenda format contains the processional songs written in square black notation on staves of four red lines for the feasts of Purification, Palm Sunday, Ascension and the Assumption of the Virgin Mary, beginning on f. 1ᵛ. Some of these songs were sung by the whole chorus, others by smaller groups of soloists. The *Gloria, laus, et honor*, the procession for Palm Sunday, which was customarily sung alternately by chanters inside and outside the church door, is marked in this manuscript *Duo fratres* suggesting an antiphonal performance by soloists. The first page of the manuscript contains Alleluias and Verses in a second but contemporary hand, apparently entered after the Processional songs had been written. The soloist character of these Alleluias is revealed by the florid nature of the melodies whereby each syllable of text carries long musical lines or *melismata*. The last two and one-half pages are completed in a later hand. Marginal musical and textual additions in a much later (seventeenth-century?) hand show that this manuscript remained in use for hundreds of years. The manuscript's slenderness and small size are traditional for processionals, which were carried for the chorus by the soloist from station to station during and between the singing, as indicated by the rubrics: *in prima statione, in secunda, in tertia, ad ingressum chori*, etc.

The manuscript is complete in its original covers, to which integral leaves of the first and last quires are pasted. Of the eight books that the Library owns whose bindings are earlier than 1300, five were presented by Philip Hofer. Of these, two are blind-stamped and represent the two main classes of such bindings produced shortly before and after the beginning of the thirteenth century. One of these, an intricately stamped tanned (*i.e.*, dark brown) leather Romanesque binding exemplifies a group of single glossed books of the Bible which were, in great part, Parisian in origin. This manuscript, MS Typ 204, was presented by Philip Hofer in 1955 in honor of William Alexander Jackson. The other class of bindings, of which our Processional is an example, were not covered with tanned but with whittawed leather, that is, leather treated with oak bark and cured with alum so that it has a creamy color. The wood boards over which the leather was stretched protrude slightly beyond the manuscript leaves and have a somewhat rounded or beveled shape, both characteristics introduced at the beginning of the thirteenth century. The tanned Romanesque binding made perhaps twenty to thirty years earlier has squared boards, flush with the manuscript leaves. The stamps of our binding have been traced to a Parisian atelier. These stamps (there are about ten) range from abstract rosettes to eagles and (perhaps) pelicans. The sudden appearance of binding stamps in Paris at the end of the twelfth century has been attributed to the influx into that city of artisans required for the construction of the cathedral of Notre Dame.

R.G.D.

REF *Illuminated and Calligraphic Manuscripts*, no. 28 and pl. 8; Faye and Bond, 270; Walters, *History of Bookbinding*, no. 108 and pl. XXVI; Ernst Kyriss, "Vorgotische verzierte Einbände der Landesbibliothek Karlsruhe," *Gutenberg-Jahrbuch* (1961), 284 and Tafel 3. For the origins of MS Typ 204 most recently, C.F.R. De Hamel, *Glossed Books of the Bible and the Origins of the Paris Book Trade* (Woodbridge, Suffolk, 1984), 66; and Light, no. 32.

No. 5. Processional songs for Palm Sunday.

6   HUGO DE FOLIETO
De Bestiis et Aliis Rebus

ST. JOHN CHRYSOSTOM
Dicta de Naturis Bestiarum
England, mid-13th century

Manuscript on vellum, including 14 leaves of drawings in tempera and ink. Model book for a bestiary. 16.3 x 11.6 cm. 15th-century brown calf, blind-stamped. Presented by Philip Hofer in July 1983 in honor of Roger S. Wieck. MS Typ 101.

"SCARCER than hen's teeth" was Philip Hofer's description of this manuscript when he showed it to visitors. He was right. Medieval model books have a very poor rate of survival. Used and abused, they were discarded when worn out or when the style of their decoration fell out of fashion.

This manuscript is remarkable for a number of reasons. First, it is the only model book to survive from the period between 1230 and 1350, the dates of the famous drawings by Villard de Honnecourt in Paris and of the Lombard sketchbook in the Pierpont Morgan Library. Second, it contains not only a complete set of illustrations for a specific text, but it also includes the complete text itself. That text is the bestiary, the most important work of natural history for the Middle Ages. The presence of the accompanying text is unusual in itself, but even rarer is the fact that it, too, is laid out like a model, written with blank ovals and rectangles that, in a finished version, would accommodate the illustrations. The empty spaces in the text, too small for the pictures provided in the front of the book, were never intended to be filled in.

Finally, this manuscript is remarkable because it contains evidence that its pictures functioned as models in two different ways. As indicated by the varying sizes of the miniatures, it is clear that, originally, they were to be copied, freehand, by the illuminator. At a later date many of the pictures were pricked with a needle producing a series of small holes. Transferred to an intermediary sheet of vellum, these perforations could be pounced with charcoal dust and the illustrations easily duplicated. The fact that not all of the pictures were pricked suggests that this was a later use of the model book. Corroborating this theory are tiny folio numbers, added to the figures, that correspond to appropriate folios in the text. Like the prickings, these added folio numbers suggest that some years after its creation, the model book had fallen into less competent, but still interested, hands that continued to make good use of it.

The Hofer bestiary is but one of a number of manuscripts that contain instructive evidence on the writing and illustrating of the medieval and Renaissance book. These include a large collection of writing manuals, in both manuscript and printed form (see No. 23) and unfinished codices such as the fifteenth-century *Vite de santi* in the bequest, which contains miniatures in four stages of completion. The Hofer bestiary is also the earliest among the manuscripts dealing with animals that Philip Hofer avidly collected. These include the lushly illustrated pair of hunting manuals, Frederick II Hohenstaufen, *Livre de la science de chasser aux oiseaux*, and Gaston Phoebus, *Livre de la chasse*, both made for the Flemish bibliophile, Louis of Bruges, and Manuel Phile, *De Animalium Proprietate* of 1565 (No. 26). Hofer himself published both the Hohenstaufen and the Phile in the *Harvard Library Bulletin*. His interest in animals did not stop with manuscripts, however. The printed animal books he amassed range from the fifteenth century—the 1485 Aesop (No. 15)—to Guillaume Apollinaire's bestiary of 1911 illustrated by Raoul Dufy (No. 86) and Marie Angel's diminutive *Bestiary* of 1958 (No. 100). See No. 15 for additional discussion of bestiaries and fables.

R.S.W.

REF *Illuminated and Calligraphic Manuscripts*, no. 22, pl. 19; Samuel A. Ives and Hellmut Lehmann-Haupt, *An English 13th-Century Bestiary: A New Discovery in the Technique of Medieval Illumination* (New York, 1942); Dorothy Miner, review of Ives and Lehmann-Haupt in *Art Bulletin*, xxv (1943), 88–89; Florence McCulloch, *Mediaeval Latin and French Bestiaries* (Chapel Hill, 1960), p. 31, no. 33, 42–43; Faye and Bond, 258; R.W. Scheller, *A Survey of Medieval Model Books* (Haarlem, 1963), p. 101–103, no. 13, figs. 53, 54; Hellmut Lehmann-Haupt, *Gutenberg and the Master of the Playing Cards* (New Haven and London, 1966), p. 70, figs. 37d, e; Dorothy Miner, "More about Medieval Pouncing," *Homage to a Bookman. Essays on Manuscripts, Books and Printing, Written for Hans P. Kraus on his 60th Birthday, Oct. 12, 1967* (Berlin [1967]), p. 87–90.

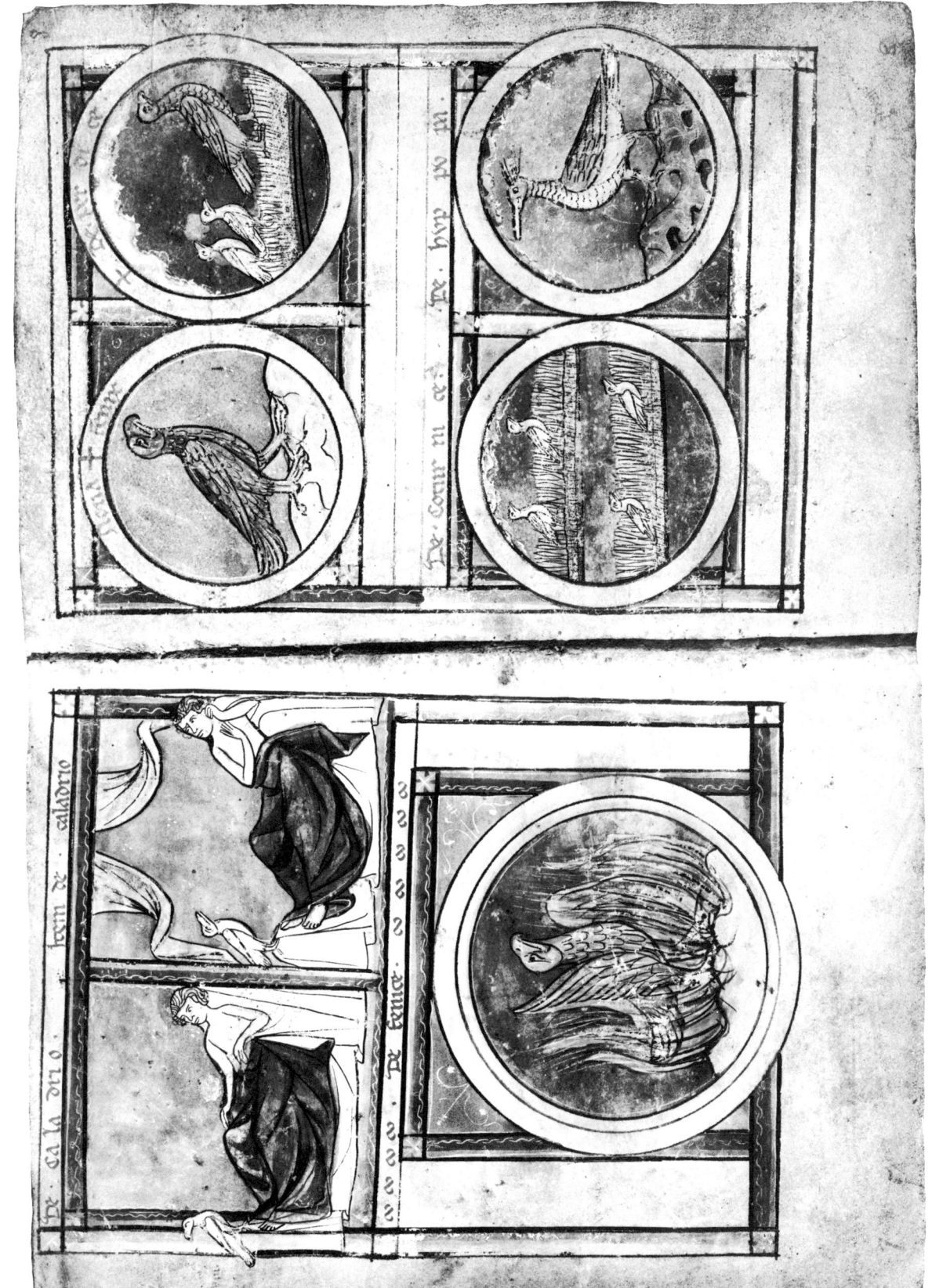

No. 6. Phoenix and other birds from Hugo de Folieto, *De Bestiis et Aliis Rebus.*

7 ❧ BIBLE FRAGMENT
Northern France, 13th century

Manuscript on vellum; 6 leaves. Square Gothic script; 1 large and 2 smaller initials decorated in gold and colors; red pen decorations with blue highlights; red and blue running titles.

48.7 x 34.4 cm. Unbound, in cloth case. Formerly in the collection of Count Gregoire Stroganoff. MS Typ 119.

THIS SPLENDID FRAGMENT from a great thirteenth-century Bible contains portions of Jerome's introductory prologues to the Old Testament and Genesis, part of Genesis and part of Deuteronomy. The initial "I" from the *In principio* which opens the Bible is often one of the most elaborate features in any given program of Bible decorations, and the "I" in this fragment, which stretches the full length of the page, is sumptuous indeed. The body of the letter encloses seven small creation scenes and a Crucifixion, stacked one above the other and set against a background of red and blue diaperwork. The borders at the top and bottom, which are formed by dragons biting the edge of the initial, support a variety of comic subjects: apes playing musical instruments, men fighting with swords, a man shooting an ape with an arrow, etc. The other two initials, though smaller in scale, are scarcely less lavish in their decoration. A few additional leaves from the same Bible are in other American collections, and other Bibles from the same workshop are in Europe. Although clearly in northern France, the exact location of this workshop remains in doubt, Arras, Lille and Cambrai all being mentioned as possibilities. It has even been suggested that these Bibles might be the work of a group of itinerant artists.

Bibles and other liturgical books of the twelfth through the sixteenth century are well represented in the Hofer collection. Some early examples, including a North Italian Psalter from the bequest (MS Typ 260), are discussed in Laura Light's catalogue of her Houghton Library exhibition, *The Bible in the Twelfth Century* (Cambridge, 1988). Later examples will be found in Roger S. Wieck's catalogue of *Late Medieval and Renaissance Manuscripts in the Houghton Library* (Cambridge, 1983). In this period, the Book of Hours gradually replaced the Psalter as the principal vehicle for illumination; among fifteenth-century Books of Hours in the Hofer collection are one attributed to the master of Morgan 453 (MS Typ 34) and one attributed to Jean Colombe (MS Typ 464). Other liturgical manuscripts are discussed in No. 2, 3, 5 and 9.

Fragments and single leaves from manuscripts were of particular interest to Hofer. These help to round out the Houghton collection and to offer a more comprehensive survey of scripts and illumination than would otherwise be possible. The bequest includes many such fragments, which supplement those already given to the Library. Examples include a cutting from a twelfth-century Bible, possibly from Pontigny in northern France, with an elaborate interlaced initial (MS Typ 315), and five leaves from a thirteenth-century Missal for Noyon Use (MS Typ 120). A sixth, especially magnificent leaf from the same Missal was given by Hofer in 1981. The figures of Ecclesia and Synagogia on this leaf have been related by scholars to the style of Villard de Honnecourt.

N.F.

REF   Light, no. 3; *Illuminated and Calligraphic Manuscripts*, no. 26; Faye and Bond, 260; Robert Branner, "A Cutting from a Thirteenth-Century Bible," *The Bulletin of the Cleveland Museum of Art*, LVIII (1971), 221–227.

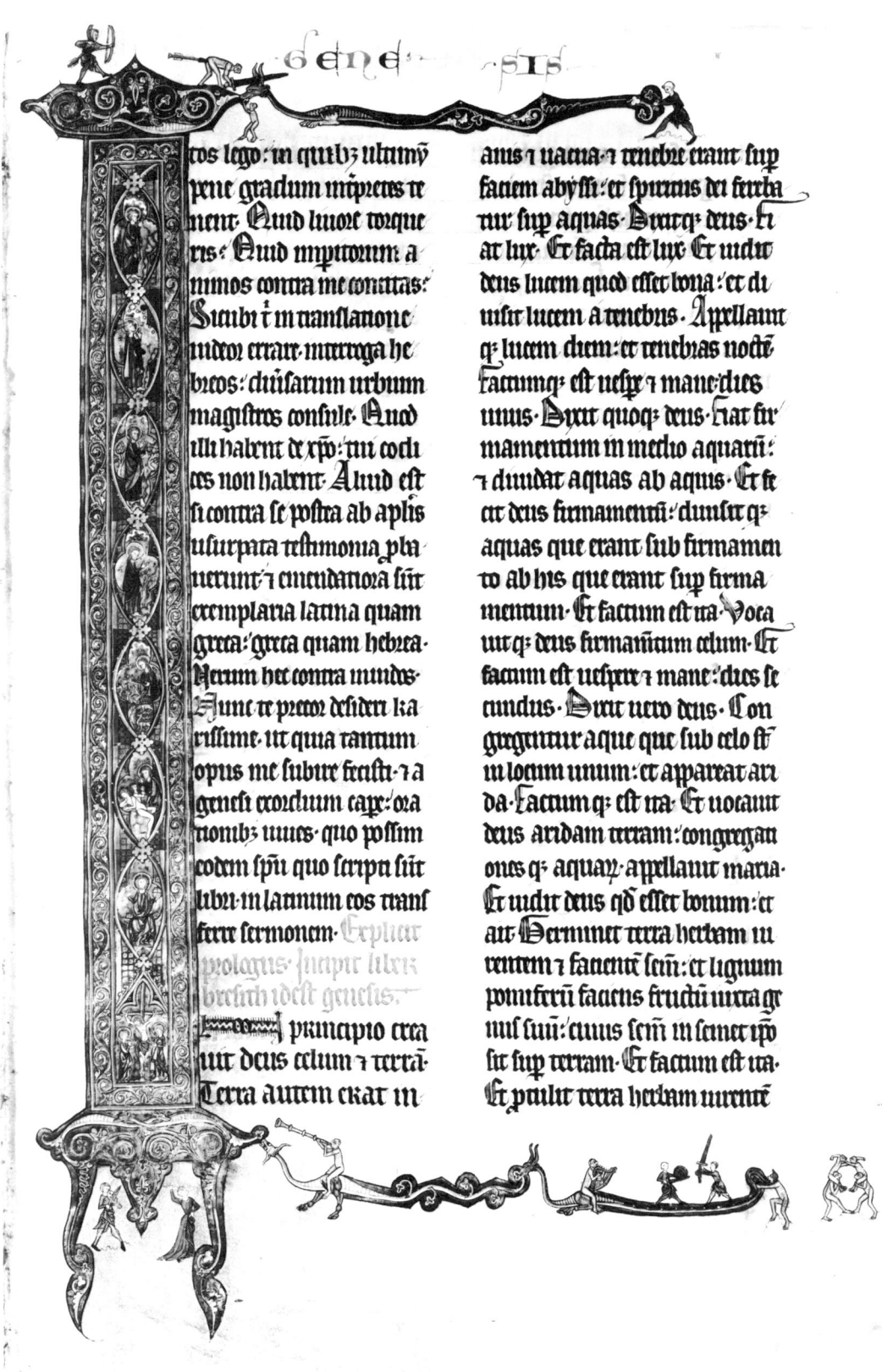

No. 7. Opening of Genesis from a Bible fragment.

8   ARISTOTLE
Magna Moralia, Ethica, Politica & Oeconomica
Italy (Bologna?), ca. 1280

Manuscript on vellum; 100 leaves. Small rounded Gothic script; 14 historiated initials.

34 x 24 cm. Red morocco, gilt, by S. Ridge of Grantham. Formerly in the collection of Sir John Thorold (sale, London, 1884, lot 168); John Hirst (sale, London, 1887, lot 304); John Gennadius (sale, London, 1895, lot 290); Harold Baillie Weaver (sale, London, 1898, lot 137); Charles Butler (sale, London, 1914, lot 3526); purchased by Philip Hofer from Giuseppe Martini, 1931. MS Typ 233.

FROM THE MONASTIC BOOKS in this exhibition (for example, No. 2 and 5) by way of a Psalter that may have had a monastic or a secular origin (No. 9), we come to one of the great number of books produced in the thirteenth century in shops around the new universities. The number of surviving manuscripts of Latin translations of Aristotle is around 2200, and the history of these translations is extremely complex. There were a number of Greco-Latin translations already available in the twelfth century that were largely superseded in the thirteenth. At this time, Robert Grosseteste translated the Ethics, and two versions of his translation spread throughout Europe in manuscripts, all apparently deriving ultimately from Paris. Our manuscript, probably from the University of Bologna, is remarkable because although it contains the second version of Grosseteste's translation, it is so contaminated by readings from the earlier translations that it is regarded as one of the two principal surviving witnesses to these earlier texts. The version of Grosseteste's text in this manuscript doubtless had a French source, but the same cannot necessarily be said of the earlier translations or the manuscripts which were copied to produce the early elements in our text. Furthermore the scribe of this manuscript, after he had finished writing the Ethics, sought out manuscripts he considered newer and more correct, and filled the margins of his own manuscript with "better readings." What results is a text very far from having claims to purity or authenticity, but one which has commanded and continues to command the special attention of scholars in a field densely populated with other source material.

Our codex, "The Hoferiana," as it is called in Aristotelian circles, is famous for its text. Philip Hofer purchased it very early in his career (1931), doubtless for its illuminations and as a beautiful instance of the "university style." It constitutes, therefore, a perfect example of one quality of his selections, a quality so consistent that one cannot attribute it to accident: his books and manuscripts almost always turned out to have previously undiscovered virtues. Looking at this manuscript, one notices, of course, the carefully written marginalia. One sees other marginalia written perhaps by the main scribe, but in a hastier hand. These are signs of intense use. Some sections are beautifully illustrated; in others there is no color, just gaps for pictures and initials. The manuscript draws the reader's attention to the process of its own creation. These, and other signs as yet unnoticed by this reader, are doubtless the clues that prompted a young Philip Hofer to acquire it.

R.G.D.

REF   De Ricci, *Census*, 1697; *Illuminated and Calligraphic Manuscripts*, no. 30 and pl. 16; *Aristoteles Latinus* pars prior (Rome, 1939), I, 74, no. 54 and 243, no. 16; *Aristoteles Latinus* suppl. altera (Bruges, Paris, 1961), 21, 48–49 and Praefatio, x; Albert Brounts, "Nouvelles précisions sur la 'pecia'," *Scriptorium* XXIV (1970), 349; *Scriptorium* XXV (1971), *Bulletin codicologique*, no. 751; R.D. Gaulthier "Ethica Nicomachea," *Aristoteles Latinus* XXVI, 1–3 (Brussels, Leiden, 1974) on Hoferiana throughout; M. Bastait, review of H.P.F. Mercken, *The Greek Commentaries on the Nicomachean Ethics*, *Scriptorium* XXX (1976), 320; M.T. d'Alverny, "Translations and Translators" [in] R.L. Benson and G. Constable, eds., *Renaissance and Renewal in the Twelfth Century* (Cambridge, Mass., 1982), p. 436, no. 63.

ethicor

temperatus autem non talis. set ut recta ratio. uoluntario autem magis assimilat intemperancia quam timor. hec quidem enim propter delectacionem. hic autem propter tristiciam. Quorum hic quidem desiderabile. hoc autem fugibile. et tristicia quidem stupefacit et corrumpit habentis naturam. delectacio autem nichil tale facit. Magis autem uoluntarium. propter quod et exprobabilius. et est assuefieri facile ad hec. multa enim in uita talia et assuetudines sine piculo in timendo autem econuerso. uidebitur autem utique non similiter uoluntarium. Timor est in hijs que secundum singula. hec quidem enim sine tristicia. hec autem propter tristiciam stupefaciunt. ut ex arma proicunt et alia deformiter faciant. propter quod et uidentur uiolenta esse in temperato autem econuerso que quidem secundum singula uoluntaria. concupiscet enim appetitus totum autem minus. nullus enim concupiscat intemperatus ut oeconomus autem intemperatae ad puerilia peccata seruamus. huic enim quandam similitudinem unum autem ab utro uocetur. nil ad ea que nunc differt. Manifestum autem quoniam posterius apriori non male autem uidetur translatum esse puniri autem orationis appetentem in multam augmentacionem habentem. Tale autem maxime concupiscencia enim uiuunt in puero. et maxime in hijs delectabilibus appetitus. signo enim persuasibilis ad cominans in multum uenierit. in castigabilis enim delectabilius appetitus uindiqua sapienti et coincupiscentie operatio auget cognatum et si magne uehementes sunt. et cogitationem praeripiunt. propter quod oportet mensuratas esse ipsas. et paucas et rationi nil contrarian. Tale autem bene persuasibilis dicimus apunitum quemadmodum enim puero oportet secundum preceptum pedagogi uiuere sic et concupiscibile secundum rationem propter quod oportet temperati concupiscabile consonare rationi. In tento enim ambobus bonum. et concupiscet temperatus: que oportet. et quando tenendum autem ordinat et ratio hec igitur nobis dicta sunt de temperancia.

Explicit tertius.

Incipit liber quartus.

Dicimus autem deinceps de liberalitate. uidetur autem esse circa pecunias medietas. laudatur enim liberalis non in bellicis in quibus temperatus. Rursus neque in iudicijs set circa dancem pecuniarum et sumptionem. magis autem in dancionem pecunias autem dicimus omnia quorum cumque dignitas nomismate mensuratur. Est autem et prodigalitas et illiberalitas circa pecunias superhabundancia et defectus. et illiberalitatem quidem copulamus semper magis quam oportet circa pecunias studentibus. prodigalitatem autem infirmius quandoque compleximus in temperabominibus in continentes enim uniciquam consumptores prodigos uocamus propter quod et prauissimi uidentur et multas simul habent malicias. non autem proprie appellantur. uult enim prodigus esse qui propter seipsum perditus uidetur autem perditio quedam ipsius esse. et sibi corruptio. uita plus existente. Sic utique prodigalitatem accipimus. quorum autem est alicuius utilitatis est hijs bene uti et male. diuicie autem sunt utiles unicuique. aut optime utitur qui habet circa singula uirtutem eorum cuius autem utetur optime qui habet circa pecuniam uirtutem iste autem est liberalis.

Usus autem et uidetur pecuniae sumptus et dacio acceptio autem et custodia possessio magis propter quod magis est liberalis dare quibus oportet qua accipere uirtutis enim magis beneficere quam bene pati. et bene operari quam turpia non operari. non in manifestum autem quoniam. non dationi quidem sequitur beneficere. et bene operari sumptioni autem bene pati ut non pati turpe operari. et gratianti non accipienti et laus magis et facilius autem non acceptori quam dare. proprium enim minus premittunt magis quam non accipit alienum. set et liberales dicuntur qui dant. Qui autem non accipiunt non in liberalitatem laudantur. set non minus in iusticia

9   PSALTER (GALLICAN)
Northern France, 2nd half of the 13th century

Manuscript on vellum; 134 leaves. Tall, pointed Gothic script; 11 large historiated initials, numerous smaller initials in gold and colors, bar ornaments in gold and colors throughout.

21.5 x 16 cm. 19th-century brown calf, blind-tooled. Written for the Abbey of St. Riquier; Simon Mathon of Arras; given to a provincial official of Artois for the public library, 1700; H.P. Kraus; purchased by Philip Hofer, 1955. MS Typ 311.

ONE of the main service books associated with the Offices of hourly prayers is the Psalter, which includes the 150 Psalms sung during the Offices as well as, often, a variety of other prayers and songs. This Psalter contains the Gallican translation of the Psalms thought to have been made by St. Jerome with reference to the Hebrew text after his earlier translation, the Roman, based entirely on the Septuagint. The Gallican version (which is the Vulgate version) dominated on the Continent outside Italy throughout the later Middle Ages. The songs in their Biblical order were sung mostly at Matins (about 2 A.M.) and Vespers (about 4 P.M.). Sunday Matins had the greatest number of Psalms, twenty-five; after that at Matins during the week from twelve to sixteen Psalms were sung. Saturday Matins concluded with Psalm 108; the Vespers Psalms commenced with 109. This custom is reflected in the Psalter's visual arrangement and decoration. The Psalms begin with an eleven-line historiated "B" for *Beatus vir*, that is, an initial tall enough to be placed next to eleven lines of text. Subsequent days' readings begin with eight-line initials on the 26th, 38th, 52nd, 68th, 80th, and 97th Psalms (our manuscript also has large initials for the 31st and 101st Psalms). Then the second major part of the book begins with a ten-line initial "D" for *Dixit Dominus*, the 109th and first Vespers Psalm. This constitutes an eight-part division of the Psalter which distinguishes the so-called non-monastic arrangement.

The manuscript begins with a liturgical calendar rich with references to the special saints and commemorations of the Abbey of St. Riquier near the town of Abbeville in the Artois, so there can be no question that it was written for this Abbey. After the calendar come the Psalms followed by minor canticles, the *Te Deum*, three greater canticles, a litany for all saints, and prayers for the dead. The manuscript concludes with three Marian Sequences in beautifully written Northern French choral notation. These Sequences, written in rhythmic and densely rhymed verse, new poems set to new melodies, were sung during the Mass after the Alleluia and as a class form one of the high points of medieval melody and lyric verse. The reason for their inclusion in an Office Book is not obvious. The last three and one-half leaves of the manuscript contain prayers in several later hands.

This Psalter is richly decorated but with an impressive simplicity. All of the initials, such as the Beatus initial illustrating scenes from the life of King David, have a plain gold background with such a high gesso underlay that the gold seems extremely thick. And the painting is expert, so much so that Robert Branner, in a letter, has questioned whether one must not assume a Parisian atelier. He also mentioned that the misspelled saints' names in the calendar suggest a non-monastic scriptorium. In any case, this Psalter represents the early Gothic style at a high level. The pointed and angular script makes the usual dark effect, but this is offset by two factors: there is slightly more space between the lines than is usual for this type of book, and every third line or so contains a line filler or bar ornament in one of an enormous variety of designs. These line fillers, which may have had their origin in legal documents, fit in with the Gothic aesthetic which demands that no spaces may be left within the bounding lines surrounding the text. In the present case, they give a great richness, even an ebullience to the appearance of the text.

The history of the Psalter is sketchy. Written either in Paris or St. Riquier, it appeared in the 1950s in New York in the possession of H.P. Kraus. Two earlier unidentified booksellers' descriptions laid in the manuscript show that it had been in the trade for some time. It appears never to have been mentioned in the scholarly literature. An inscription on one of the flyleaves partially tells and partially conceals a story:

> Ce livre a esté trouvé dans une concavité pratiquée entre deux murailles d'une très ancienne maison de la Ville d'Arras dans la Rue des Trois Visages, appartenante a Monsieur Mathon Receveur general des. . . .

The rest has been carefully washed off. A hasty reading with ultra-violet light resulted in the following partial reading:

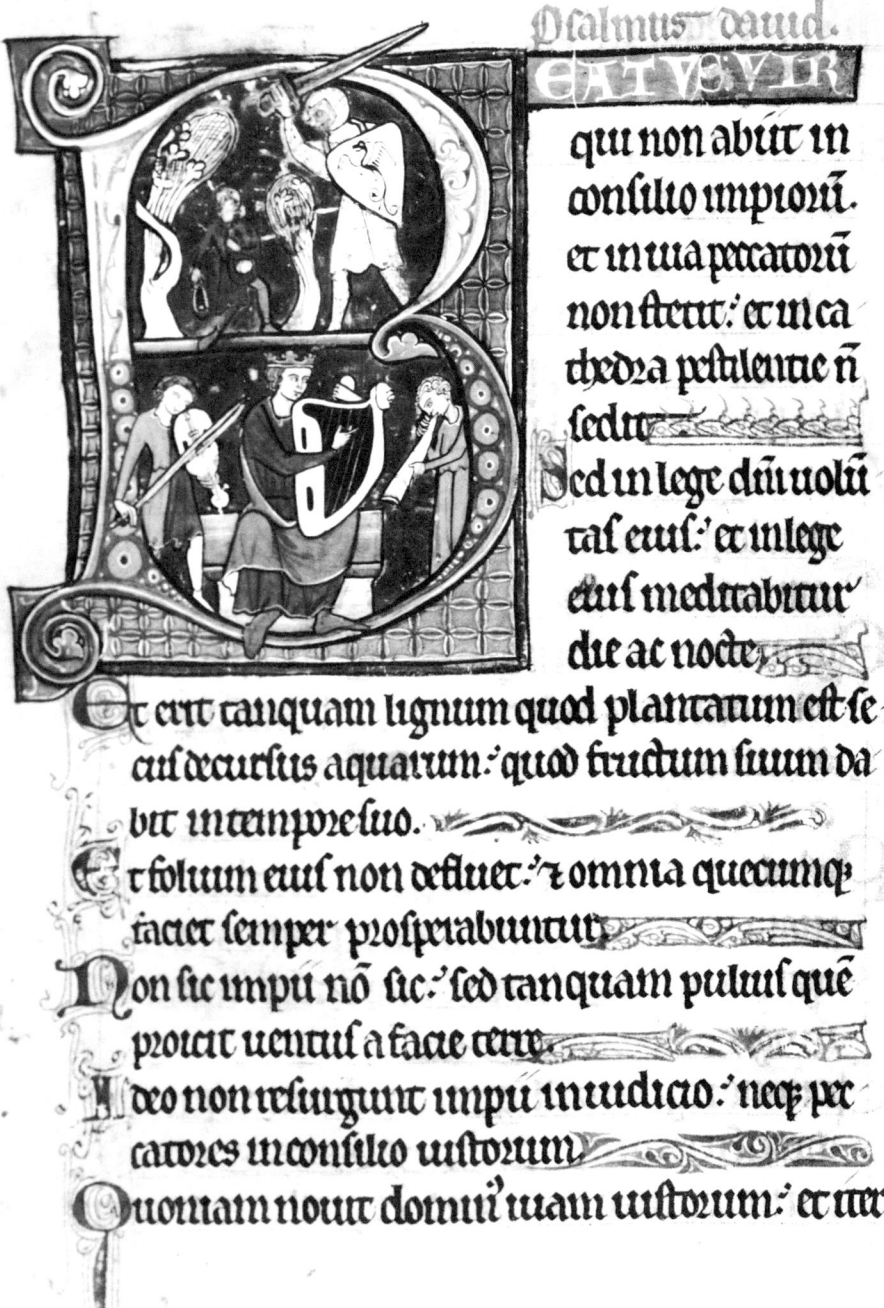

Psalmus dauid.

BEATVS VIR qui non abiit in
consilio impiorum.
et in uia peccatorum
non stetit: et in ca
thedra pestilentie non
sedit.
Sed in lege dñi uolun
tas eius: et in lege
eius meditabitur
die ac nocte.
Et erit tanquam lignum quod plantatum est se
cus decursus aquarum: quod fructum suum da
bit in tempore suo.
Et folium eius non defluet: et omnia quecumq;
faciet semper prosperabuntur.
Non sic impii non sic: sed tanquam puluis quem
proicit uentus a facie terre.
Ideo non resurgunt impii in iudicio: neq; pec
catores in consilio iustorum.
Quoniam nouit dominus uiam iustorum: et iter

No. 9. Opening of a Psalter with scenes from David's life.

... Etats d'Artois et donné par le dit Simon Mathon a notre ... Pere et Dieu Frere Jean D ... Abbé de D ... pour [...] (?) Deputé Ordinaire des ... d'Artois ... lequel ... enrichi notre Bibliothèque comme d'une antiquité curieuse. l'Année 1700.

So our Psalter has had its adventures.

R.G.D.

10   COMPUTISTIC CALENDAR
France (Diocese of Bourges), first half of the 14th century

Manuscript on vellum; 19 leaves folded to ⅙ size. Rounded Gothic script; illuminated throughout in gold and colors. 6.2 x 3 cm. closed; each leaf opens to 12.5 x 12 cm. Original ornamental velvet and cloth binding. Purchased by Philip Hofer from Blumka Galleries in 1955. MS Typ 278.

IN THE MIDDLE AGES, two types of books which were shaped for easy portability were certain service books such as the slender Processional (No. 5) in this catalogue and a class of calendars, mainly computistic calendars, that were folded into an extremely small format and attached to triangular tabs that could be suspended by a thong attached to the owner's belt.

Medieval calendars were essentially lists of saints' days arranged throughout the year according to the Julian calendar, which was introduced by Julius Caesar in 45 B.C. In the liturgical calendars found at the beginnings of most of the principal service books, the saints' days were usually preceded by the day of the month, which in turn followed two columns giving the Sunday Letters (days of the week designated A–G) and the Golden Numbers (an ancient technique for dividing time into nineteen-year cycles which, it was discovered, could be used accurately to predict the Paschal moon). To these elements, the computistic calendars added other tables for computing astronomical and astrological elements: the moon, stars, weather, and good luck.

Computistic girdle calendars are not common. Hermann Degering knew of seven; Howard Nixon added about seven more; S.J.P. Van Dijk listed three in the Bodleian Library. Of these, most are from the late fourteenth and fifteenth centuries. The earliest has been dated (but not certainly) to 1294. Only one of these has been described as being illuminated. The present example appears to be of considerable relative antiquity (the earliest year named in the table showing the conjunction of the sun and moon is 1292) and of superior workmanship. Each leaf, excepting the damaged eighteenth, has a small illumination relating to the contents of the leaf; *i.e.*, January has a two-headed Janus drinking from two cups next to the words *Pocula Janus amat* from a long hexameter poem about the months. There are also zodiacal drawings in color, without gold, for each month, and handsome capitals for the Sunday Letters.

The page arrangement for each month is in thirteen columns of differing widths, from left to right: lunar tables with letters, numbers and points; Golden Numbers; Sunday Letters; the days of the month; saints' days; Egyptian days (or *Dies mali*, unlucky days) with occasional astronomical (*i.e., sulstitium*) or astrological (*i.e., in piscibus*) remarks; length of the day; altitude of the sun. The seven leaves not containing the monthly calendars have a variety of computistic tables: conjunction of the sun and moon; table showing which sign the moon is in on a given day; zodiacal poem in hexameters beginning "*Nil capit facias ...* " known in many other manuscripts; opening of the Gospel according to John (the favored creation story), and miscellaneous related tables.

This calendar is in extraordinary condition for a manuscript that had to be unfolded for use and that was, in fact, used. The same must be said of the binding in red velvet, one panel of which is torn, with linings of red and white striped silk, each cover attached at the bottom to three green silk balls with tassels (only one missing) and at the top to the triangular attachment of red velvet with green embroidery which connected formerly to the thong (now missing) that made it fast to the girdle. The entire object is only 11.5 cm. in length.

R.G.D.

REF Faye and Bond, 275; Walters, *History of Bookbinding*, no. 112a; Hermann Degering, "Ein Calendarium Pugillare mit Computus aus dem Jahr 1294," *Buch und Bucheinband ... zum Geburtstage von Hans Loubier* (Leipzig, 1923), 77–88; S.J.P. Van Dijk, *Latin Liturgical Manuscripts and Printed Books* (Oxford, 1952), nos. 94, 95, 96; H.M. Nixon, *Broxbourne Library; Styles and Designs of Bookbindings* (London, 1956), no. 3.

No. 10. Velvet and cloth binding of a Computistic Calendar.

No. 10. Page for January from a Computistic Calendar.

11   JEAN DE MEUN, d. 1305?
Testament

JEAN CHAPPUIS
Les sept articles de la foi
France, ca. 1400

Manuscript on vellum. Illuminated initial with bar and ivy leaf border at the beginning of each work; small illuminated initial at the beginning of each verse.

27.5 x 19.5 cm. Brown morocco, blind-tooled, by Trautz-Bauzonnet. Written for Joan of Navarre, second queen of Henry IV; subsequently in the library of Lord Fairfax, Leeds Castle; bought by Richard Heber at the *Sale of Printed Books and Manuscripts from Leeds Castle*, Christie's, 10–12 January 1831; bought by Thomas Thorpe, Bookseller, February 1836; presumably acquired by a French owner and rebound in Paris; bought by William Morris, Sotheby's, 14 December 1894; bought by H. Yates Thompson, Sotheby's, 10 December 1898; sold by him to Sydney C. Cockerell, 4 May 1905; bought by Quaritch at Cockerell Sale, Sotheby's, 3 April 1957; bought by Philip Hofer, November 1961.

THE LENGTHY PROVENANCE of this manuscript was painstakingly unraveled by Sydney Cockerell. Cockerell, better known as the secretary and historian of the Kelmscott Press and the Director of the Fitzwilliam Museum, had worked with William Morris on the catalogue of his library at Kelmscott House and with M.R. James and others on the catalogue of Henry Yates Thompson's collection. The Jean de Meun *Testament* belonged to both Morris and Yates Thompson and contains their bookplates; in 1905, Cockerell acquired the manuscript for himself. It remained in his possession until 1957, when he sold the bulk of his collection for the benefit of his children. His researches into the history of the manuscript are summarized in three long notes dated October 3, 1917; April 4, 1918; and August 5, 1937, inside the front cover.

It was Cockerell who identified Joan of Navarre as the original owner of the manuscript. The title-page bears the inscription "Cest livre est a Jehan [two letters and the following words erased]" and the word "Royne" is just legible at the end of each poem. The widowed Joan, accused of conspiring against Henry V, was held captive for a time in Leeds Castle. Cockerell suggested that this manuscript was left behind when she was transferred to Pevensey—and remained at Leeds until the sale of the Fairfax Collection in 1831. Cockerell also noted the resemblance of the writing, with its extravagant flourishes, to that of Nicolas Flamel, the librarian of Jean, Duc de Berry. Millard Meiss, drawing on a musical vocabulary, compared these embellishments to trills, arpeggios and cadences (*French Painting in the Time of Jean de Berry*, London, 1969, p. 290).

A second manuscript from the library of William Morris, a twelfth-century German St. Augustine, with numerous corrector's emendations, is also included in the Hofer bequest.

N.F.

REF   Sotheby and Co., London, *Catalogue of Nineteen Highly Distinguished Medieval and Renaissance Manuscripts* (April 3, 1957), no. 19; Quaritch, Catalogue 767, no. 15.

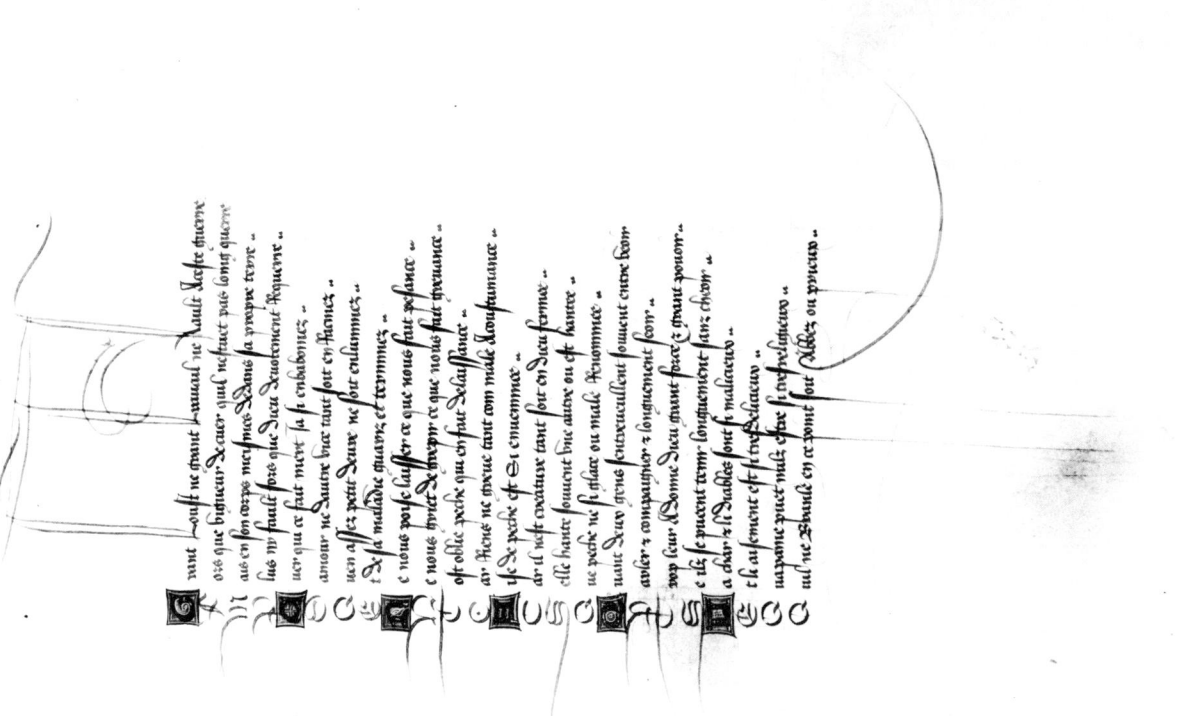

No. 11. Jean de Meun, *Testament*.

12 ONOSANDER
De Optimo Imperatore

FRONTINUS
De Re Militari
Italy (Naples?), ca. 1480

Manuscript on vellum; 174 leaves; italic script; two title-pages in capital script in blue and gold with green borders; two first text pages with white vine-leaf initials and full vine-leaf borders in gold and color; f. 2ʳ has an unfilled circle for arms on the lower margin. Signed by the scribe on f. 174ʳ: *P. Hippolyti lunensis manu.*

21.5 x 14.5 cm. 19th-century blue morocco. Formerly in the possession of Guglielmo Libri (sale 1859, lot 740); Sir Thomas Phillipps (no. 23619); purchased by Philip Hofer from William H. Robinson Ltd. in 1947. MS Typ 179.

THE RADICAL CHANGE in handwriting and book design that occurred in Italy at the beginning of the fifteenth century and engendered the humanist manuscript was prompted by the rediscovery of Carolingian bookmaking and expressed itself as a self-conscious reaction against the excesses of the dark and illegible Gothic style. The humanists thought they were recovering an antique form. Their manuscripts, which appear at first glance to form a homogeneous group, seem in fact to divide, very roughly, into three periods: the first, in which Carolingian techniques are closely imitated and in which production is mainly in major centers, Florence, Rome, or Naples; the second, in which standards slacken, occasional Gothic practices reassert themselves and production spreads to numerous less important centers; and a third, after the introduction of printing, when a number of ateliers strove to produce luxuriously decorated manuscripts which could be seen at a glance to be different from and superior to printed books. MS Typ 179 appears definitely to fall into the third category. Philip Hofer was particularly attracted to humanist manuscripts of all kinds and they form one of the great and unusual strengths of his collection.

Two ancient treatises on soldiery, one of them a translation dedicated in other manuscripts as well as ours to Alphonse of Aragon, King of Naples, are written here partly in capitals and partly in a very elegant and free italic hand and signed by the scribe, Hippolytus de Luni, who (Albinia De La Mare informs us) did much work for the Royal Court in Naples between 1470 and 1485. The condition of the manuscript is splendid. The very white vellum often bears that particular Italian sign of beauty, sooty cloudy formations on the hair-side resulting from hair follicles left from scraping both sides of the vellum equally instead of favoring the hair-side. The scribe expressed his personality not only by signing his name but also by adding in red marginal comments, sarcastic or outraged about the state of the text he is copying: "Thrameus: in other sources he is called Thisamenius," or "I don't know whether to correct this or not, the exemplar is mad."

There is an interesting point illustrating the development in manuscript production around the time of the introduction of printing. The humanist scribes, in laying out their pages, rejected the Gothic practice of tracing text guidelines and bounding lines in ink or color. They returned to the older practice of scratching them on with a stylus. This manuscript employs a fifteenth-century invention (recently brought to light by Albert Derolez), a ruling board tied with slender cords that could impress all the lines at once, and uniformly, on the soft flesh-side of the vellum. In this way they produced their old-fashioned effect with modern mechanical means.

For other Renaissance manuscripts, see No. 21 and 23.

R.G.D.

REF Faye and Bond, 267; Walters, *Manuscripts*, no. 187; *Illuminated and Calligraphic Manuscripts*, no. 73 and pl. 37; *Two Thousand Years of Calligraphy*, no. 50; T. de Marinis, *La Biblioteca Napoletana dei Re d'Aragona* (Milan, 1952), I, 57, no. 17; Portland Art Association, *Calligraphy; the Golden Age and its Revival* (Portland, Oregon, 1958), no. 9 and pl. 5; Alfred Fairbank and Berthold Wolpe, *Renaissance Handwriting* (London [1960]), pl. 5; Nicholas Mann, "Petrarch Manuscripts in the British Isles," *Italia medievale e umanistica*, XVIII (1975), 218, note 1; Adriana Marucchi, "Note su un nuovo manoscritto Carafa scritto da Ippolito Lunense nel Fondo Reginense," *Revue d'Histoire des Textes*, III (1973), 299 and 302. For ruling boards, see Albert Derolez, *Codicologie des manuscrits en écriture humanistique sur parchemin*, 2 vols. (Turnhout, 1984).

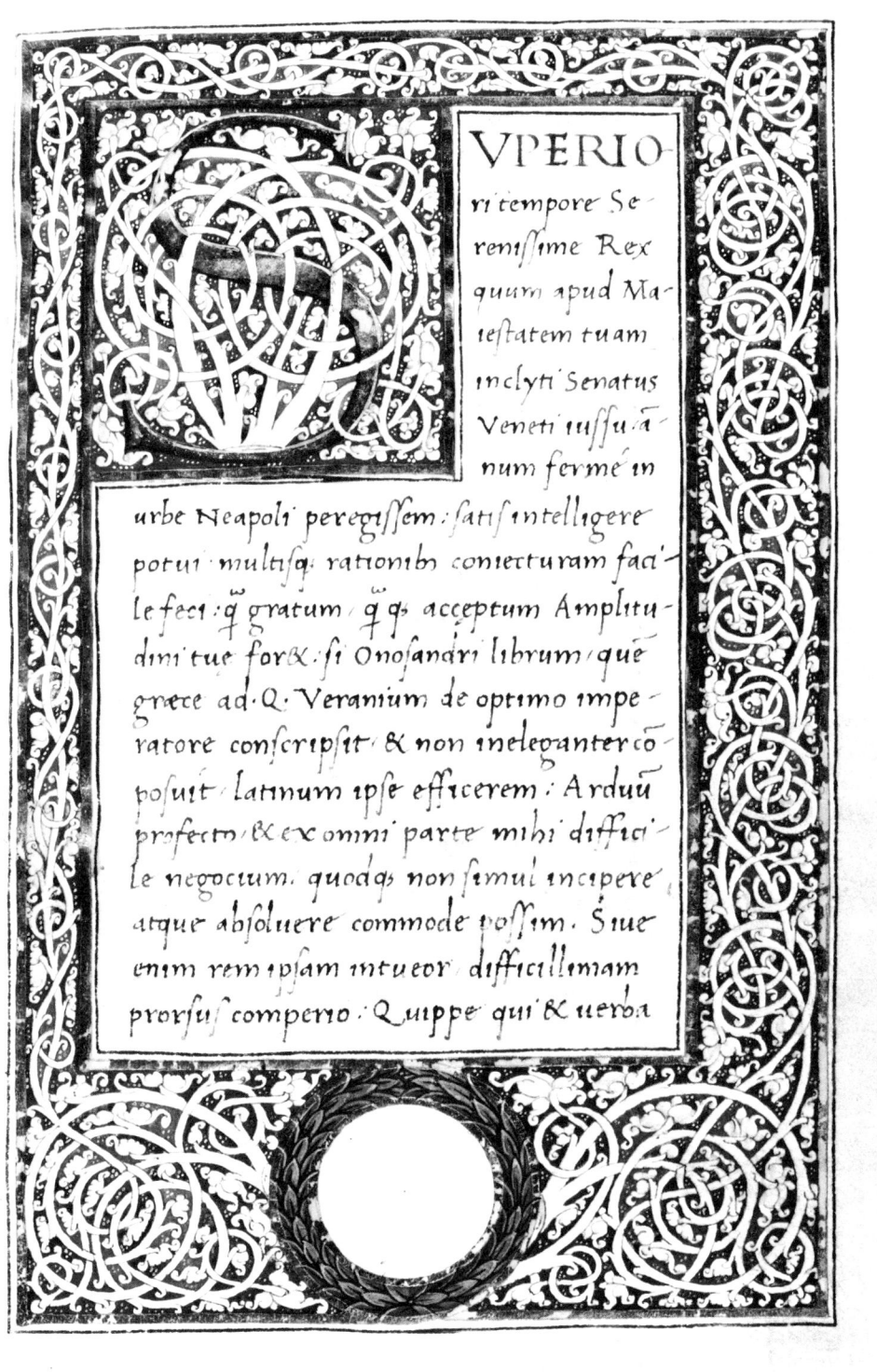

No. 12.   Dedication page from Onosander, *De Optimo Imperatore*.

13 ❦ GIOVANNI BOCCACCIO, 1313–1375
De Claris Mulieribus
Ulm, Johann Zainer, 1473

81 woodcuts, hand-colored; woodcut initials and a woodcut border.

29.8 x 21 cm. Red sheep, blind-ruled. Signatures of Antonius Kress, Christophorus Kress, and André de Montferrand, the last dated 1824.

THE ARTISTIC MERITS of the earliest books printed in Ulm and Augsburg have long been recognized. The brothers Günther and Johann Zainer learned the craft of printing in Strassburg in the 1460s. Günther then went on to establish a press in Augsburg about the year 1467; Johann later moved to Ulm, where his first book, a plague tract by Dr. Heinrich Steinhöwel, appeared in January 1473. It was evidently Steinhöwel who encouraged Zainer to produce the series of richly illustrated humanist texts which issued from his press between 1473 and 1478. Boccaccio's *De Claris Mulieribus* ("On Famous Women") was the first of these. With its eighty-one woodcuts, its foliated initials and its magnificent initial "s" incorporating figures of Adam and Eve and the seven deadly sins, it is a remarkably lavish and handsome book, which was to prove influential, not only for its own time, but also for the revival of fine printing at the end of the nineteenth century. William Morris named it as one of his favorites and identified it as the first book to give him a clear insight into the essential qualities of "medieval" design.

Despite a sprinkling of worm holes, the Hofer copy is a fine one, with attractive hand-coloring and especially wide margins. It is of further interest because of two early owners: Anton Kress (1478–1513) and his younger brother Christopher Kress (1484–1535), whose signatures appear on the fly-leaf. Christopher Kress, a patron of Albrecht Dürer, was also a delegate to the Diet of Worms and one of the publishers of the Augsburg Confession. Bound in at the front is a seventeenth-century reprint of Christoph Scheurl's 1515 *Vita Antonii Kressen*.

Other German incunabula in the bequest include the Latin Aesop printed at Augsburg by Anton Sorg in 1480, using the woodblocks from Johann Zainer's edition of 1476–1477; Konrad von Megenburg's *Buch der Natur* (1481), one of the most individual productions of Johann Bämler, another Augsburg printer; and Ptolemy's *Cosmographia* (1482), the earliest collection of printed maps in Germany, the masterpiece of Ulm printer Lienhart Holle. Another book printed by Anton Sorg, the *Buch der natürlichen Weiszheit* (1490), a collection of fables attributed to Cyrillus de Quidenon, is also in the bequest. Petrus Berchorius, *Liber Bibliae Moralis* may be cited from among many previous gifts of German incunabula, since it was printed at Ulm in 1474 by Johann Zainer. Books illustrated by Albrecht Dürer are discussed separately in No. 18.

N.F.

REF Goff B-716; William Morris, "On the Artistic Qualities of the Woodcut Books of Ulm and Augsburg in the XV Century," *Bibliographica*, I (1895), 437–455; Hind, II, 304–310; Peter Amelung, *Der Buchdruck im deutschen Südwesten 1473–1500*, I: *Ulm* (Stuttgart, 1979); Ruth Schwab-Rosenthal, trans., *Peter Amelung's Johann Zainer the Elder & Younger* (Los Angeles, 1985).

.xiiij.

relictis aliquibus filiabus, cum parte copiarū cesa est.
Quid aūt ex lampedone secutū sit legisse non memini.

De Tisbe babilonia virgine. Capitulū duodecimum

Tisbes babilonia virgo infelicis amoris
exitu magis q̃ opere alio inter mortales ce
lebris facta est. Huius & si non a maioribꝰ
nr̃is qui parentes fuerint baburim? intra
tn̄ babiloniam habuisse cum piramo etatis sue puero
contiguas domos satis creditum ē. Quoꝑ cū esset iure
conuicinij, quasi conuictus assiduus, & inde eis adhuc
pueris puerilis affectio egit iniqua sors vt crescentibꝰ
annis (cum ambo formosissimi essent) puerilis amor in
maximum augeretur incendium illudq̃ inter se nutibꝰ
saltem apirent aliqñ, iam in puberem ꝑpinquantes
etatem. Sane cum iam grandiuscula fieret tisbes a pa
rētibꝰ in futuros hymeneos domi detineri cepta ē. Q ᷣ
cū egerrime ferrent ambo, q̃rentesq̃ solliciti q̃ via pos
set saltē aliqñ colloq̃ n̄ isi adhuc visā cois pietria inuenē

No. 13. "Pyramus and Thisbe." Illustration from Boccaccio, *De Claris Mulieribus*.

14 ❧ ENRIQUE DE VILLENA, 1384–1434
Los trabajos de Hercules
Zamora, Antonio de Centenera, 1483

11 woodcuts (or metalcuts).

27.3 x 20.3 cm. Brown morocco by C. & C. McLeish. Formerly in the library of James P.R. Lyell.

IT SEEMS APPROPRIATE that the first Spanish book acquired by Philip Hofer should have been *Los trabajos de Hercules* by Enrique de Villena (Zamora, 1483), the first important illustrated book in the Spanish language. Hofer acquired his copy from James P.R. Lyell in 1931, following a first trip to Spain in 1927. It is the copy which Lyell described in *Early Book Illustration in Spain* (London, 1926) as "one of the rarest books in the world." It certainly is a wonderful book. The illustrations, which combine decorative and bizarre elements in a way that is characteristic of much later Spanish work, are almost certainly by a native Spanish artist, though Hind suggests a possible influence from either early Lyons woodcuts or the Ulm Boccaccio (No. 13). They depict eleven of the twelve labors of Hercules, which Villena, in his text, discusses from an allegorical, an historical and a moral point of view, as well as recounting the traditional versions of the myths. Hercules appears as a Renaissance knight, wielding a mace as a club, and his adversaries—the lion of Nemea, the Cretan bull, the Hydra, etc.—are transformed by the Spanish artist into unfamiliar and fantastic monsters. Curiously, these cuts must have been printed separately from the text, since in several instances the illustrations overlap the letterpress. The initial letters would also have been added separately by hand, the places where they would have appeared being left blank, and the appropriate letter indicated in small type.

Other early Spanish books from the Hofer collection include two books printed in Seville in 1494 by Meinardo Ungut and Stanislao Polono (Stanislas "the Pole"): Egidio Colonna's *Regimiento de los principes* (bequest) and the *Processionarium ordinis praedicatorum* (previous gift). The latter, handsomely printed in red and black, contains some of the earliest music printing in Spain. Two other previous gifts are books that are known only from the Hofer copies. Both are without date, printer or place of printing, but the *Tractado breve de confession* has been ascribed to the Burgos printer Juan de Burgos and dated ca. 1495–1499; Plutarch *De liberorum educatione*, which must also date from the later 1490s, was probably printed at Valencia by the peripatetic German printer Nicolás Spindeler.

The Hofer bequest also includes nine sixteenth-century Spanish books, which join the large group described in Anne Anniger's catalogue of *Spanish and Portuguese 16th-Century Books in the Department of Printing and Graphic Arts* (Cambridge, 1985). Most of the 250 items in that catalogue were previous gifts of Philip Hofer (see also No. 20).

N.F.

REF   Goff v-275; Palau XXVII, 272–273; Conrad Haebler, *Early Printers of Spain and Portugal* (London, 1897), no. 688; James P.R. Lyell, *Early Book Illustration in Spain* (London, 1926), p. 7–15; Martin Kurz, *Handbuch der iberischen Bilddrucke des XV Jahrhunderts* (Leipzig, 1931), no. 367; Hind, II, 748.

ya concordia paresçe la significaçion enla manera que se sygue.

❡ Hystoria nuda. ❡ Es en greçia vna grande selua z espesura de arboles antigua z espantable z esquiua z no abitada z aspera de peñas z afoyada de cueuas sombrosas z escuras dicha mornia. acõpañada de fieras z saluajes bestias. ẽtre las quales auia vn leon muy grãde z brauo gastador delos pobladores z delos de alli vezinos por miedo del qual los viandantes desmãparauã los caminos q̃ pasauan açerca de aquel lugar z los labradores cõ los bueyes no osauã reboluer la tr̃a dura ni ẽcomẽdar las simientes al labrado campo. Los pastores dexauan los ganados sin osar los boluer quãdo se llegauan a aq̃l lugar. E los moradores enlas caserias z aldeas dexauan su labrança ençerrãdose enel fuerte muro delos mayores lugares recogiendose enlas fortalezas z casas altas tanto era el temor q̃ del dicho leon auia z no menos daño auido z conçebido auian. Oyendo esto el virtuoso hercules z cauallero valiente corrio z ayudo al hermamiento z daño que resçebiã los de aq̃lla tierra. no auiendo miedo maguera oyera dezir de otros muchos caualleros que antes del auian dubdado matar el dicho leon z avn algunos quelo prouarõ fenesçieron ay sus dias ẽtre los dientes del leon. z la suya syn defesion perdieron arrebatada mẽte vida. Hercules con vtud sobrada ãdudo ala selua ya dicha buscãdo el espãtable leon conbidãdolo que veniese a el por bozes z amenazas fasta q̃ llego

No. 14. "Hercules and the Nemean Lion." Illustration from Enrique de Villena, *Los trabajos de Hercules*.

15 ❧ AESOP
[Vitae et Fabulae]
[Naples, Francesco del Tuppo, 1485]

88 woodcuts, woodcut borders and initials; lightly ruled in red.

27.5 x 19.5 cm. Brown levant, blind-stamped, edges gilt. Label of C.W. Dyson Perrins.

THE NAPLES AESOP is one of a remarkable trio of early Italian fable-bestiary books in the Hofer collection. It joins previous gifts of the 1508 Mondovi *Libellus de natura animalium* and the Verona Aesop of 1479, a palimpsest and the only recorded copy on vellum. That was the first Latin-Italian edition, a smaller and simpler book than the Naples edition, also in Latin and Italian and containing an illustrated life of Aesop, as well as sixty-six fables, each with four separate explanations or morals.

Considered the most important South Italian illustrated incunabulum, the Naples Aesop is distinguished by its vivid woodcuts, black and crisp, with a clear two-dimensional design. The fable images, cut with strong outlines reinforced with parallel hatching, are silhouetted against low horizons with pattern in the foreground and white space above, which focuses attention on the outlines. Each of these images is set within an ornamental, architectural frame composed of many elements carefully joined together. The central feature of the border is a lunette in the upper part with scenes from the Labors of Hercules. This richness of pattern, black against white in the images and white against black in the frames, may reflect Arabic influences from neighboring Sicily. The figures, dependent in part on the Verona edition, are more northern in character, yet with an Italian concern for volume and space. At the beginning of the fables, an additional border in a different, freer style, white scroll work with figures on a black ground, appears in a slightly different version in a previous gift of a Neapolitan incunabulum, Moses ben Nahman's Commentary on the Pentateuch of 1490. Bestiaries and fables with their humor and wry comment on human behaviour were favorites of Philip Hofer, and he collected them widely. The authors might be Aesop, Faerno, La Fontaine, La Motte, Phaedrus, or the anonymous bestiary or physiologus collections. Examples are too numerous to list, but a few items may be mentioned to indicate their range.

Among the manuscripts are the thirteenth-century Hugo de Folieto, *De Bestiis et Aliis Rebus* (No. 6) the sixteenth-century *De Animalium Proprietate* by Manuel Phile (No. 26), and two great fifteenth-century Flemish hunting manuscripts, Gaston Phoebus, *Livre de la chasse* and Frederick II Hohenstaufen, *Le livre de la science de chasser aux oiseaux*. The incunabula include Gerard Leeu's 1480 Gouda *Dialogus Creaturarum*, Anton Sorg's Aesop of ca. 1480 and his Cyrillus, *Buch der natürlichen Weiszheit* of 1490, both colored copies.

On the sixteenth-century shelves are Denis Janot's Paris Aesop of 1542, Jean de Tournes' Lyons Aesop of 1547 with woodcuts after Bernard Salomon, the 1563 Roman Faerno with engravings after designs attributed to Titian, Sigmund Feyerabent's 1566 Aesop with woodcuts after Vergil Solis, and Marcus Geeraert's 1579 Bruges engraved Aesop.

The seventeenth century begins with Aegidius Sadeler's Prague *Theatrum Morum* of 1608, and from England are several editions of both John Ogilby's and Francis Barlow's Aesops (No. 35). At this time La Fontaine begins to appear; two distinguished examples are the Paris 1668 edition illustrated by François Chauveau, and the Amsterdam 1685 edition with engravings by Romeyn de Hooghe.

In the eighteenth century there is a wide representation of engraved examples, including La Motte's *Fables nouvelles* of 1719 with designs by Charles Antoine Coypel and Claude Gillot and Giorgio Fossati's 1744 Venetian *Raccolta di varie favole* printed in color. Two La Fontaines are the 1762 Fermiers Généraux Paris edition with the false imprint of Amsterdam containing engravings by C.N. Cochin the Younger after Charles Eisen and the 1755 Paris edition engraved by Cochin after J.-B. Oudry, with a set of engraver's proofs in early stages in the bequest. Wood-engraved versions include Thomas Bewick's various editions of his fables (see No. 58) and his blocks for John Gay's *Fables*. Bodoni's Faerno of 1793 and his Aesop of 1800 are handsome typographic versions, unillustrated.

Russia is represented in an 1815 edition of Krylov's fables illustrated by Ivanov, a copy with the stamp of the imperial Library of Tsarkoe Selo.

No. 15. "The Ox and the Frog." Illustration from Aesop, *Vitae et Fabulae*.

Nineteenth-century wood-engraved examples include Grandville's Florian and La Fontaine (see No. 70) and Wilhelm von Kaulbach's illustrations for Goethe's *Reineke Fuchs* of 1857. At the end of the century are Boutet de Monvel's color illustrations for an 1890 Paris La Fontaine and Peter Newell's for Guy Wetmore Carryl's *Fables for the Frivolous, with Apologies to La Fontaine* of 1898. Hofer's great favorite was Jules Renard's *Histoires naturelles* of 1899 with lithographs by Toulouse-Lautrec. In 1954 Hofer translated and published a selection of these texts and illustrations as Fogg Museum Picture Book No. 3.

In the twentieth century this genre has continued, and a few examples may be mentioned. The most important is Guillaume Apollinaire's *Le bestiaire* of 1911, a proof copy with drawings by Raoul Dufy (No. 86). The 1931 Harrison of Paris Aesop illustrated by Alexander Calder is accompanied by four drawings in the Frances L. Hofer bequest (Becker no. 49). The French are further represented with Picasso's aquatints in the 1942 *Eaux-fortes originales pour textes de Buffon* and Jean Lurçat's 1948 *Géographie animale*. Among the Germans are Gerhard Marcks' 1940 Aesop, and among the Americans, Leonard Baskin's 1951 *A Little Book of Natural History*.

In a special category are two items in which Hofer worked with contemporary artists he admired. In 1957, when Ben Shahn was in Cambridge as the Charles Eliot Norton Lecturer, he and Hofer collaborated in producing Fogg Museum Picture Book No. 8, *A Portion of Jubilate Agno* by Christopher Smart, which reproduces twelve little bestiary drawings by Shahn. The original drawings were a later gift to the Department of Printing and Graphic Arts from Prof. and Mrs. José Luis Sert. A few years later, Hofer commissioned Walter Stein to make a set of lithographs to illustrate a new edition of Renard's *Natural History*, which was published by the Department of Printing and Graphic Arts in 1960 in an edition of 600 copies, including fifty with a set of trial proofs and an extra set of the lithographs.

E.M.G.

REF Goff A-155; British Museum, p. 8; Hind, II, 405–408; Sander, I, no. 52; Alfredo Mauro, *Francesco del Tuppo e il sue "Esopo"* (Città di Castello, 1926); Lamberto Donati, "Di alcune ignote zilografie del XV secolo nella Biblioteca Vaticana," *Gutenberg Jahrbuch* (1934), 73–106.

16 ❧ MISSALE MAGDEBURGENSE
Magdeburg, Simon Koch, 1486

Initials and Canon picture hand-painted in gouache; blind impression of a woodcut on recto of Canon picture.

39.5 x 27.5 cm. Contemporary pigskin, blind-stamped. Bookplate of Charles Louis de Bourbon, Duke of Parma.

AT FIRST GLANCE, the lavish Missal printed in Magdeburg, Prussia in 1486 by Simon Koch might almost be taken for a manuscript. The Gothic type is closely based on handwritten models, and while the printer has replaced the scribe insofar as the production of the text is concerned, he has not yet subsumed the traditional roles of rubricator, illuminator and binder. In fact, this early printed book still contains a good deal of handwork. As in the Gutenberg Bible and many other fifteenth-century books (see, for example, No. 14 and 19), the initial letters are entirely the work of a professional rubricator, and were added by hand after the text had been printed. The blue and red of these hand-painted initials contributes significantly to the decorative appearance of the page.

In addition, this copy of the Missal includes four large illuminated initials and a Canon picture of the Crucifixion, entirely executed in gouache by an artist of some ability. This miniature has not been inserted, but was painted directly on the verso of the original leaf, which has fourteen lines of text on its recto. A blind impression of a very curious woodcut is only just visible in the large blank space below these fourteen lines: the block was evidently one that was lying about Koch's shop and was selected at random for use as make-ready. The subject of the cut has been identified as a butcher making sausages. A similar blind impression—of four lines of type—occurs in the blank space following the colophon. In other known copies of the Missal, a woodcut occupies the place of the painted Crucifixion. The ten leaves of the Canon are printed on vellum, while the rest of the book is on paper.

The binding further contributes to the monumental effect of the Missal. In the fifteenth century, the same

No. 16. Canon picture from *Missale Magdeburgense*.

binders would have been employed on both manuscripts and printed books: it was indeed impossible to judge a book by its cover. The binding of the Magdeburg Missal is a splendid one, in white pigskin, blind-stamped with Gothic ornaments (tendrils, small acorn in a rhomb, lion in a rhomb), over heavy wooden boards. Two brass clasps with pigskin throngs serve to hold it shut, and woven index markers colored red and green are attached to the front edges of the leaves. Inserted at the end are two vellum proof sheets of leaf LXXX, which were apparently once pasted down on the insides of the front and back covers. This suggests that the binding, though generally accepted as early, is probably not contemporary with the Missal itself. In any case, it dramatically enhances the book's effect as a physical object, not totally dissimilar to certain late twentieth-century bookworks.

Missals and Horae were the two categories of ecclesiastical books most likely to receive this sort of special treatment. An exquisite little Book of Hours (Naples, Mathias Moravus, 1487), presented by Hofer in 1984 in honor of Eleanor Garvey, was enhanced through the addition of elaborate illuminated initials and borders and extra miniatures of Christ and various saints. Even the woodcut illustrations have been painted over in gold and colors. Other early ecclesiastical books in the bequest include two additional Books of Hours printed at Paris ca. 1499, one by Philippe Pigouchet and one by Thielman Kerver (No. 19). Previous gifts include the Bibles printed by Anton Koberger in Nuremberg in 1483 and by Steffen Arndes in Lübeck in 1494.

N.F.

REF Goff M-672; W.H.J. Weale and H. Bohatta, *Bibliographia Liturgica: Catalogus Missalium Ritus Latini* (London, 1928), p. 100; L. Giraud-Badin and Ulrico Hoepli, *Livres de liturgie imprimés aux XVe et XVIe siècles faisant partie de la bibliothèque de son Altesse Royale le Duc Robert de Parme* (Paris and Milan, 1932), no. 98; Curt F. Bühler, *The Fifteenth-Century Book* (Philadelphia, 1960).

17 ❧ VBERTO & PHILOMENA, TRACTA D'AMORE
[Florence, Lorenzo Morgiani and Johannes Petri, ca. 1495]

Woodcut title-page.

20.5 x 13.5 cm. Red straight-grain morocco, blind-tooled, gilt fillets, by C. Haring, London. With signature of Richard Heber.

THE FLORENTINE QUATTROCENTO woodcut is seen at its finest in this rare little book, the only recorded copy in America. (Another copy is recorded in the library of Erlangen University.) The freedom of the figure style and the spaciousness of the architectural setting suggest that the design, like a number of others in Florentine Renaissance books, came from the hand of a painter. The *passe-partout* border in which it is framed is typically Florentine; this particular one, with tilting putti mounted on pigs at the bottom, hare and hound above, and candelabra at the sides, appears in other publications of the same period, some from Morgiani and Petri and some with other imprints, for such decorative features were customarily borrowed and copied by other publishers. In this copy, black wash has been added to the lower border, possibly to cover breaks in the block.

Vberto & Philomena is divided into two sections, "Pri[m]o Duberto & Philomena & poi desso Uberto & alba figlia del Duca di borgogna." Uberto's adventures in love are recounted in verse, in *ottava rima*, with four stanzas to a page. The description in the Heber catalogue does not agree with this copy, which lacks an imprint (supplied by Goff). Brunet lists the Crevenna copy and cites a 1492 Venice edition (copy in the Herzog August-Bibliothek, Wolfenbüttel).

Florentine illustrated incunabula are simpler than their Venetian contemporaries. Woodcut illustrations were featured in the last decade of the century, and Morgiani and Petri issued a number of them. Secular subjects were popular—poetry and romance—as well as devotional tracts and sermons. They have a genre character, many of them with domestic or street settings, thus preserving a record of contemporary interiors and exteriors. Because of their popular and ephemeral nature, they survive in very small numbers.

Both secular and sacred Florentine books of this genre with woodcut illustrations are represented in the Hofer collection, especially among previous gifts, and several were published by Morgiani and Petri. These

No. 17. Title-page of *Vberto & Philomena*.

include *El contrasto di carnesciale et la quaresima* of ca. 1495, an Aegidius Assisiensis of ca. 1493, a St. Anthony of Florence, *Tractato* of 1493, Antonio Bettini, *Libro del monte di dio* of 1491, Domenico Cavalca, *Libro molto devoto & spirituale della lingua* of 1493. Similar woodcut books from other Florentine publishers include the *Epistole et Evangelii* of ca. 1500 (a fragment of 88 leaves, but the only copy recorded); Jacobus de Cessolis, *Libro di giuocho di scacchi* (Antonio di Bartolommeo, 1494); Jacopone da Todi, *Laude* (Francesco Bonaccorsi, 1490); a number of Savonarolas; and Luigi Pulci's *La confessione* of ca. 1495, the latter with the same border as *Vberto & Philomena*. A number of illustrated Venetian incunabula are among previous gifts, including both the Malermi Bibles, the Jenson Pliny of 1472, the St. Jerome of 1485, and the Herodotus of 1494, both with the white-figured border, the 1482 Regiomontanus with the diagrams in color, and the Sacro Bosco of 1485, the Petrarch *Trionfi* of 1490, the Bergomensis *Supplementum Chronicarum* of 1490, the Livy (1493), and the Bonaventura (1500). A fine colored copy of the Verona Valturio of 1472 is in the bequest.

E.M.G.

REF Brunet, v, 998; Goff u-56; Richard Heber, *Biblioteca Heberiana* [London, Sold by Messers. Sotheby and Sons, 1834–1837], pt. 2, no. 6159; Pietro Antonio Crevenna, *Catalogue des livres de la bibliothèque de Pierre Antoine Bolongaro-Crevenna* (Amsterdam, 1789), III, no. 4591; Hermann Varnhagen, *Uber eine Sammlung alter italienischer Drucke der Erlanger Universitätsbibliothek* (Erlangen, 1892), p. 56; Erhard Lommatsch, "Uberto e Philomena," *Akademie der Wissenschaften und der Literatur*, 6 (1964); Hind, II, 555; Sander, III, no. 7416; Paul Kristeller, *Early Florentine Woodcuts* (London, 1897), 421a.

18 ❧ APOCALYPSIS CUM FIGURIS
[Nuremberg, Published by the artist] 1498
Woodcuts by ALBRECHT DÜRER, 1471–1528

15 woodcuts by Dürer, hand-colored. Initials and paragraph marks added in red and blue, capital strokes in yellow, underlining in red.

44.1 x 30.5 cm. 19th-century tan calf, blind-stamped. Inscribed "E codicibus P.E. Sporey."

DÜRER's 1498 *Apocalypse* was a milestone in the history of book illustration. The large-scale woodcuts with their elaborate though unified compositions were unlike anything that had been seen before for intricacy of design and naturalism of detail. It is difficult to believe that less than twenty years separate this monumental achievement from the vigorous but crude woodcut books of the 1470s and 1480s.

The son of a goldsmith, Dürer served his apprenticeship in the workshop of Michael Wolgemut, an artist well-known for his designs for woodcut book illustrations. Many of these were published by Dürer's godfather, Anton Koberger. The earliest book illustrations attributed to Dürer date from the period of his apprenticeship and the succeeding *Wanderjahre* when he designed illustrations for books published at Basel, Freiburg and Strassburg. Following his return from Italy in 1495, he turned naturally to book illustration as a means of disseminating his work. The immediate outcome was the *Apocalypse*, a book which, according to its colophon, was printed at Nuremberg by Albrecht Dürer, painter [in the] year of our Lord 1498. The book exists in two versions, one with a Latin text from the Vulgate of St. Jerome, the other with the German text from Koberger's 1483 Bible. The type used was also designed by Koberger. Copies of both versions are in the Hofer bequest, the German version with the woodcuts trimmed and matted, the Latin version in an exemplar with magnificent hand-coloring. It has even been suggested that the coloring of this copy may have been ordered by Dürer himself, since it differs from the conventional coloring of Nuremberg at this time.

A second Latin edition of the *Apocalypse* was issued in 1511, with the addition of a cut of St. John with the Virgin and Child on the title-page. A copy of this second edition was a previous gift. In the same year, Dürer issued two additional series on a scale similar to that of the *Apocalypse*: the *Great Passion* and the *Life of the Virgin*, both of which were also previous gifts. Although many of the blocks had been cut and printed separately much earlier, 1511 marked their first appearance with a text. These "Three Great Books" of Albrecht Dürer, through their monumentality and sheer artistic quality, look ahead four centuries to modern *livres de peintre*.

In an altogether different vein, Dürer, a true Renaissance man, also wrote and illustrated treatises on

No. 18. Albrecht Dürer, "The Four Horsemen of the Apocalypse." Illustration from *Apocalypsis cum Figuris*.

human proportion, geometry and fortification. Of these, only *Underweysung der Messung* (1525) was published in the artist's lifetime. Two copies of variant issues are in the Department of Printing and Graphic Arts, one a previous gift of Philip Hofer, the other the gift of William Bentinck-Smith. *Etliche Unterricht zu Befestigung der Stett* (bequest) was published in 1527, *Vier Bücher von Menchlicher Proportion* (previous gift) in 1528. The Hofer copy of the *Befestigung* includes the rare folding cut of the siege. Taken together, these three books constitute a major contribution to scientific thought in Northern Europe. Dürer was encouraged in these pursuits by his friend and patron, the humanist scholar Willibald Pirckheimer. A book from Pirckheimer's library, a Latin Aesop printed at Venice by Aldus Manutius in 1505 (previous gift) contains painted decorations which may be by Dürer himself.

Numerous previous gifts combined with the important items in the bequest give the Department of Printing and Graphic Arts an almost complete collection of books illustrated by Dürer. Dürer's contemporaries Hans Sebald Beham, Hans Burgkmair, Lucas Cranach, Hans Baldung Grien, Hans Schäufelein and Wolf Traut are also all well-represented; Hans Weiditz is represented in more than eighty books. Indeed, although the bequest contains only about a dozen sixteenth-century German books, this area is one of the richest in the Hofer collection, by far the greatest number of such books having been given previously, in 1941 and in 1975.

N.F.

REF   Goff J-226; Bartsch 60–75; Joseph Meder, *Dürer-Katalog: Ein Handbuch über Albrecht Dürers Stiche, Radierungen, Holzschnitte* (Vienna, 1932), X2, no. 164–178; Erwin Panofsky, *Albrecht Dürer* (Princeton, 1943), no. 280–295; Museum of Fine Arts, *Albrecht Dürer, Master Printmaker* (Boston, 1971), no. 28–46; Hind, II, 379–388; Philip Hofer, "The Three Great Books of Albrecht Dürer," *Bulletin of the New York Public Library*, XXXV (1931), 459–464; Philip Hofer, "A Newly Discovered Book with Painted Decorations from Willibald Pirckheimer's Library," *Harvard Library Bulletin*, I (1947), 66–75.

19 ❧ HORAE B.M.V.
Hore intemerate Virginis Marie secu[n]dum vsum Romanu[m]
[Paris] Thielman Kerver for Guillaume Eustache [1499?]

Illuminated copy on vellum.

21 x 14 cm. 18th-century red morocco, gilt pointillé borders, decorated gilt endpapers.

FIFTEENTH-CENTURY Paris printers who reproduced in type, woodblock, and metalcut the *Horae Beatissimae Mariae Virginis*, the Hours of the Virgin Mary, were concerned with the transition not simply from manuscript to printed book but from illuminated manuscript to illustrated and decorated printed book. In its traditional manuscript form, the Book of Hours, intended for private devotions, was elegantly written, delicately painted, and ornamented with generous application of gold. Among printed Books of Hours, the link to the manuscript is strongest in copies such as this Hofer copy, printed on vellum instead of paper and hand-painted. The painting of initial letters is common in fifteenth- and sixteenth-century vellum copies of Books of Hours. Unusual in the Hofer copy is the extent of the additional ornamentation—paragraph marks and strips filling out the short lines of text, gold on alternating red and blue ground. Special care was taken with the floral initials on each page containing an illustration. Capital letters are highlighted in yellow, a subtle touch which further animates the page. Text lines and margins are hand-ruled in red.

The phenomenal success of the Paris trade in printed Books of Hours can be measured in the Hofer collection in examples of the work of printers and publishers who sustained and perfected the particular art of the Book of Hours in the fifteenth and sixteenth centuries, Antoine Vérard, Philippe Pigouchet, Simon Vostre, Thielman Kerver and his wife Yolande Bonhomme and son the younger Thielman, Simon de Colines, and Geoffroy Tory. Thielman Kerver is the printer at the center of the Paris trade who responded most sensitively to the developing national styles in printed images. For the illustration of the Book of Hours, the printer inherited a fixed sequence of subjects determined in the manuscript. Kerver began printing with blocks derivative of the stock of other printers, but this edition, coming at the end of the fifteenth century,

No. 19. *Hore intemerate Virginis Marie.*

displays eighteen large illustrations (including one repeated block) newly designed. From scene to scene, Kerver's anonymous artist has created crowds of expressive figures in richly ornamented settings.

This Kerver volume, marking the height of achievement in the fifteenth-century style, finds its true counterpart in the sixteenth-century portion of the Hofer collection in the fully illuminated copy of the 1525 Hours redesigned by Geoffroy Tory in the Italianate manner. On another level of comparison, the consistent architectural framework of the Kerver illustrations—the decorated arch through which each scene is viewed and the miniature arches on the border scenes and figures of saints present in the text—reflects the French fascination with architectural detail and anticipates in the Hofer collection the splendid sixteenth-century folios illustrating architectural theory and practice.

R.M.

REF This edition is not recorded in the standard sources. The Introduction to the Horae B.M.V. section of the Hofer French catalogue contains a bibliography relevant to the Kerver edition and the Kerver illustrations are charted there together with those in all other editions at Harvard; see Harvard College Library, Department of Printing and Graphic Arts, Catalogue of Books and Manuscripts, Part I: *French 16th Century Books* by Ruth Mortimer (Cambridge, 1964), II, 363–378.

20 ❦ MARCO POLO, 1254–1323?
Ho livro de Marco Paulo
Lisbon, Valentim Fernandes, 1502

Woodcut on title-page, woodcut initials.

28.5 x 19 cm. Red morocco, gilt fillets and corner pieces, by Francis Bedford. Bookplates of the Huth Library and John Arthur Brooke.

VALENTIM FERNANDES printed the *Livro de Marco Paulo* in Lisbon where he was active from 1495 to 1518. Little is known of Fernandes before his Lisbon years except for his Moravian origins which he claimed proudly in his colophons. By the time of the publication of the *Marco Paulo* in 1502, Fernandes was recognized as the most prominent printer in Lisbon. The *Marco Paulo* is one of the best examples of Fernandes's talents as a skillful editor and shrewd entrepreneur. It shows his personal interest in the Portuguese discoveries of the time and his awareness of the general public's intense curiosity about the navigators and their tales. The publication of the *Marco Paulo* came only two years after Vasco da Gama's triumphant return from India. Fernandes wanted to give his readers a description of the geography, natural resources, population and mores of the distant lands to which the Portuguese navigators had just discovered the maritime route.

The account of Marco Polo's voyage to Asia in the late thirteenth century was translated anonymously into Portuguese from the Latin version prepared in Marco Polo's lifetime by Francesco Pipino, a Dominican friar from Bologna. This account constitutes the core text of the book. Fernandes personally added and translated two other texts by Italian travelers: an account by Poggio Bracciolini of Niccolò dei Conti's journey to India at the beginning of the fifteenth century and a letter by the Genoese Girolamo di S. Stefano describing his journey with his companion, Girolamo Adorno, to the East Indies in the 1490s.

In anticipation of a strong market for the *Marco Paulo*, and perhaps out of fear of competition from João Pedro Bonhomini de Cremona, a gifted newcomer on the Lisbon printing scene, Fernandes sought and obtained a royal privilege for the *Marco Paulo*, the second of its kind in Portugal. The work is printed in the generously spaced and leaded round Gothic type favored by the Peninsula, using two of the three fonts of Sevillan origin which constituted Fernandes's basic stock. The woodcut ornaments were executed locally, but for the most part after German models such as the large capitals copied after those of Peter Wagner of Nuremberg.

Previously in the library of Alfred H. Huth, John Arthur Brooke and Sir Leicester Harmsworth, Philip Hofer's copy is one of only five extant copies of Fernandes's *Marco Paulo*, and the only one on this continent. Previous Hofer gifts are listed in Anninger, *Spanish and Portuguese 16th Century Books in the Department of Printing and Graphic Arts* (Cambridge, 1985). Early Spanish books are discussed in No. 14.

A.A.

No. 20. Title-page of *Ho livro de Marco Paulo*.

REF   Brunet, III, col. 1406; Antonio Joaquim Anselmo, *Bibliografia das obras impressas em Portugal no século XVI* (Lisbon, 1926), no. 551; Biblioteca Nacional, Lisbon, *Reimpressoes II. Marco Paulo, com introduçao e índices por Francisco Maria Esteves Pereira* (Lisbon, 1922); Konrad Burger, *Die Drucker und Verleger in Spanien und Portugal von 1501–1536* (Leipzig, 1913), p. 37; Manuel, King of Portugal, *Early Portuguese Books 1489–1600 in the Library of His Majesty* (London, 1929–1935), no. 8; José V. de Pina Martins, "Para a história da Cultura Portuguesa do Renascimento: a iconografia do livro impresso em Portugal no tempo de Dürer," *Arquivos do Centro Cultural Portugues* (Paris, 1972) v, 143–44; F.J.A. Norton, *A Descriptive Catalogue of Printing in Spain and Portugal, 1501–1520* (Cambridge, 1978), P3; Pedro Salvá y Mallén, *Catálogo de la Biblioteca de [Vicente] Sálva* (Valencia, 1872), no. 3278.

21   PANEGYRIC TO SULEIMAN THE MAGNIFICENT
Venice? 1520–1530?

Manuscript on vellum; 10 leaves. Italic hand. Illuminated borders in gold and color.

19 x 13 cm. 19th-century Italian red calf, gilt and blind-tooled. MS Typ 145.

VENICE and the Ottoman Empire were traditional enemies in the eastern Mediterranean, and the conquests of Suleiman the Magnificent (1520–1566) marked the beginning of the decline of Venetian power. In an attempt to negotiate, Venice sent numerous missions to Constantinople, and it is probable that this little manuscript was designed as a peace offering. It recounts Suleiman's early victories, including Belgrade in 1521, Rhodes in 1522, and Hungary in 1526. It also refers to earlier Turkish heroes and conquests in the Mediterranean and the Aegean. The only Venetian mentioned is Andrea Gritti, who negotiated peace with Bayezid, Suleiman's grandfather, in the first decade of the century. This suggests that the manuscript may have been executed while Gritti was Doge (1523–1538), at a time when his peace efforts were intensified.

With its richly decorated pages, the panegyric was designed as a special gift for an imperial ruler versed in the arts and a great patron of Islamic calligraphy and illumination. The text is written on pages that give the illusion of scrolls with curling tabs, which are set against a gold ground decorated with birds, fish, insects, animals, fruit, flowers, and jewels. Cameos in grisaille, rose, and blue picture scenes from the life of the sultan and his ancestors. Each opening is essentially symmetrical with slight variations in detail. This illusionistic treatment of the page in the Italian Renaissance manuscript may be seen in a previous Hofer gift in memory of his classmate, Thomas S. Lamont: a large Ferrarese Breviary of the late fifteenth century (MS Typ 219) with bold juxtapositions of *trompe l'oeil* leaves of torn vellum and hovering insects set against decorated portals.

The italic hand of the Suleiman manuscript has been a challenge to expert opinion. In 1960 Alfred Fairbank and Berthold Wolpe attributed it to the Spanish-born Ferdinando Ruano, an opinion Fairbank revised in 1978 in supporting Vera Law's attribution to the more renowned Ludovico degli Arrighi (Vicentino). Law further suggested a comparison of the decoration of this manuscript with a Book of Hours in the Bodleian Library made ca. 1530–1538 for Eleanora Gonzaga, wife of Duke Francesco Maria I of Urbino (MS Douce 29), attributed by Fairbank to Arrighi and with miniatures, borders, and initials by Vincenzo Raimondi (Raymond of Lodève).

The study of Arrighi, the Vatican chancery scribe, publisher, printer, type designer, and author of the first printed handwriting manual, owes much to Stanley Morison, James Wardrop, Berthold Wolpe, Fairbank, and Law, and a dozen manuscripts have now been attributed to Arrighi. A native of Vicenza, he was trained in Venice before assuming his duties in Rome; for a brief time he returned to Venice, where his second book was published in 1523. All records of his activity cease in 1527, and he is presumed to have been a victim of the sack of Rome.

Hofer's interest in Arrighi is attested to by six printed manuals by this writing master in the bequest. There is the first issue of the first edition of his 1522 *La operina da imparare di scrivere littera cancellarescha*, printed from woodblocks cut by Ugo da Carpi, along with the second edition of 1525 and the third of 1532; the first edition of his second book, *Il modo de temperare le penne* of 1523; and the 1532 and 1533 Venice editions combining both the first and second treatises in a single volume, *Regola da imparare scrivere . . . Et il modo di temperare le penne*. In 1954 Hofer sponsored the publication in the Harvard College

No. 21. Panegyric to Suleiman the Magnificent. Italic script attributed to Arrighi.

Library-Newberry Library series, *Studies in the History of Calligraphy*, of John Howard Benson's *The First Writing Book: An English Translation & Facsimile Text of Arrighi's Operina* (see No. 96). Arrighi the publisher, printer, and type designer is represented in a number of sixteenth-century Italian books among previous gifts (see index of printers and publishers in Mortimer). Among these is *Epistola de le lettere nuovamente aggiunte ne la lingua italiana* (1524), by Gian Giorgio Trissino, Arrighi's Vicenzan patron with a special interest in letters and orthography. The modern typographic influence of Arrighi is demonstrated in *The Calligraphic Models of Ludovico degli Arrighi*, a facsimile with introduction by Stanley Morison printed in Frederic Warde's Arrighi type, a publication directed by Warde and printed by Giovanni Mardersteig at the Officina Bodoni in Montagnola di Lugano (see No. 99), but with a Paris imprint, 1926.

E.M.G.

REF   Faye and Bond, 263; *Illuminated and Calligraphic Manuscripts*, no. 131; Alfred Fairbank and Berthold Wolpe, *Renaissance Handwriting* (London [1960]), no. 43; Alfred Fairbank, "Another Arrighi Manuscript, Douce 29," *The Book Collector*, XXIII (1974), 551–552; Vera Law, "Two More Arrighi Manuscripts Discovered," *The Book Collector*, XXVII (1978), 368–379; Philip Hofer, "Variant Issues of the First Edition of Ludovico Arrighi Vicentino's Operina," *Harvard Library Bulletin*, XIV (1960), 334–342.

22 DESIDERIUS ERASMUS, d. 1536
Precatio Dominica in Septem Portiones Distributa
Basel, Johann Froben, 1524
Metal cuts after HANS HOLBEIN THE YOUNGER, 1497–1543

15.5 x 10 cm. Dark blue morocco, gilt; edges gilt.

THE *PRECATIO DOMINICA* of Erasmus was first printed by Johann Froben in Basel late in 1523 without illustrations. The present edition, also by Froben, appeared early in 1524 with eight magnificently composed illustrations cut on metal by the unidentified monogrammist "CV" after designs by Hans Holbein the Younger. They rank among his most impressive productions. Their dark tone and often flickering light are unusual compared with the brightness one associates with Holbein's compositions, but there can be no doubt that they reflect a facet of the artist's genius, perhaps helped by the nature of the medium itself, which allows a more concentrated cutting than wood. The "CV" signature of the cutter has been mistaken for the monogram of Urs Graf, but the style of these illustrations is very different from the work of that artist. The same plates were used by Johann Bebel of Basel for another edition of this work published in the summer of 1524, and that is also in the Hofer collection.

Hans Holbein was a favorite object of Philip Hofer's collecting interest, and indeed Hofer was on one occasion instrumental in adding a hitherto unrecognized work to the Holbein canon, a very fine woodcut border used for a rare edition of Philipp Melanchthon's *Loci communes* printed at Antwerp in 1536. One of Holbein's best-known series of designs, the Dance of Death, is represented in the Hofer collection by nine different editions in several languages; his Old Testament cuts are also present in several editions. His famous roundel portrait of Erasmus occurs in the 1533 Basel edition of the *Adagia*. On the Hofer shelves are also the *Missale speciale* of 1521, while a great many works containing title-page borders and initials by Holbein are interspersed throughout the sixteenth-century collections in the Department of Printing and Graphic Arts. Formerly in the Hofer collection was Holbein's color roundel drawing of Tantalus, from which Rudolph Ruzicka made a wood-engraved bookplate for Hofer (see No. 95).

Bound with *Precatio Dominica* is the first edition of another short work of Erasmus, his *Virginis Matris apvd Lavretvm cultae liturgia* (Basel, Froben, May 1525).

J.E.W.

REF   Campbell Dodgson, "The Engravers on Metal after Holbein," *Burlington Magazine*, LXXXIII (1943), 282–285; Hans Reinhardt, "Einige Bemerkungen zum graphischen Werk Hans Holbeins des Jüngeren," *Zeitschrift für Archäologie und Kunstgeschichte*, XXXIV (1977), 229–260; James E. Walsh and Philip Hofer, "A New Holbein Attribution," *Harvard Library Bulletin*, XXXIII (1975), 42–48; Hans Reinhardt, "Ein unbekannter Holzschnitt Hans Holbeins d. J. von 1536 und Holbeins Melanchthon-Bildnis," *Zeitschrift für Archäologie und Kunstgeschichte*, XXXII (1975), 135–140.

PRECATIO DOMINICA

gnitati gratias agimus, qui per filium tuum ac spiritū
sanctum tantis beneficijs nos dignaris in gloriam san
ctissimi tui nomnis perennem. Amen.

No. 22. Hans Holbein. Illustration from Erasmus, *Precatio Dominica*.

23   VESPASIANO AMPHIAREO, 1501–1563
Writing Manual
Italy (Venice?), ca. 1548

Manuscript on vellum; 19 leaves. Examples of handwriting in brown and red ink.
16 x 22 cm. Half calf, marbled boards. MS Typ 166.

SO INFLUENTIAL and imitated was the handwriting developed in the papal chancery that in the sixteenth century manuals of instruction, often by the Roman scribes, were printed in large numbers. The first was Ludovico degli Arrighi's *La operina da imparare di scrivere littera cancellarescha* of 1522, followed by his *Il modo de temperare le penne* of 1523 (see No. 21). The books were printed from woodblocks on which the letters were first drawn in reverse, and the role of the block cutter was crucial, for on his skills depended the quality of the model. A variety of hands was presented, many of them very demanding of the student. Decoration and fancy often crept in, and the simple italic was succeeded by more mannered hands. By the end of the century, the pages were engraved rather than woodcut.

A Franciscan and a native of Ferrara, Vespasiano Amphiareo had a long career as a writing master in Venice. He exercised considerable influence through his manual, *Uno novo modo d'insegnar a scrivere* (Venice, 1548), entitled *Opera . . . nella quale si insegna a scrivere varie sorti di lettere* in later editions, which continued to appear till the end of the century. This manuscript, signed on f.2^r and 8^r, was probably executed just before the publication of the manual, since on f.5^v of the manuscript, Amphiareo refers to the projected book ("molto occupato nella stampa che io fatto stampare un mia opereta de imparere a scrivere...."). The manuscript makes an interesting comparison with the printed manual (1554 and four subsequent editions in the Hofer collection), for a number of the same writing styles are illustrated in each, including the *lettera bastarda del frate* in which Amphiareo attempted to combine elements of the chancery and mercantile forms. In the manuscript, the examples are written in an ink now brown in color, with elaborate red or brown initials and an occasional blue capital. It contains none of the fanciful letters of the printed manual, such as the tree trunk and historiated letters, but a number of lively variations on basic forms. Each opening in both manuscript and printed book is a double page; in both cases the format is oblong, a common shape for this genre.

Amphiareo's manuscripts are uncommon, and the Department of Printing and Graphic Arts is fortunate to have another signed example (MS Typ 13), the gift of Mrs. Charles B. Perkins, a little address to one Luca, written in a hand that varies from italic to upright and enlivened with red and blue initials. Two other Italian manuscript handwriting manuals of this period in the Hofer collection are by Bernardo Spina of Perugia (MS Typ 167) and by Bernardo Cataneo (MS Typ 246), the latter a gift from Philip Hofer to his son and, in 1981, a gift to the Library from Dr. Myron A. Hofer. It was reproduced in facsimile, with an introduction by Stephen Harvard, as no. 8 in the Harvard College Library-Newberry Library series, *Studies in the History of Calligraphy*, published in association with Taplinger. Other manuscripts in the hands of Italian scribes of this period are Onosander signed by Hippolytus of Luna (No. 12), Quintus Curtius, signed by Laurenziano Leone (MS Typ 137), and a Book of Hours attributed to Bartolomeo San Vito (MS Typ 104).

The Hofer bequest contains about 175 printed writing manuals, in addition to some 200 previous gifts, ranging from the sixteenth to the twentieth century. Of this group, about 35 are from Italy in the sixteenth century. They include the major masters, beginning with Arrighi. The range of the Italian examples, on which the rest of Europe depended in developing its own scribal conventions, may be studied in Sigismondo Fanti, *Theorica et pratica . . . de modo scribendi* (Venice, 1514) and *Thesauro de scrittori* (Rome, 1535); Giovanni Antonio Tagliente, *Libro maistrevole* (Venice, 1524) and *Lo presente libro* (Rome, 1525); Giovanni Battista Palatino, *Libro nuovo d'imparare a scrivere* (Rome, 1540); Ferdinando Ruano, *Sette alphabeti di varie lettere* (Rome, 1554); Giovanni Francesco Cresci, *Il perfetto scrittore* (Rome, 1570) and *Essemplare di più sorti lettere* (Venice, 1578); Conretto da Monte Regalo, *Un novo et facil modo d'imparar' a scrivere* (Venice, 1576); Giuliantonio Hercolani, *Essemplare utile di tutte le sorti di l're cancellaresche* (Bologna, 1571); Lodovico Curione, *Lanotomia delle cancellaresche corsive* (Rome, 1588) and *Il teatro delle cancellaresche corsive* (Rome, 1593); Simone Verovio, *Issemplare di lettere cancellaresche corsive* (Rome, 1593); and Marco Antonio de Rossi, *Giardino de scrittori* (Rome, 1598).

In domino Confido quomodo dicius aīe

Jorgio di Bernadino altouiti e Carlo strozi e Compagni di londra demo dar
questo di xxviiij di Ott. Duc. Cinquecento Cinquanta cinq̃ doro dittalia
gli sono p la valuta di tanti e medsmi hauuti questo di sopdetto e qual di
nazi sono da pagassi p tutto nouembre posmo che uiene' come apre al
libro D. a carte. 1. Et piu demo dare questo di sopradetto Ducati Cento
uintiquatro doro dit quali sono p tanti panni monachini hauuti gr =

Lettera cancellarescha e bastarda

A A a a B b b b C C c D D d
E E e e F F f f G H H h I i j
K k l l Ll M m̃ m N n O o P p Q q R r S s
R s S ss T T t V v v Y y Z z ʒ

No. 23. Vespasiano Amphiareo. Autograph manuscript writing manual.

The sixteenth century writing book in other parts of Europe is represented by a number of distinguished masters, including Jean de Beauchesne (No. 27), Guillaume Le Gagneur, Wolfgang Fugger, Urbanus Wyss, Robert Granjon, Jodocus Hondius, Clément Perret, Francisco Lucas, Pedro de Mandariaga, and Juan de Yciar.

E.M.G.

REF   A.F. Johnson, "A Catalogue of Italian Writing-Books of the Sixteenth Century," *Signature*, n.s. 10 (1950), 34–36; A.S. Osley, *Scribes and Sources* (Boston [1980]), p. 98–104; James Wardrop, "Six Italian Manuscripts in the Department of Graphic Arts," *Harvard Library Bulletin*, VII (1953), 224; *Two Thousand Years of Calligraphy*, no. 68.

24   JAN STEPHAN VAN CALCAR, 1499–1546/1550, attributed to
Standing Écorché Male Figure
Northern Italy, mid-16th century

Pen and brown ink drawing over black chalk on cream antique laid paper.

43.7 x 23.9 cm. Formerly in the collection of Comte de Robiano? (Inscribed on verso "259/C. de R.")

REPRESENTATIVE of Philip Hofer's intense interest in all aspects of book production is the large number of drawn studies for book illustrations he collected over many years. Some fifty of these are illustrated and discussed in Becker's 1980 catalogue, *Drawings for Book Illustration—the Hofer Collection*. That publication further includes a checklist of the entire group of some 1,500 drawings bequeathed by his wife Frances to the Library in 1978. Hofer retained several albums (see No. 42, 48 and 84) and single drawings of particular interest which are included in his own bequest.

As book illustrations most often involved a collaborative effort, the determination of a drawing's place in the creative process can at times be complex and stimulating. Such a case is the sheet exhibited here, which was acquired by Hofer as a study related to the famed series of anatomical woodcuts for Andreas Vesalius, *De humani corporis fabrica libri septem*, published in Basel in 1543. It was a revolutionary book for both anatomists and artists, and is the ultimate source for modern anatomical studies. In addition, it physically comprises one of the most handsome examples of Renaissance book production and illustration.

The very fame and influence of the *Fabrica* illustrations have served to stimulate a lively search for their artistic sources and manufacture. Most scholars attribute the primary artistic collaboration with Vesalius to Jan Stephan van Calcar, a Netherlandish artist who had worked in Titian's studio. None of the woodcuts in the *Fabrica* is signed, nor does Vesalius mention his collaborators in his text. However, Jan Stephan had signed the blocks for an earlier set of six anatomical woodcuts issued by Vesalius in 1538, the *Tabulae anatomicae sex*, and Giorgio Vasari mentioned several times in his *Vite* that Stephan was the draftsman for the more sophisticated *Fabrica* illustrations. Recently, Konrad Oberhuber has ventured that the Hofer sheet was indeed executed by a northern artist within Titian's immediate influence, therefore bringing it into the right place at the right time, for Jan Stephan's period of study in Titian's studio corresponded to that of the execution in Venice of the woodcuts. There are weaknesses of the pen draughtsmanship in the Hofer sheet, however, and its specific authorship and relation to the *Fabrica* woodcuts are in the end difficult to prove, since it does not relate directly in pose to any of the illustrations.

Hofer's interest in anatomical subjects was very strong, and he gathered a sizable number of such illustrated books. One cannot help but relate them to his enthusiasm for Dance of Death subjects, as many anatomical illustrations are graphic reminders of the vanity and frailty of human life. Among previous gifts of Vesalian texts are the first edition of the *Fabrica* itself, the second Basel edition of 1555, the London Geminus version of 1545 (and the Nuremberg 1551 and Paris 1565 copies of that), the Venice 1568 edition, and the Juan de Valverde engraved versions of the plates issued in Rome in 1560 (the latter with a macabre title page). Included in his bequest are the Latin and German editions bound together of the 1543 *Epitome*, issued by Vesalius as a digest of the most significant plates from the *Fabrica*, plus two woodcuts of the "ideal" nude woman and man. Numerous volumes of post-Vesalian anatomical illustration given by Hofer include Giulio Casserio's *De Vocis Auditusque Organis* (Ferrara, 1600), with its famous engraved title-page

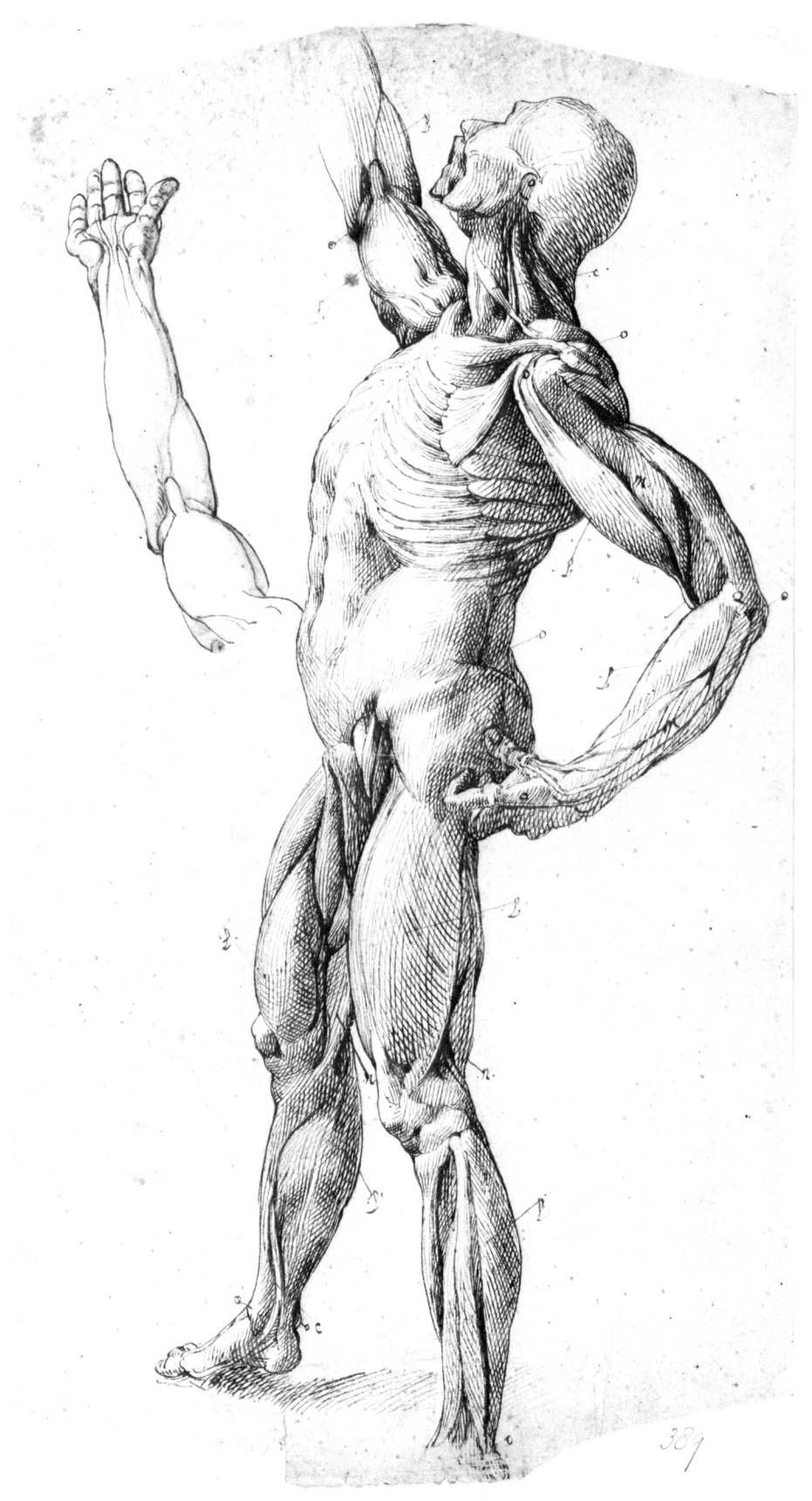

No. 24. Attributed to Jan Stephan van Calcar. Standing écorché male figure.

swarming with human and animal skeletons; the same author's *Tabulae anatomicae* (Venice, 1627); Govert Bidloo's *Ontleding des menschelyken Lichams* (Amsterdam, 1690); Jan L'Admiral's *Anatomische voorwerpen* (Leiden, 1741?); and several treatisees illustrated with color mezzotints by Jacques-Fabien Gautier d'Agoty. Included in the bequest is Jacques Gamelin's *Nouveau recueil d'ostéologie et de myologie* (Toulouse, 1779) with several disquieting Dance of Death prints among the straightforward anatomical depictions.

D.P.B.

REF David Rosand and Michelangelo Muraro, *Titian and the Venetian Woodcut* (Washington, D.C., the National Gallery of Art, 1976), p. 211–215; M. Kemp. "A Drawing for the *Fabrica*; and some thoughts upon the Vesalian Musclemen," *Medical History*, XIV (1970), 277–288.

25 ❧ CHRISTIANAE JUVENTUTIS CREPUNDIA
Zürich, Christoph Froschauer, 1559

Title-page with woodcut border, printed in red and black.

15.9 x 10.2 cm. Vellum wrappers.

CHRISTIANAE JUVENTUTIS CREPUNDIA is one of twenty sixteenth-century Swiss books included in the Hofer bequest. An early children's book, it is a great rarity. The title-page, somewhat crudely printed in red and black, may be the work of Heinrich Vogtherr (1490–1556), who contributed designs to several Froschauer publications. This colorful title-page with its lively representation of the seven virtues is the only thing about the book likely to appeal to young readers. The text, which is in Latin, is entirely made up of prayers and scripture lessons. The first page, which combines an alphabet in large type with the text of the Lord's Prayer, exactly prefigures the layout that would be used for hornbooks well into the nineteenth century.

Most of Philip Hofer's Swiss sixteenth-century books were given to the Department of Printing and Graphic Arts as long ago as 1941. Another large group was added in 1977. Unfortunately, no printed catalogue comparable to Ruth Mortimer's two catalogues of French and Italian sixteenth-century books (Cambridge, 1964 and 1974) or Anne Anniger's catalogue of Spanish and Portuguese sixteenth-century books (Cambridge, 1985) exists to chronicle the riches of this area of the collection. The sixteenth century was the great age of Swiss printing, due in part to the impact of the Reformation. While Protestant refugees streamed across the borders fleeing religious persecution, Swiss presses issued vernacular editions of the Bible and other books that were banned or restricted elsewhere. Christoph Froschauer set up his press in Zürich in 1521. His many religious publications were of less interest to Hofer than his illustrated books, including the 1548 Swiss Chronicle of Hans Stumpf, which contains an early illustration of a printing press (previous gift). In Basel, Johann Froben printed the works of Erasmus with decorations by Urs Graf and Hans Holbein (see No. 22); Johann Oporin, who had worked for a while as a corrector for Froben, was the publisher of Vesalius's Anatomy (see No. 24). Other Basel printers included Michael Isengrin, the publisher of Fuchs' Herbal and Agricola's *De re metallica* (both previous gifts) and Adam and Heinrich Petri, the latter best known as the printer of the Cosmography of Sebastian Münster (several editions; previous gifts). In Geneva, the Protestant cause was served by Robert Estienne, who arrived from Paris in 1550. Although any overview of the period is necessarily dominated by great names such as Froben, Froschauer and Estienne, it is salutary to remember that at one time in the sixteenth century more than 300 printers and booksellers were active in Geneva alone. The diversity—as well as the quality—of Swiss printing of this period is well-represented by previous Hofer gifts.

N.F.

REF Edmund Camillo Rudolphi, *Die Buchdrucker-Familie Froschauer in Zürich, 1521–1595* (Nieuwkoop, 1963), no. 503; Paul Leemann-Van Elck, *Die Offizin Froschauer* (Zürich and Leipzig, 1940); Joachim Staedtke, *Anfänge und Erste Blütezeit des Züricher Buchdrucks* (Zürich [1965]); F.C. Lonchamp, *Manuel du Bibliophile Suisse* (Paris and Lausanne, 1922).

No. 25. Title-page of *Christianae Juventutis Crepundia*.

26   MANUEL PHILE, ca. 1275 – ca. 1340
De Animalium Proprietate
Paris? 1565

Manuscript on paper. Greek script, by Angelo Vergezio. 3 illuminated headbands and 106 illustrations in gouache and gold, possibly by Vergezio's daughter.

23.5 x 16.5 cm. Contemporary French dark green morocco, gilt and inlaid with red morocco; central medallions replaced with plain vellum. Formerly in the collection of A. Chester Beatty (MS.Gr. 10); presented by Mrs. Beatty to Philip Hofer. MS Typ 222.

THE MANUSCRIPT of Manuel Phile's *De Animalium Proprietate* in the Philip Hofer bequest (MS Typ 222) was written by Angelo Vergezio, the most famous Greek scribe of the sixteenth century. Vergezio was summoned to France in 1538 by François I, and continued to serve the Valois kings for the next thirty years. During this period he produced at least nine copies of the Manuel Phile. Besides the Hofer copy, six similar illuminated copies survive in the Bodleian, Vatican and British Libraries, the Bibliothèque Sainte-Geneviève and the Preussische Staatsbibliothek. The fact that so many different copies are known suggests that there was a considerable demand for such manuscripts in sixteenth-century France, and that even after the invention of printing, they continued to be sought after and collected.

Manuel Phile's *De Animalium Proprietate* is yet another example of Hofer's interest in bestiaries and natural histories (see No. 6 and 56). The text is based on the *De Animalium Natura* of Aelian and includes descriptions of many mythical creatures, including a manticore (a lionlike creature with a human face), two kinds of unicorn, and a dragon. The depictions of actual animals, however, are even more remarkable in their way than these depictions of prodigies. They are touched with a realism and a precision which suggest direct observation on the part of the artist. Several of the birds might have served as models for Bewick (see No. 58) and even such exotics as the lion and the elephant are portrayed with an accuracy that would rarely be surpassed before the nineteenth century. A persistent tradition of doubtful origin identifies the artist of these illustrations as the scribe's daughter.

Vergezio's script with its elaborate flourishes and ligatures served as the basis for the Greek types cut for Robert Estienne by Claude Garamont. The first complete text printed in the first font of these "grecs du roi" was a folio Eusebius, published in 1544, followed by Greek New Testaments in 1546 and 1550 (all previous gifts). The very first appearance of this type, however, was in an *Alphabetum Graecum* of 1543. Although this book is so rare that it was long believed to be a "ghost," a copy was presented to the Department of Printing and Graphic Arts in 1951 by William Bentinck-Smith. Garamont's "grecs du roi" dominated the printing of Greek for more than two centuries before they were abandoned in favor of a simpler and more legible style. They are still admired for their beauty. Hofer's previous gifts to the Houghton Library include many other examples of Greek printing.

At her first meeting with Philip Hofer in London, a few weeks before her death, Mrs. A. Chester Beatty spontaneously presented him with the Manuel Phile manuscript. In the same year, 1952, Hofer presented a fifteenth-century Florentine manuscript of Cicero, *Le questione tuscalane* (MS Typ 69), to the Library in her memory.

N.F.

REF   *Illuminated and Calligraphic Manuscripts*, no. 133: Philip Hofer and G.W. Cottrell Jr., "Angelos Vergecios and the Bestiary of Manuel Phile," *Harvard Library Bulletin*, VIII (1954), 323–339; John W. Bradley, *A Dictionary of Miniaturists, Illuminators, Calligraphers, and Copyists*, III (London, 1889), 373–375.

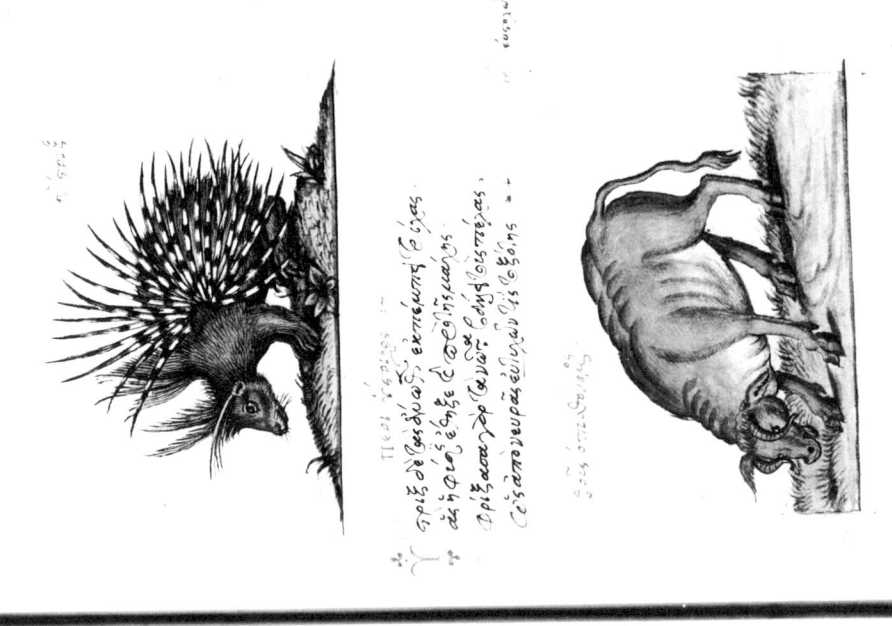

No. 26. Manuel Phile, *De Animalium Proprietate*. Greek script by Angelo Vergezio.

27 ~ JEAN DE BEAUCHESNE, 1528?–1620
Calligraphic Specimen
England (London?), 1575

Pen and black ink on laid paper. 7 different scripts in Latin and French on one folio sheet. Signed and dated in mirror writing: *Johannes de Beau Chesne scribebat A° 1575*.

47.3 x 32.1 cm.

A FRENCH HUGUENOT, Jean de Beauchesne, presumably having apprenticed with the Parisian writing master Pierre Hamon, settled in London in 1565, taking employment as a servant. He undertook work for William Bowyer, the keeper of the Royal Archives at the Tower of London, for whom he wrote a manuscript in 1567. He gave the Elizabethans of England their first native printed writing book, *A Booke containing divers sortes of hands* (London, Thomas Vautroullier, 1570). This book is a small oblong quarto with forty-two specimen alphabets and texts, mainly cut on wood, ranging from formal black letters and their derivatives to Roman capitals and lower case in the italic hand. The three known copies in the British Library, the Pepys Library in Cambridge, and the Plimpton Library at Columbia seem to belong to slightly variant issues.

The Hofer specimen is dated 1575, five years after the publication of this first English writing book. It displays seven scripts, including Gothic, upright Roman and cursive with flourishes and elaboration of two initial letters. It was Beauchesne who gave the Elizabethan cursive hand the name *bastard secretary*, the elegant and legible script known on the continent as *bastarde angloise*. The broadsheet was found by E.P. Goldschmidt of London in a copy of Hartmann Schedel's *Nuremberg Chronicle* (1493) and sold to Hofer in the spring of 1946. Only one other original specimen of Beauchesne's calligraphy is recorded, a copy-book in French and Italian written for Princess Elizabeth, the daughter of James I, in 1610. This was described in 1885 by D.W. Kettle ("Pens, Ink and Paper," Sette of Odd Volumes, *Opuscula*). Its present location is unknown.

Also in the Hofer bequest is a copy of *Le trésor d'escriture*, a book written, designed and published by Beauchesne in 1580, during a stay in Lyons. Stanley Morison considered it one of the finest books of its period. A previous gift was a volume of forty-one decorated initials copied from *A Booke containing divers sortes of hands*. Other near-contemporary items in the bequest include a copy of Jean de Beaugrand, *Panchrestographie, Exemples de toutes les sortes d'escritures* (Paris, 1604), with a dedication to Louis XIII, written in gold on purple-tinted paper by the author's son Jean II de Beaugrand, and *Argumenta in librum psalmorum*, written and illuminated by Esther Inglis Kello in 1606 for Sir Thomas Egerton, Lord Chancellor of England. One of three Esther Inglis manuscripts already in the Department of Printing and Graphic Arts was another previous Hofer gift; the remaining two are from the bequest of Charles Sumner.

P.A.W.

REF *Illuminated and Calligraphic Manuscripts*, no. 135; *Two Thousand Years of Calligraphy*, no. 105; Ambrose Heal, *English Writing Masters* (London, 1931); Anthony G. Petti, *English Literary Hands from Chaucer to Dryden* (Cambridge, 1977); A.S. Osley, ed., *Scribes and Sources, Handbook of the Chancery Hand in the Sixteenth Century, With an Account of John de Beauchesne by Berthold Wolpe* (Boston [1980]), p. 227–240.

Sexta etas mundi   CCLVIIII

**Tres hominis digiti scribunt animusq; laborat,
Scribe qui nescit nullum putat esse laborem.**

Celuy qui n'a d'escrire la science, dit que celuy qui escrit ne labeure,
Trois de l'homme en font l'experience, mesme l'esprit qui traueille a tout heure.

Audite filium disciplinam patris, et attendite vt sciatis prudentiam: Donum bonum
tribuam vobis, legem meam ne derelinquatis. Nam et ego filius fui patris mei tenell?
Et vnigenitus coram matre mea, et docebat me atq; dicebat, Suscipiat verba mea cor
tuum, custodi precepta mea, et viues. Posside sapientiã: posside prudentiam: Ne
obliuiscaris neq; declines a verbis oris mei. Ne dimittas eam et eus todiet te. Sal. Pro.

Omnia tempus habent: z suis spacijs transeunt vniuersa sub celo tempus
nascendi: z tempus moriendi: tempus plantandi z tempus euellendi
quod plantatum est. tempus occidendi et tempus sanandi. tepus
destruendi z tempus edificandi. tempus flendi et tempus ridendi.
tempus plangendi z tempus saltandi. tempus spargendi lapides
et tempus coligendi. tempus amplexandi: z temp' longe fieri z cf.

Bien heureux est celuy qui droictement chemine
A la sentier du Seigneur qui apres mort nous donne
Le vray loyer que Dieu a tous les siens ordonne
Qui purement suyuront sa tressaincte doctrine.

NON IS PENNA, SED VSVS.

Joannes de Beau Chesne scribebat A. 1572.

No. 27. Jean de Beauchesne. Calligraphic specimen.

28 ❧ CHRISTOPHER SAXTON, ca. 1543–ca. 1611
[Atlas of the Counties of England and Wales]
[London, ca. 1590]

34 double-page and one folded maps; engraved frontispiece; double-page with engraved coats of arms and list of cities; letterpress table of contents; all hand-colored.

42.7 x 30.5 cm. Contemporary calf, gold-blocked and tooled, with the name I. Panton within the centerpiece of both covers; his signature, Ioh[ann]es Panton, appears in the upper margin of the frontispiece. Formerly in the collections of Lt.-Col. Walter R. Tyrell, Robert Hoe, Huntington Library (duplicate), John Camp Williams.

A COLORED COPY of Saxton's altas—particularly one in contemporary binding like the present example—ranks today as the handsomest publication of late sixteenth-century England, a true feast for the eyes. It should not be forgotten, however, that the origin and sponsorship of the project came from government circles and from Elizabeth I herself. The purpose of the atlas was not aesthetic but rather to gather and co-ordinate information useful to the government in defending the realm from enemies within and without and undoubtedly in strengthening the central bureaucracy's influence in local affairs. The atlas is the earliest published national survey. Individual maps are dated from 1574 to 1579, and proofs were sent to Lord Burghley, the Lord Treasurer, as the plates were completed. Other copies known to have belonged to government officials are those of Sir Christopher Hatton, member of the Privy Council and ultimately Lord Chancellor, and Sir Francis Walsingham, Secretary of State. The copy of Thomas Seckford, Master of Requests, has not been identified; he was Saxton's patron, and his arms, in addition to the Queen's, appear on each of the maps.

Although Saxton may have been working on a related project by 1570 under John Rudd, a Yorkshire cleric and amateur cartographer, 1574 is the earliest date documenting the government survey. Saxton surely consulted whatever earlier local manuscript maps were available to him in addition to doing a great deal of surveying himself. He was granted a ten-year patent for sale of the maps from 1577, but the definitive issue to which the Hofer copy belongs was not published until ca. 1590, probably by Augustine Ryther, the engraver of five of the maps and also a printseller in London. By this time Saxton was working as a private surveyor on projects involving estate management or disputes of ownership. His plates had an extended life, the last collective issue as an atlas being ca. 1770.

Saxton's maps were conceived of and issued strictly as an atlas, without text throughout their existence. They are mentioned in Holinshed's *Chronicles*, 1577, as partly completed and of use in compiling the description of Britain. Latin descriptions of counties were published in Camden's *Britannia* from 1586, but the first combination of text with a full complement of county maps largely based on Saxton's was the Camden Latin folio of 1607 and the English translation of 1610. Then followed a rash of such editions: Drayton's *Poly-Olbion*, 1612, 1622, and Speed's *Theatre of the Empire of Great Britaine*, 1612, 1616 (editions in English and in Latin), 1627, 1631. The results of Saxton's labor were at last available in a form the reading public could enjoy.

Although maps were never one of Hofer's major interests, a few significant early atlases were acquired because of the great beauty of their illustrations. Besides the Saxton atlas, the Hofer bequest includes French and Latin editions of Abraham Ortelius, *Theatrum orbis terrarum* (Antwerp, 1595 and 1598); the German edition (Antwerp, 1573) and Gerardus Mercator's *Galliae tabulae geographicae* (Duisburg, 1585) were previous gifts. Simon Grynaeus, *Novus orbis regionum* (Basel, 1532) contains a double-page woodcut map by Hans Holbein the Younger, which Hofer described as "probably the most artistically attractive early world map." Both the book (with the map in state "B") and a separate framed copy of the map (in state "A") are in the bequest. In 1976, a facsimile of the Holbein World Map was published as part of the Reproduction Series of the Department of Printing and Graphic Arts. For other books illustrated by Holbein, see No. 22.

K.F.P.

REF   A.M. Hind, *Engraving in England; Part I: the Tudor Period* (Cambridge, 1952), p. 85f.; R.A. Skelton, *County Altases of the Britsh Isles* (London, 1970); Ifor M. Evans and Heather Lawrence, *Christopher Saxton, Elizabethan Map-maker* (Wakefield, West Yorkshire [1979]); Sarah Tyacke and John Huddy, *Christopher Saxton and Tudor Map-making* (London, 1980).

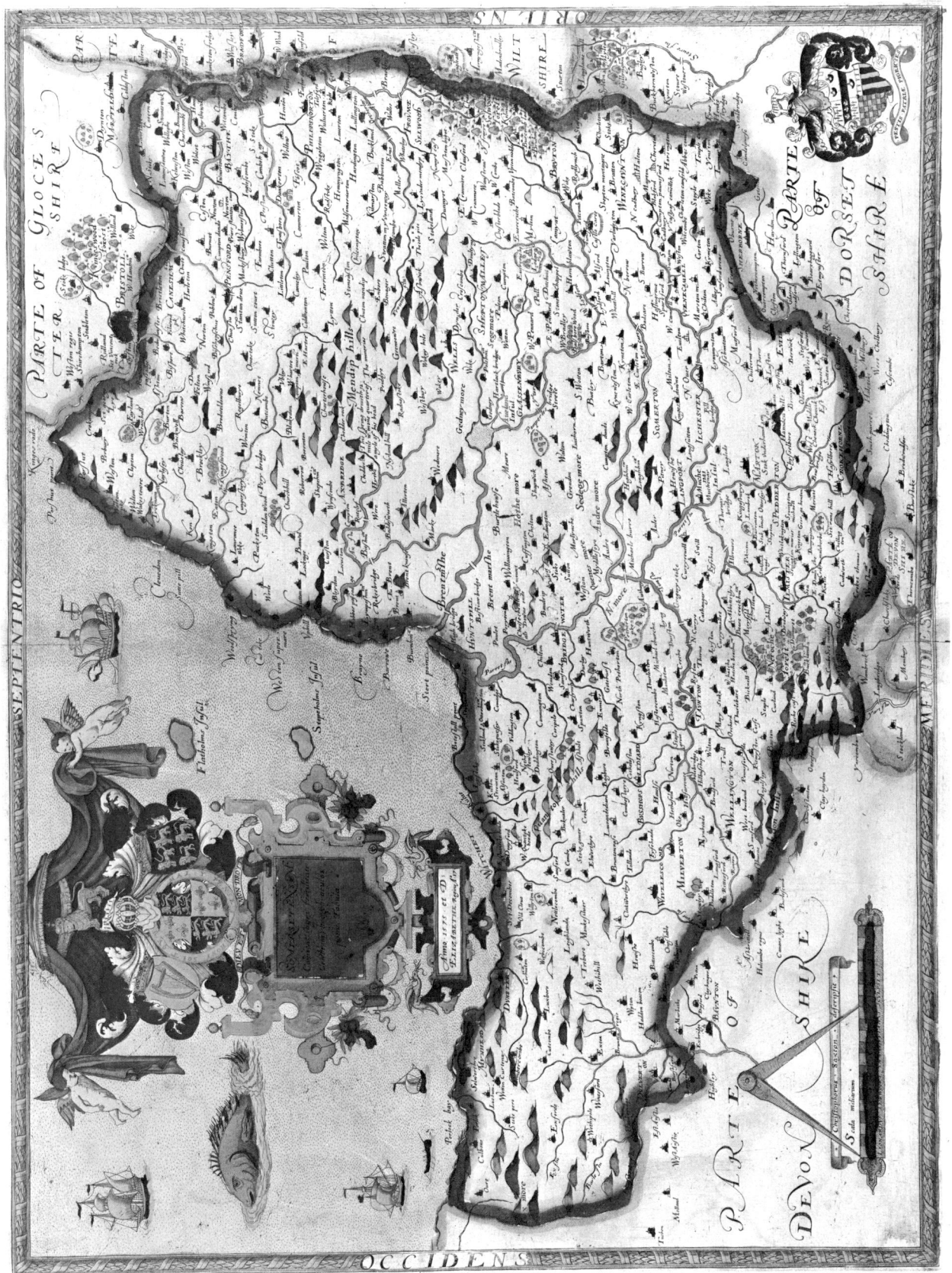

No. 28. Christopher Saxton. Map of Somerset.

29 ❧ BREVIARIUM ROMANUM
Antwerp, Officina Plantiniana, 1614
Intaglio plates after PETER PAUL RUBENS, 1577–1640

Title-page and 10 full-page engravings by Theodore Galle after Rubens.

41.4 x 28 cm. Red morocco, gilt, with the arms of Cardinal Scipione Borghese.

THE 1613 *Missale* and the 1614 *Breviarium* printed at Antwerp by Jan Moretus, the grandson and successor of Christopher Plantin, contain some of the most important religious illustrations of the seventeenth century, all expressly designed for these publications by Peter Paul Rubens. This copy of the *Breviarium* was bound in an Italian imitation of the French fanfare style for Cardinal Scipione Borghese (1576–1633). Borghese, the patron of Bernini and Caravaggio and the builder of the Villa Borghese, was also the librarian of the Vatican and a famous book collector.

Rubens was a close friend of Balthasar, the son of Jan Moretus, and provided many drawings for title-pages and illustrations for books printed by the Plantin Press. Such a close collaboration between a great artist and a great printing house was rare before the twentieth century. The illustrations for the *Missale* and the *Breviarium* were Rubens' most ambitious projects as a book illustrator. Although he contributed only two borders and two large illustrations to the 1613 *Missale*, the title-page and all ten full-page illustrations in the 1614 *Breviarium* are entirely his designs. Later editions, beginning in 1616, combined illustrations from both works. A 1630 edition of the *Missale* in the bequest incorporates the two borders and two illustrations from the 1613 *Missale*, seven illustrations from the 1614 *Breviarium* and one additional illustration, expressly designed for the 1616 edition of the *Breviarium*. Additional ornamental borders were engraved by Theodore Galle after his own designs. The Hofer copy of the 1630 *Missale* was bound in red morocco for Cardinal Franz von Wartenberg, bishop of Regensburg and Osnabruck (1593–1661).

A Rubens drawing for the title-page of Cornelius à Lapide, *Commentaria in Pentateuchum Mosis* (Antwerp, The Heirs of Martin Nutius and Johannes Meursius, 1616) is part of the Frances L. Hofer bequest (Becker no. 1). The Philip Hofer bequest includes several additional books with title-pages or illustrations by Rubens. *Electorum Libri II* (Antwerp, 1608), a book on life in ancient Rome, was written by the artist's brother, the humanist and scholar Philip Rubens. The Hofer copy of Herman Hugo, *Obsidio bredana* (Antwerp, 1626) has a contemporary pink satin binding with the painted arms of Isabella Clara Eugenia, Vice Regent of the Netherlands. Seneca, *Opera Omnia* (Antwerp, 1632; first published in 1615) includes a dramatic portrait of the dying philosopher, based on the statue known as *The African Fisherman*, formerly in the collection of Scipione Borghese and now in the Louvre, Paris. Other books with title-pages or illustrations by Rubens in the bequest include François d'Aguilon, *Opticorum libri sex* (Antwerp, 1613); Agostino Mascardi, *Silvarum libri IV* (Antwerp, 1622); Maciej Kazimierz Sarbievski, *Lyricorum libri IV* (Antwerp, 1632); Maffeo Barberini (Pope Urban VIII), *Poemata* (Antwerp, 1634); Diego de Aedo y Gallart, *Le voyage du prince don Fernande* (Antwerp, 1635) and Frederik van Marselaer, *Legatus* (Antwerp, 1666). The bequest also includes Rubens' *Palazzi di Genova* (2 vols. 1622), *Palazzi antichi di Genova* and *Palazzi moderni di Genova* (Antwerp, 1663). Previous gifts include Dionysius Areopagita, *Opera* (Antwerp, 1634), Silvestro Pietrasanta, *Da symbolis heroicis* (Antwerp, 1634) and Jan Casper Gevaerts, *Pompa Introitus Ferdinandi* (Antwerp, 1641), all with title-pages or other illustrations by Rubens. These join additional books with engravings after Rubens, acquired from a variety of other sources.

For additional fine bindings, see No. 39 and 45.

N.F.

REF Walters, *History of Bookbinding*, no. 438; *Baroque Book Illustration*, no. 117; *Mostra Storica della Legatura Artistica* (Florence, 1922), no. 641; Nicolas Rauch, *Catalogue de Beaux Livres* (Geneva, 1948), no. 142; J. Richard Judson and Carl van de Velde, *Corpus Rubenianum Ludwig Burchard Part XXI: Book Illustrations and Title-Pages* (London and Philadelphia, 1978), nos. 18–28.

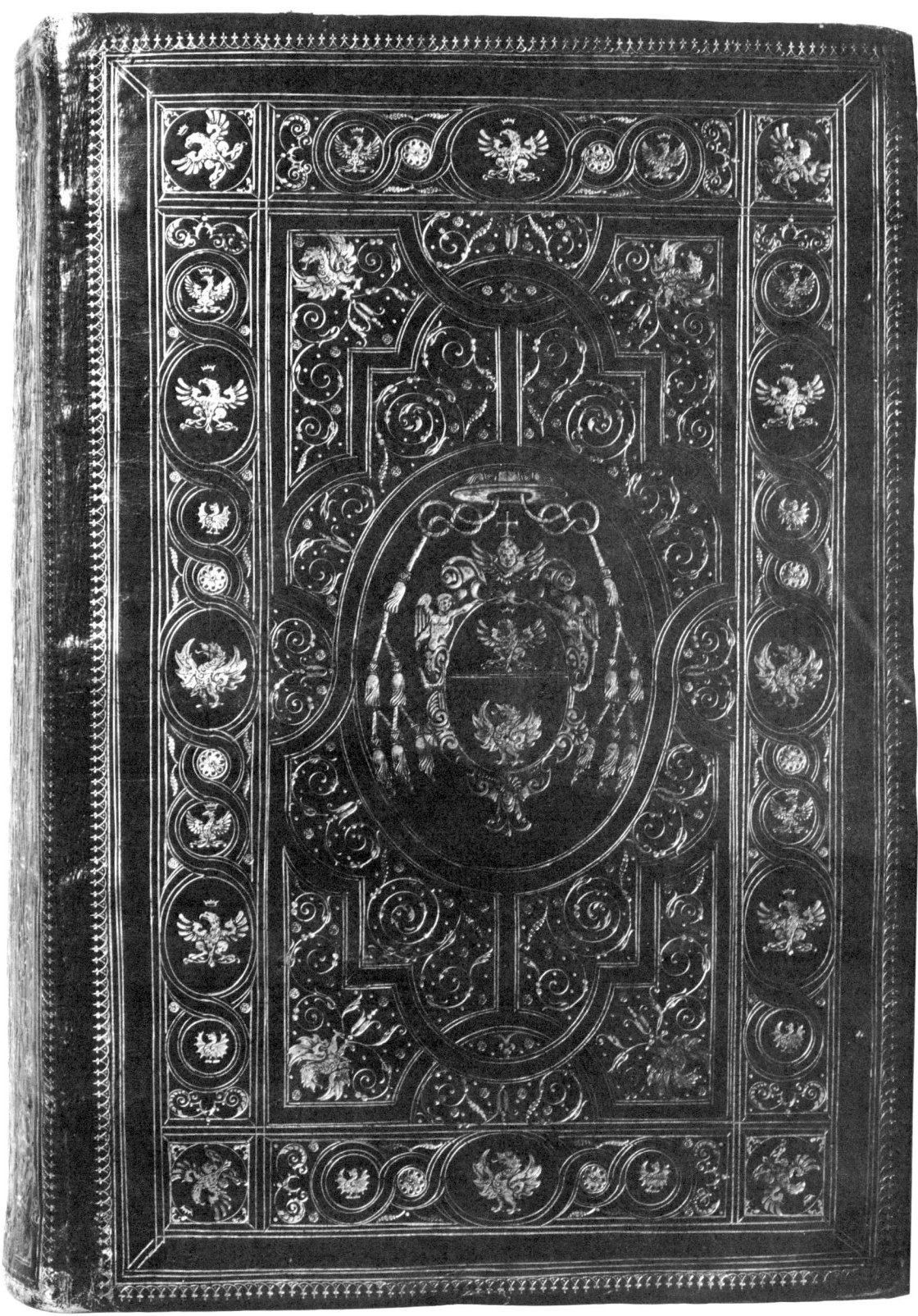

No. 29. Binding of *Breviarium Romanum*.

30   HENRI HUMBERT
Combat à la barrière faict en cour de Lorraine
Nancy, Sebastien Philippe, 1627
Intaglio plates by JACQUES CALLOT, 1592–1635

Added etched title and 9 double-page etchings by Callot.

20 x 15 cm. Contemporary mottled calf.

FESTIVAL BOOKS such as the *Combat à la barrière* display an important phase of Jacques Callot's extensive *oeuvre*. He first worked in this genre in Florence, where the young French artist was associated with the Medici court for nearly ten years. One of those commemorations, of a sombre nature, is in the Hofer bequest, Giovanni Altoviti's *Esequie della Sacra Cattolica e Real Maestà di Margherita d'Austria* of 1612, containing etchings that are probably Callot's earliest. His fine portrait of Francesco de' Medici appears in the account of the latter's funeral in 1614, *Esequie dell' ill. & ecc. principe Don Francesco Medici*, also in the bequest. Previous Hofer gifts of Medici festival books are Andrea Salvadori's *Guerra di Bellezza* of 1616, an equestrian ballet with etchings by Callot after Giulio Parigi, and Prospero Bonarelli's theatrical piece, *Il Solimano* of 1620. Other Florentine Callots among previous gifts are the *Capricci di varie figure* of ca. 1617, Bernardino Amico's *Trattato delle piante & immagini de sacri edifizi di Terra Santa* of 1620 and Giovanni Domenico Peri's *Fiesole distrutta* of 1621.

The *Combat à la Barrière* is Callot's only French festival book. He had returned in 1621 to his native Nancy in Lorraine. In 1627 he was an organizer and designer of floats, as well as the engraver of record, for the tourney in honor of the Duchesse de Chevreuse, in exile from Paris at the court of Lorraine. The book is dedicated to her, with florid words from both Callot and Humbert, whose pages describe the event so carefully recorded in the artist's plates. They illustrate the combat and the entry into the ducal palace of the courtiers in mythological guise, borne by mythological animals—fantastic constructions that glided along, powered by men walking beneath them. The combat was staged at a barrier in the great hall, and the victors of this nostalgic memento of chivalry were Duke Charles IV and his cousin the Marquis de Moüy. The range of dark and light and the variety of line in these plates demonstrate Callot's mastery of the etching medium, a skill he taught to Abraham Bosse, who communicated many of Callot's methods to subsequent generations in his *Traicté des manières de graver* (No. 32). Unlike many festival books with large and cumbersome folding plates, the *Combat* is a compact little book of sixty pages, the plates measuring ca. 155 x 235 mm. with generous margins, each folded in the center to open as a double-page spread.

Festival books, which are memorials of political and public events and of the ephemeral architecture and decoration specially constructed for them, are amply represented in the Hofer collections. Earlier French ones are recorded in Ruth Mortimer's catalogue of *French 16th Century Books*, nos. 200–207, and many Renaissance and Baroque examples from France, Italy, Spain, the Netherlands and Germany are present. One of the most lavish is Jan Casper Gevaerts' *Pompa Introitus Ferdinandi Austriaci*, Antwerp, 1641, engraved by Theodor van Tulden after Peter Paul Rubens, who designed much of the event. One of the most picturesque and one of the last of its kind is the *Voyage de S.M. Louis-Philippe Ier ... au Château de Windsor* of 1844, illustrated with lithographs, including one depicting the French king with Queen Victoria and Prince Albert seated in her private railway carriage.

Bound with the bequest copy of the *Combat* (another copy was a previous gift) are two additional Callot items: the *Vita Beatae Mariae* of 1626 and the *Lux Claustri* of 1646, both collections of religious emblems. Of the same genre is the first issue of *Les images de tous les saints et saintes* of 1636 (the Destailleur copy). Callot's powerful record of the Thirty Years War, *Les misères et les malheurs de la guerre* of 1633, was a previous gift.

E.M.G.

REF   Brunet, III, 371; Edouard Meaume, *Recherches sur la vie et les ouvrages de Jacques Callot* (Paris, 1860), no. 492–501; Edmond Bruwaert, *Vie de Jacques Callot* (Paris, 1912), p. 110–112; Pierre-Paul Plon, *Jacques Callot* (Brussels and Paris, 1914), no. 556–569; Jules Lieure, *Jacques Callot* (New York, 1969), no. 575–586; H. Diane Russell, *Jacques Callot* (Washington, National Gallery of Art, 1975), p. 78 and no. 112–127.

No. 30. Jacques Callot. Illustration from Henri Humbert, *Combat à la barrière*.

31 ❧ [ANDREA CAVALCANTI, 1610–1672]
Esequie del serenissimo principe Francesco
Florence, Giovanni Battista Landini, 1634
Intaglio plates by STEFANO DELLA BELLA, 1610–1664

Etched portrait, folding plate, and 8 etched emblems by Stefano della Bella.

20.5 x 14.5 cm. Contemporary vellum.

THE YOUNG FLORENTINE Stefano della Bella, a follower of Jacques Callot (see No. 30), was also employed as an artist at the Medici court. Like his French colleague, Stefano recorded official celebrations of life and death—weddings and funerals and festivals of church and state. One of the former occasions, the marriage of the Grand Duke Ferdinando II, elder brother of Prince Francesco, to Vittoria della Rovere of Urbino in 1637, is recorded by Stefano in two previous Hofer gifts, Gian Carlo Coppola's *Le nozze degli dei* with etchings after Alfonso Parigi, and Ferdinando Bardi's *Descrizione delle feste* with an equestrian ballet and its choreography etched by Stefano. (Alessandro Carducci's *Il mondo festeggiante* of 1664, etched by Stefano for another Medici wedding, is in the Harvard Theatre collection.) An elevation to sainthood is Benedetto Buommattei's 1632 *Descrizione delle feste fatte in Firenze per la canonizzazione di S. Andrea Corsini* (copy in the bequest). The bequest includes a second copy of the Cavalcanti.

The Department of Printing and Graphic Arts has a Stefano drawing from his stay in Paris, "Apollo and Daphne," for one of the playing cards in the series designed for the young Louis XIV. It was the gift of the Spanish painter, Fernando Zobel y Montojo, Harvard '49, a student and colleague of Philip Hofer.

Stefano della Bella's dramatic imagination brilliantly expressed the subject of death in some of his last prints of the 1660s. Thirty years earlier, for the *Esequie*, Alfonso Parigi had designed the decorations of the Medici church of San Lorenzo for the funeral of Francesco, who had died at the siege of Regensburg. Stefano's portrait of the young prince recalls Callot's portrait of Francesco's uncle, another young Francesco, who was buried from San Lorenzo in 1614 (see No. 30). Callot, at age twenty-two, was perhaps more assured than Stefano at twenty-four, but already the latter's personal style was asserting itself in his first portrait. Parigi's decorations for the church formed a theatrical setting for the funeral, for at each column was placed the figure of a skeleton, robed with the vestiges of fine clothes and holding the weapons of war. Embellished with black draperies and the Medici arms, such a tableau heightened and dramatised the occasion, expressing the dual Baroque concern for rank and splendor and the constant presence of death. Philip Hofer has pointed out the relation of these attitudes to aesthetic expression in such works of anatomy as Giulio Casserio's *De Vocis Auditusque Organis* (Ferrara, 1601) a previous gift, and Teodoro Filippo di Liagno's series of etchings (Rome, ca. 1620, Zobel gift); Dutch copy of 1626 by Hendrik Hondius, a previous Hofer gift.

E.M.G.

REF Alessandro Baudi de Vesme, *Stefano della Bella, catalogue raisonné*, with additions by Phyllis Dearborn Massar [New York, 1971], no. 36, 74, 971–978, Phyllis Dearborn Massar, *Presenting Stefano della Bella* (New York [1971]), p. 38–39; Anna Forlani Tempesta, *Stefano della Bella incisioni* (Florence [1972]), no. IX–XIII; Anna Forlani Tempesta, *Mostra di incisioni di Stefano della Bella* (Florence, Gabinetto Disegni e Stampe degli Uffizi, 1973), no. 5–7; Philip Hofer, "Some Little Known Italian Illustrations of Comparative Anatomy," *De Artibus Opuscula XL, Essays in Honor of Erwin Panofsky* (New York, 1961), I, p. 230–237; Arthur R. Blumenthal, *Theatre Art of the Medici* (Hanover, N.H., Dartmouth College, 1980), p. 152–153.

No. 31. Stefano della Bella. Illustration from Andrea Cavalcanti, *Esequie del serenissimo principe Francesco*.

32 ▰ ABRAHAM BOSSE, 1602–1676
Traicté des manières de graver en taille douce sur l'airin
Paris, Charles-Antoine Jombert, 1645

19 engravings by Bosse.

17.4 x 11 cm. Contemporary calf.

AS MASTER-PRINTER and theoretician as well as artist-printmaker, Abraham Bosse published a number of illustrated manuals in a period eager for instruction. Academies were flourishing, and students and amateurs sought experienced guidance, which is presented with precision and practicality in Bosse's books, the written instruction always supplemented with detailed illustration. The *Traicté*, dedicated "Aux amateurs de cet art," is one of the first manuals on engraving, and an indispensible handbook, often reprinted.

In his introduction, Bosse cites his debt to the printmakers Simon Vries, Matthaeus Merian, and especially Jacques Callot (No. 30). He goes on to discuss both engraving and etching, illustrating the tools and their handling, the preparation of plates, the construction and operation of the roller press. Included in the bequest is the Hofer copy of the 1758 edition of the *Traicté*, entitled *De la manière de graver à l'eau forte et au burin*, with a section on Sebastien Le Clerc's new method of biting an etching (see No. 38) and additional sections on the *manière noire* or mezzotint (No. 34), including Le Blon's color work in this new medium (No. 44).

Bosse the theoretician and teacher was also concerned with the study of perspective and its application to painting and architecture, and this phase of his work is represented in the bequest by his *Moyen universel de pratiquer la perspective sur les tableaux* of 1653 and *Le peintre converty aux précises et universelles règles de son art* of 1667, which includes an account of his quarrel with Charles Le Brun and the Académie. A previous gift in this area is his *Traité des pratiques géométrales et perspectives* of 1665. (The copy of *Sentimens sur la distinction des diverses manières de peintre* of 1649 was the gift of another great Harvard benefactor, Thomas Hollis.)

A folio volume in the bequest contains three of the architectural treatises: *Représentations géométrales de plusieurs parties de bastiments faites par les reigles de l'architecture antique* of 1659, *Traité des manières de dessiner les ordres de l'architecture antique* of 1659, and *Des ordres de colōnes en l'architecture*, both of 1664. His engraved portrait of Alexandre Francini decorates the latter's *Livre d'architecture* of 1631. Bosse's interest in mathematics is represented in one of the books by his friend Gérard Desargues that the artist illustrated and published after the mathematician's death: *La manière universelle pour poser l'essieu . . . aux cadrans au soleil*, a book about sundials, also in the bequest.

In his huge output of prints (over 1500), Bosse was a chronicler of seventeenth-century French society in the age of Louis XIII, and an illustrator of literature. The bequest contains a copy of Jean Desmarets de Saint Sorlin's *L'Ariane* of 1643, with engravings by Bosse after Claude Vignon, the plates repeated from the 1639 edition. Also engraved after the designs of Vignon are the illustrations of Jean Chapelain's *La Pucelle ou la France délivrée* of 1656. Ascribed to Bosse are four of the engravings after François Chauveau for Desmaret de Saint Sorlin's *Clovis* of 1657, one of the more elaborately ornamented of Baroque books. A previous Hofer gift is a colored copy bound with the arms of Louis XIV. The role of Bosse in the classics is represented in the illustrations for *L'Eneide de Virgile* of 1648, and an unusual author portrait is that of James Howells in his *Dendrologie* of 1642, signed by Bosse and Claude Mellan.

E.M.G.

REF André Blum, *L'oeuvre gravé d'Abraham Bosse* (Paris, 1924), no. 403–421; Blum, *Abraham Bosse et la société française au dix-septième siècle* (Paris, 1924), ch. 7; Smith College Museum of Art, *Abraham Bosse, An Exhibition* (Northampton, Mass., 1956), no. 47.

No. 32. Abraham Bosse. Illustration from *Traicté des manières de graver*.

33   [HENRI D'AVICE]
La pompeuse et magnifique cérémonie du sacre du roy Louis XIV
Paris, Edmé Martin, 1655
Intaglio plates by ROBERT NANTEUIL, 1623–1678
and JEAN LE PAUTRE, 1618–1682

One engraving by Robert Nanteuil; 3 etchings by Jean Le Pautre.

40.6 x 27.4 cm. Brown morocco, gilt, with the arms of Anne of Austria.

LOUIS XIV was thirteen years old when he was crowned at Rheims on June 7, 1654. Louis XIII had died in 1643, and the early years of his son's reign, troubled by wars on the frontiers and the internal difficulties of the Fronde, had been dominated by the policies of his great minister Cardinal Jules Mazarin. The young king himself would not assume personal rule until the death of Mazarin in 1661. Nanteuil's portrait of Mazarin, though rarely present in known copies, was apparently executed specifically for *La pompeuse et magnifique cérémonie du sacre du roy Louis XIV*, which was dedicated to the Cardinal. The three great folding plates are also sometimes found separately, although they, too, were executed as illustrations for this book. They depict the preliminary séance while the King and his officials await the arrival of the holy oil from Saint-Rémy, the actual coronation ceremony, and the subsequent high mass. In all three scenes, the tiny figure of the king is almost lost amid the crowds and panoply of the spectacle, despite the assurance of an inscription on the third plate that "l'éclat qui vient de luy/Releue de beaucoup l'éclat qui l'environne." The unusual completeness of this copy of *La pompeuse et magnifique cérémonie* may be due to the fact that it was a royal copy and originally belonged to Anne of Austria, the mother of Louis XIV and queen regent during his minority.

    The prosperity of Louis XIV's later reign did much to encourage the arts of etching and engraving. Nanteuil was appointed royal portrait engraver in 1659 and proceeded to produce portraits of nearly all the great personages of the court. A small group of these portraits is included in the bequest, as is a copy of Georges de Scudéry's *Alaric* (Paris, 1654) with an author portrait by Nanteuil. The festivals, theatrical performances, ballets and concerts at Versailles were illustrated by Le Pautre and Israel Silvestre in *Les plaisirs de l'isle enchantée* (Paris, 1673), *Les divertissemens de Versailles* (Paris, 1676) and *Relation de la feste de Versailles* (Paris, 1679). All three are included in the bequest, together with five volumes of engravings by Silvestre. A collection of Le Pautre's architectural works (Paris, 1761) in the bequest contains many designs for interior decorations and suggests Le Pautre's importance for later artists. Silvestre's *Recueil de cent vues différentes* and *L'Entrée triomphante de Louis XIV* (Paris, 1662) with illustrations by Jean Marot, were two previous gifts. Another previous gift was the *Cabinet du roi*, fourteen volumes containing representations of monuments, palaces and art treasures by Silvestre, Le Pautre, Marot, François Chauveau, Claude Mellan and others. Hofer greatly admired this work and called special attention to it in *Baroque Book Illustration* (1951). The bequest also includes seven drawings by Chauveau for the *Métamorphoses* of Ovid (Paris, 1676), and two manuscripts, *Les premières monnoies et les poids des anciens Romains pour servir de préliminaire aux Médailles antiques du Cabinet du Roy* and *Eloge de Louis XIII et Vie de Louis XIV* (Phillips MS. 866). The Frances L. Hofer bequest includes drawings by Charles Nicolas Cochin, Charles Monnet and Jean Michel Moreau.

N.F.

REF   Nagler, XII, 166–168; Vinet, no. 497; Charles Petitjean and Charles Wickert, *Catalogue de l'oeuvre gravée de Robert Nanteuil* (Paris, 1925), no. 156.

No. 33. Jean Le Pautre. Illustration from *La pompeuse et magnifique cérémonie du sacre du roy Louis XIV.*

34   [JOHN EVELYN, 1620–1706]
Sculptura: or the History and Art of Chalcography and Engraving in Copper
London, Printed by J.C. for G. Beedle and J. Collins, 1662

Engraved frontispiece signed with monogram AH (A. Hertochs) after Evelyn; engraved plate; tipped-in mezzotint plate, by Prince Rupert, signed with his monogram.

15.5 x 10 cm. Dark blue morocco, gilt fillets, edges gilt.

SCULPTURA represents one of the many areas in which Evelyn published his exploration of specialized interests. In it he is concerned not with three-dimensional plastic art, but with two-dimensional graphic art, the cutting of the printmaker's knife or graver, not the sculptor's knife or chisel.

Five chapters—144 pages—of this slender book of 148 pages are devoted to a survey of graphic art and incised lettering from ancient times. Only in the last four pages does Evelyn discuss the mezzotint, the "new manner of engraving," as stated on the title-page. He offers no technical details, but promises a future demonstration should the description he is preparing for the Royal Society be considered insufficient.

More eloquent than any verbal instruction is the fine mezzotint head by Prince Rupert (1619–1682) Count Palatine of the Rhine and son of the Winter King and Queen of Bohemia, Friedrich I and Elizabeth, the daughter of James I. Often lacking in copies of *Sculptura*, the plate is referred to by the author as an integral part of the book. One of a dozen pieces by Rupert, this early mezzotint depicts the head of the executioner, a detail copied by the artist from his 1658 print, "The Great Executioner," a three-quarter length male figure holding the head of John the Baptist after a painting by Ribera or his School. The strong contrast of the highlighted face emerging from the dark background is a dramatic example of the essential character of the mezzotint, a method in which the artist works from dark to light, beginning with a plate roughened with a roulette or rocker, then scraped and burnished for lighter tones.

Although Evelyn credits the invention of the mezzotint to Prince Rupert, the latter learned it on the continent from Ludwig von Siegen. Settling in England with the Stuart Restoration, Rupert, also Duke of Cumberland, shared his knowledge of the new technique with Evelyn. Subsequent research into the Evelyn papers indicates that he intended to correct this misattribution and that Rupert's contribution to the new medium was the invention of the rocker, an improvement over the roulette in roughening the surface of the plate.

The strong lights and darks of the mezzotint made it a popular medium for portraits and for reproductive prints after paintings, and Jakob Christof Le Blon experimented with printing mezzotints in color (No. 44). Because the burr of the copper mezzotint plate quickly wears, only a limited number of good impressions can be pulled, so it was not a practical medium for book illustration in the seventeenth- and eighteenth-centuries. With the introduction of steel plates in the 1820s, the mezzotint was put to brilliant use by John Martin in his illustrations for Milton's *Paradise Lost* of 1827 (both quarto and folio editions, the latter the Holford copy, were previous Hofer gifts).

E.M.G.

REF   Eichenberg, p. 347; A.M. Hind, "Studies in English Engraving VI. Prince Rupert and the Beginnings of Mezzotint," *Gazette des Beaux-Arts*, XCII (1933), 382–391; Orovida C. Pissarro, "Prince Rupert and the Invention of the Mezzotint," *The Walpole Society*, XXXVI (1960), 1–9; Geoffrey Keynes, *John Evelyn, A Study in Bibliophily* (Oxford, 1968), no. 33, p. 116–119; Jane Bayard and Ellen D'Oench, *Darkness into Light, the Early Mezzotint* ([New Haven, Conn.] 1976), no. 4–5.

No. 34.   Prince Rupert, "Head of the Executioner."   Illustration from John Evelyn, *Sculptura*.

35   AESOP
Aesop's Fables with his Life
London, Printed by William Godbid for Francis Barlow, 1666
Intaglio plates by FRANCIS BARLOW, 1626?–1702

Added engraved title, frontispiece, and 110 etchings by Barlow.

36 x 23.5 cm. Large paper copy. Contemporary paneled calf, gilt tooled with bookplates of Sir Thomas Hanmer, Henry Edward Bunbury, and John Jay Paul.

THE AESOP of Francis Barlow, the "first master of English book illustration," had an honored place in the Hofer collection of bestiaries and fables (see his *Baroque Book Illustration*, p. 8). Accomplished as a sporting artist and skilled in the depiction of animals and birds, Barlow was best known as a painter, and it is uncertain where he acquired his etching skills, which he minimized. In 1652 he illustrated Edward Benlowes' *Theophila* (a previous Hofer gift) and in 1653, William Denny's *Pelicanicidium* (copy in the bequest), and both those books display his facility.

The illustrated fable tradition in England was shaped by Marcus Geeraerts the Elder, whose etchings for a Flemish Aesop, *Die Warachtighe Fabulen der Dieren* (previous Hofer gift) appeared in Bruges in 1567, the year before the artist fled to London at the time of religious upheavals in the Low Countries. His powerful images of the traditional tales were very influential in his adopted country, and he contributed additional illustrations to English books. Although he returned to Antwerp for a time, he died in England, where his son Marcus the Younger became a leading Elizabethan and Jacobean portraitist. Two other Europeans, the German Franz Cleyn and the Bohemian Wenceslaus Hollar, participated in the illustrations for John Ogilby's two Aesops of 1651 and 1665, which established the native Aesopic tradition in England, for earlier editions, such as Caxton's of 1484 and Pynson's of 1497, were illustrated with cuts borrowed or copied from continental editions.

The first edition of Barlow's Aesop was planned for 1665, the date on the etched title. Actual publication was in 1666, the year of the Great Fire. The book includes an illustrated life of Aesop and a text in English, French, and Latin, the English limited to rhymed couplets with a moral engraved below the illustrations. These unsigned etchings are not full-page plates, but text illustrations (ca. 155 x 160 mm.) on the letterpress pages. Barlow's foreword records his modesty as a printmaker: "I am no professed Graveer or Eacher [sic] but a Well-wisher to the Art of Painting; and therefore Designe is all we aim at, and cannot perform Curious Neatness without losing the Spirit which is the main." Despite his disclaimer, Barlow's etchings are skillful transcriptions of his original drawings, many of which are in the Department of Prints and Drawings at the British Museum, and they transcribe some of the atmospheric qualities of those wash drawings. The plates owe much to the tradition of Geeraerts and Cleyn, but Barlow's compositions have greater animation. Set in a compact and luxuriant landscape, his animals and birds are presented with a remarkable naturalism and freshness of observation.

A second large paper variant copy and a small paper copy of this first edition are in the bequest; additionally included in the bequest, as well as among previous gifts, is a large paper copy of the 1687 second edition with thirty-one new plates illustrating the life of Aesop designed by Barlow and etched by himself and by Thomas Dudley, and with new verse couplets and morals by Aphra Behn. Also present in the bequest is Ogilby's 1665 *The Fables of Aesop*, and his 1668 *Aesopics*, to which Barlow contributed designs, is a previous gift. The Frances L. Hofer bequest contains an early Barlow drawing for the title-page of James Ussher's *The Annals of the World*, London, 1658 (Becker, no. 2).

E.M.G.

REF   Brunet, I, 102; Walter Shaw Sparrow, *British Sporting Artists* (London and New York, [1922]), ch. 1; Edward Hodnett, *Aesop in England* (Charlottesville, Va. [1979]); Edward Hodnett, *Francis Barlow, First Master of English Book Illustration* (London, 1978); Philip Hofer, "Francis Barlow's Aesop," *Harvard Library Bulletin*, II (1948), 179–295.

No. 35. Francis Barlow, "The Cock and the Jewel." Illustration from *Aesop's Fables*.

36   CERTAMEN EQUESTRE
Stockholm, Johann Georg Eberdt [1672]

Engraved title and 62 engravings and etchings by Georg Christoph Eimmart after David Klöcker.
26.4 x 37 cm. Half vellum, marbled paper sides.

THIS rare Swedish festival book depicts the celebrations that took place in 1672 when Charles XI, king since 1660, assumed personal rule upon reaching the age of seventeen. The three large folding plates show Charles's mother and tutors conferring supreme authority on the young king, the royal feast in the palace, and the hall in which the festival took place. Most of the remaining plates are devoted to the procession of richly caparisoned horses and riders, but four depict the fireworks which were an indispensable part of such ceremonies in the seventeenth century.

Georg Christoph Eimmart (1638–1705) and David Klöcker were both German artists. Eimmart was a pupil of Joachim Sandrart and spent most of his life in Nuremburg. Klöcker, who had studied with Pietro da Cortona in Italy, settled in Stockholm, where he became court painter. Both Eimmart and Klöcker are included in Sandrart's *Teutsche Academie* (Nuremburg, 1675; I, 334–335, 375). A copy of the 1683 Latin edition of this important early reference book is in the bequest.

A small but choice group of Scandinavian books is included in the bequest. Among them are Eric Dahlberg, *Suecia antiqua et hodierna* (Stockholm, ca. 1689); Johann Täntzer, *Der Dianen Jagtgeheimnüss* (Copenhagen, 1682–1689); Holger Jacobaeus, *Museum regium* (Copenhagen, 1696); and Gottfried Fuchs, *Glückliche Dämpfung* (Copenhagen, ca. 1700). All of the above books are illustrated in Hofer's *Baroque Book Illustration*. They join another small but choice group of previous gifts including André Mollet, *Le Jardin de Plaisir* (Stockholm, 1651); Ole Worm, *Fasti Danici* (Copenhagen, 1643); Olaus Rudbeck, *Atland eller Manheim* (Upsala, 1675–1698); and Laurids Thurah, *Den danske Vitruvius* (Copenhagen, 1746–1749). Some of Hofer's Scandinavian gifts, including a Danish translation of Don Quixote by Charlotte Dorothea Biehl (Copenhagen, 1776–1777) and Ludvig Holberg's *Niels Klims Underjordiske Reise* (Copenhagen, 1789), are described in Nancy S. Reinhardt's Houghton Library exhibition catalogue, *Danish Literature, Saxo Grammaticus to Isak Dinesen* (Cambridge, 1986).

Other festival books in the bequest are discussed in No. 30, 31, 33, and 41. A number of these feature representations of fireworks displays. In *Divertissemens de Versailles* (Paris, 1676), Jean Le Pautre depicted the elaborate firework machine designed by Le Brun to celebrate Louis XIV's reconquest of the Franche-Comté. *Description des festes données par la ville de Paris* (Paris, 1740) includes Jacques-François Blondel's representations of the fireworks over the Seine celebrating the recent marriage of Elizabeth of France with Philip of Spain. Copies of both books are in the bequest. Previous gifts include *Roma Festeggiante* (Rome, 1687), in which a fireworks display was staged as part of the celebrations; and *Voyage de sa Majesté britannique en Holland* (The Hague, 1692) with etchings by Romeyn de Hooghe of the fireworks honoring William III.

N.F.

REF   Thieme-Becker X, 420–422, XX, 533–536; *Baroque Book Illustration*, no. 91; Gabriel René Mennessier de la Lance, *Essai de bibliographie hippique* (Paris, 1915–1921) I, 241; Arthur Lotz, *Das Feuerwerk, Seine Geschichte und Bibliographie* (Leipzig [1940]), p. 49, 106.

No. 36. Illustration from *Certamen Equestre*.

37   [JAN SIX, 1618–1700]
Medea, Treurspel
Amsterdam, Jacob Lescailje, 1679
Intaglio plate by REMBRANDT HERMANSZOON VAN RIJN, 1606–1669

Etched frontispiece.

24.4 x 18.7 cm. Contemporary vellum.

THE BURGOMASTER JAN SIX was Rembrandt's friend and patron, the subject of both etched and painted portraits by the artist. His tragedy *Medea* was performed in Amsterdam in 1647 and published in 1648 with the fourth state of Rembrandt's etching of the marriage of Jason and Creusa as the frontispiece. The fifth state of the print appears in presentation copies of the second edition of 1679. Some scholars have doubted whether the print was made specifically for the book, both because the etching is in such a late state and because the scene depicted does not occur in the play. A direct connection appears likely, however, since the original etched copperplate is still in the Six Collection. Medea's costume also corresponds closely to Six's stage directions, which describe the figure of the sun beneath her breast. It has been suggested that the scene of the marriage, although not part of the play itself, may have been included as a *tableau vivant* between the second and third acts.

Although Rembrandt was scarcely a prolific illustrator, his etchings do appear in a handful of contemporary books. The earliest of these, *Der Zee-vaert Lof* (In Praise of Navigation), by the sailor-poet Elias Herckmans, was published in 1634, fifteen years before the first edition of Six's *Medea*. Rembrandt's etching, traditionally known as "The Ship of Fortune" (Bartsch 111), was only one of eighteen illustrations, the others being by the minor artist Willem Bosse. A copy of Herckmans' book is included in the bequest. Another book for which Rembrandt designed illustrations is *La piedra gloriosa o de la estatua de Nebuchadnesar* (Amsterdam, 1655) by the Hebrew scholar Manesseh ben Israel. As in the case of *Medea*, the exact relationship between book and etchings was long in doubt; however, the discovery in the Leiden University Library of an uncut copy with Rembrandt's illustrations confirms that they were included in at least some copies of the first edition. Copies of all four etchings (Bartsch 36), but not the book, are included in the Frances L. Hofer bequest. Also in the Philip Hofer bequest is *Den grooten emblemata sacra* (Amsterdam, 1654), a collection of 352 prints assembled by Jan Philipsz Schabaelje. Included is Rembrandt's "Student at a table by candlelight," which Schabaelje interpreted as a portrait of Hermes Trismegistus.

A previous gift was Rembrandt's 1658 portrait etching of the writing master Lieven Willemsz van Coppenol (Bartsch 283), together with two specimens of Coppenol's calligraphy, one written in Dutch and one in French. Additional examples of calligraphy are discussed in No. 21, 23, and 27.

N.F.

REF   Bartsch 112; *Baroque Book Illustration*, no. 136; Arthur M. Hind, *A Catalogue of Rembrandt's Etchings* (London, 1923), no. 235; Clara Bille, "Rembrandt and Burgomaster Jan Six: Conjectures as to their relationship," *Apollo*, LXXXV (1967), 260–265; Herman de la Fontaine Verwey, "Rembrandt as a Book-Illustrator," *Quaerendo*, III, 1 (January 1973), 3–19; Clifford S. Ackley, *Printmaking in the Age of Rembrandt*, Museum of Fine Arts (Boston, 1981).

No. 37. Rembrandt van Rijn, "Wedding of Jason and Creusa." Frontispiece of Jan Six, *Medea*.

38   [CHARLES PERRAULT, 1628–1703 and ISAAC DE BENSERADE, 1613–1691]
Labyrinte de Versailles
Paris, Imprimerie Royale, 1679
Intaglio plates by SEBASTIEN LECLERC, 1637–1714

40 etchings.

20.7 x 13 cm. Red morocco, gilt, with the arms of Louis XIV.

AS HOFER REMARKED in *Baroque Book Illustration*, Leclerc's smaller illustrations prefigure the grace and elegance of the best French rococo. This certainly is true of the etchings in *Labyrinte de Versailles*, which depict a whimsical series of garden ornaments based on subjects from Aesop's Fables. Thirty-nine fountains designed by Le Brun were set at key points within a maze in the gardens of the Château. The scale throughout is intimate, many of the compositions are asymmetrical, and extensive use is made of decorative rockwork, for example in "The Hare and the Tortoise" where a small cascade separates the two animals, and in "The Council of Rats," in which twelve little rats perch on *rocaille* outcroppings around a central leader. The accompanying prose description of the labyrinth is by Charles Perrault and the verses are by Benserade. Only a few copies are known of the 1677 first edition; even this 1679 second edition is an extremely rare book. A previous gift, a set of illustrations only on large paper, is later in date and was made after the plates were cut down.

Leclerc is well represented in the bequest, which includes his illustrations for Isaac de Benserade's *Métamorphoses d'Ovide en rondeaux* (Paris, ca. 1676), *Fables d'Esope* (Paris, ca. 1683) and a collection of *Oeuvres choisies* (Paris, 1783). Examples of his work on a larger scale include Philippe Bardin, *Le Triomphe de Son Altesse Charles III* (Nancy, 1664) and Denys Dodart, *Recueil de Plantes* (Paris, 1676), both previous gifts. Leclerc also contributed large folding plates to the *Cabinet du roi* (see No. 33). He was the author, as well as the illustrator, of a charming and influential little treatise, *Pratique de la géometrie*, first published in 1668. French, English, and Dutch editions of this work were previous gifts. Leclerc also developed a new method of etching which was included in Abraham Bosse's manual, beginning with the edition of 1701. For a discussion of this book, see No. 32. Leclerc's *Divers desseins de figures dediés à Monsieur Colbert* (Paris, 1679) is discussed in No. 39.

N.F.

REF   *Baroque Book Illustration*, no. 57; Maxime Préaud, *Bibliothèque Nationale, Inventaire du fonds français, Graveurs du XVIIIe siècle*, IX: *Sébastien Leclerc II* (Paris, 1980), nos. 2818–2858.

No. 38.   Sébastien Leclerc, "The Council of Rats."   Illustration from *Labyrinte de Versailles*.

39 ❧ SEBASTIEN LECLERC, 1637–1714
Divers desseins de figures dediés à Monsieur Colbert d'Ormoy
Paris, Chez N. Langlois [1679]
Intaglio plates by SEBASTIEN LECLERC

23 etchings plus etched title-page.

10.9 x 14.4 cm. Contemporary red morocco, gold-tooled with the Colbert arms.

LOUIS XIV's finance minister Jean-Baptiste Colbert and his two oldest sons Jean-Baptiste and Jacques-Nicolas were all great book collectors and patrons of the arts. Colbert's fourth son, Jules-Armand, has been described as "le moins intelligent de tous les fils du ministre." Nevertheless it was this fourth son, the Marquis de Blainville et Ormoy, who was responsible for the creation of Sébastien Leclerc's *Divers desseins de figures*. In 1679, the minister engaged Leclerc to teach drawing and mathematics to fifteen-year-old Jules-Armand. The *Divers desseins de figures*, executed at this time, were intended as an instruction manual for the young Colbert. The plates show men and women in contemporary costumes, engaged in a variety of activities.

This copy differs from other known examples in the number and order of the plates. Although it includes only twenty of the usual twenty-nine plates, it contains, in addition, three plates usually associated with the contemporary series, *Divers desseins de figures dediés à monsieur de Boucoeur*. This copy is also of special interest because it originally belonged to a member of the Colbert family, possibly the dedicatee's brother, Jean-Baptiste Colbert de Seignelay. For other books illustrated by Leclerc, see No. 38.

Like many book collectors, Hofer was fascinated by volumes with illustrious pedigrees. The bequest includes a number of books with royal bindings and from famous collections. Seventeenth-century France is especially well-represented by books bound for Louis XIII, Louis XIV, and their queens Anne of Austria and Marie Thérèse. Examples include *L'Office de la Semaine Saincte* (Paris, 1655; Walters no. 398) with a fine sombre binding for Anne of Austria as dowager queen, and a series of classics (Horace, Juvenal, Terence and Virgil) printed at the Imprimerie Royale for Louis XIII and bound for the young Louis XIV. Hofer's copy of Giovanni Antonio Magini, *Trigonometria* (Bologna, 1609) is from the library of the bibliophile J. A. de Thou; Michel de Marolles, *Temple des Muses* (Paris, 1655) and *La Sainte Bible* (Amsterdam, 1707) are from the library of Count Hoym. A copy of Alessandro Brandano, *Historia delle guerre di Portogallo* (Venice, 1689) was bound for Queen Christina of Sweden and later belonged to William Beckford, the author of *Vathek*. A copy of Nicolás Antonio's *Bibliotheca hispana* was also bound for Queen Christina and contains a marginal note in her hand. Later examples include a copy of *Freudengang der Judenschaft zu Sclow* (n.p., 1780) in an embroidered velvet binding for Catherine the Great, and Giuseppe Hagen, *Illustrazione d'uno zodiaco orientale* (Milan, 1811), bound in Italy for Eugène de Beauharnais. For another Beauharnais binding, see No. 59. Additional fine bindings are listed under No. 29 and 45.

The Hofer bequest also includes a document dated January 1, 1683, signed by Louis XIV and countersigned by Colbert.

N.F.

REF Maxime Préaud, *Bibliothèque Nationale, Inventaire du fonds français, Graveurs du XVIIIᵉ siécle*, VIII: *Sébastien Leclerc I* (Paris, 1980), nos. 1087–1116; Edouard Meaume, *Sébastien Leclerc et son oeuvre* (Paris, 1877), p. 120–121; Pierre Berès, Catalogue 40; (Paris, 1946), no. 180.

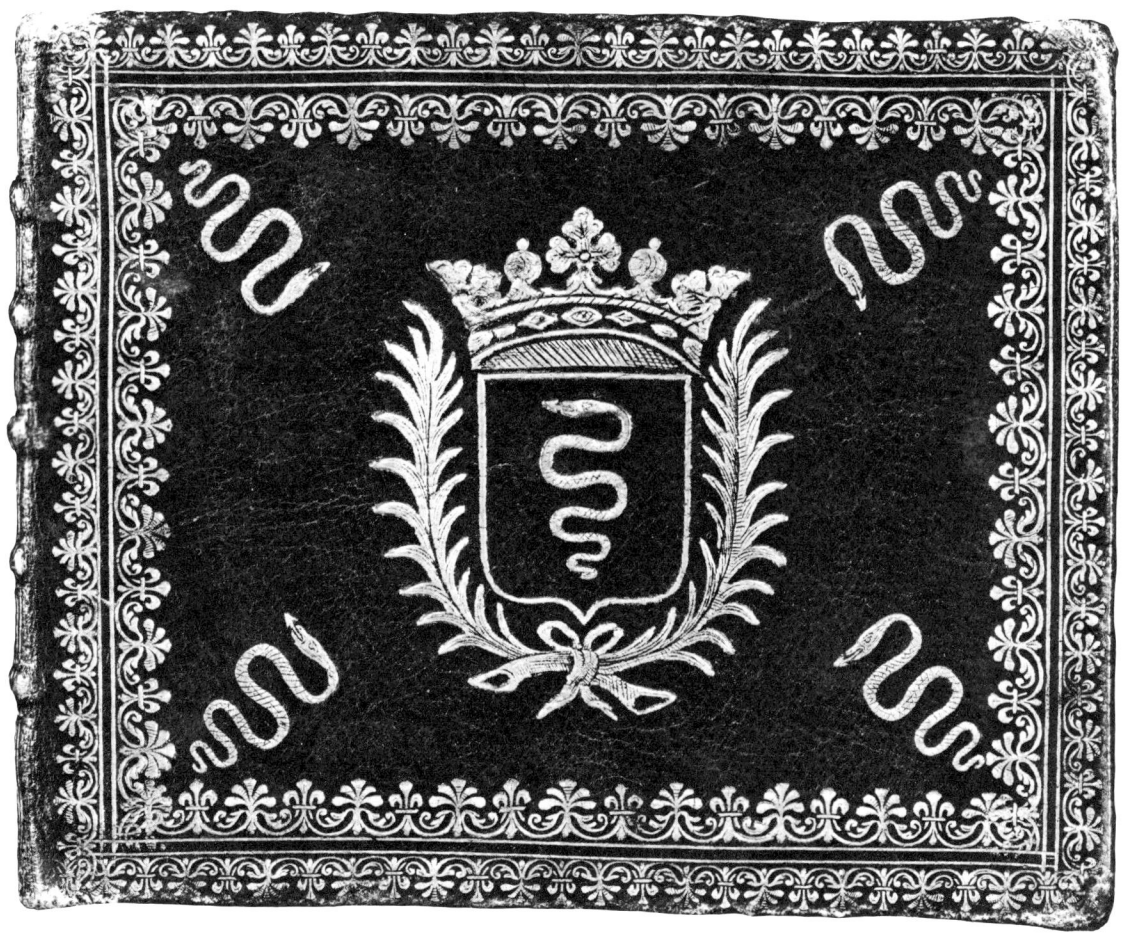

No. 39. Binding of Sébastien Leclerc, *Divers desseins de figures dediés à Monsieur Colbert d'Ormoy.*

40 ❧ JOHN MILTON, 1608–1674
Paradise Lost
London, Printed by Miles Flesher, for Jacob Tonson, 1688

Frontispiece and twelve engravings by Michael Burghers after John Baptist Medina and Henry Aldrich; by Peter Paul Bouche after Bernard Lens the elder; by Robert White after William Faithorne the elder.

37 x 23.5 cm. Contemporary paneled red-brown morocco, gilt extra, marbled endpapers.

THIS "Fourth Edition, Adorn'd with Sculptures," is the first illustrated edition of the classic work in English literature and a turning point in Milton's readership and reputation. Having purchased the copyright, Tonson was encouraged to publish this sumptuous and elegant English folio by John Somers (later Lord Somers), the poet Dryden, Henry Aldrich (then canon, later Dean of Christ Church, Oxford), and some five hundred subscribers named in the six-page list bound at the end. The frontispiece portrait by White after the oil painting by Faithorne embodies Dryden's celebrated six-line tribute to Milton, here published anonymously and for the first time.

The engraver Burghers lived in Oxford and engraved for the University Press, to which he was appointed "sculptor" in 1692. Much of his work there, including the Oxford Almanacs, consisted of copying motifs selected for him by Henry Aldrich from his extensive personal collection of engravings. The frontispiece to book two of the Milton, for instance, is copied in part from Mantegna's Descent into Limbo, and that for book twelve from Raphael's Expulsion—both prints having been discovered in Aldrich's collection by Suzanne Boorsch, the authority on this work. The most celebrated image of the book, the frontispiece to the first book which shows Satan and his legions dramatically lighted from below, must also derive from Aldrich, but the original, perhaps a St. Michael in a printed book, has not yet been found.

The frontispiece to book four was engraved by Bouche after the elder Lens, and the remainder are engraved by Burghers after Medina, whose eight original drawings for them were bequeathed by Alexander Dyce to the Victoria and Albert Museum, where they were located by Boorsch. Students of English literature, glad for the attention of any artist to their classics, have applauded Medina's concepts, enjoying his depiction of several episodes in a single plate, while art historians have criticized the work as bland and diffuse. The persistent influence of Medina's illustrations cannot be argued, as prints from the original coppers or from reduced copies adorned no fewer than eighteen reprints from 1692 to 1784.

A second copy in the Hofer bequest includes, as commonly found, Randal Taylor's editions, unillustrated, of *Paradise Regain'd* and *Samson Agonistes*, both dated 1688 and printed on the same paper stocks—bunch of grapes or arms of France and Navarre—as the *Paradise Lost*; the existence of large-paper copies remains an unfulfilled hope of the trade. The 1827 edition of *Paradise Lost*, with mezzotints by John Martin, was another favorite of Hofer's. Both quarto and folio editions were previous gifts.

R.E.S.

REF C.H. Collins-Baker, "Some Illustrators of Milton's *Paradise Lost*, (1688–1850)," *The Library*, 5th ser. III (1948–49), 1–21, 101–19; Helen Gardner, "Milton's First Illustrator," *Essays and Studies* (1956), 27–38; Suzanne Boorsch, "The 1688 *Paradise Lost* and Dr. Aldrich," *Metropolitan Museum Journal* VI (1972), 133–50.

No. 40. John Baptist Medina, "Fall of the Rebel Angels." Illustration from Milton, *Paradise Lost*.

41   FÜRSTLICHE BAU-LUST
[Glücksburg] Georg Heinrich Oppermann, 1698

10 parts in 1 vol. 158 etchings, some double-page, some folding, most by Johann Schuster; additional woodcut ornaments. 31 x 18.8 cm. Modern half-calf.

PART FESTIVAL BOOK, part architectural book and part emblem book, *Fürstliche Bau-Lust*, or the *Princely Builder's Delight* of Duke Heinrich of Saxony, provides a unique glimpse of German court life of the late seventeenth century. The illustrations by court painter Johann Schuster (1666?–1724) depict the architecture and decorations of the grottoes and pavilions which Duke Heinrich had constructed in the gardens of his castle at Glücksburg between 1692 and 1698 to celebrate the birthdays and name-days of his wife. Many of these incorporate heraldic and emblematic devices; the last part of the book is totally devoted to more than 500 emblems. Although the architectural plates lack the refinement of contemporary work by Sébastien Leclerc and Jean Le Pautre (No. 33 and 38), and the emblematic plates are positively clumsy in execution compared to the treatment of similar subjects by such artists as Crispin de Passe and Albert Flamen, Schuster's illustrations are not without a certain crude charm and vividly evoke the atmosphere of Duke Heinrich's provincial Versailles.

Most of the architectural books and emblem books from the Hofer collection were given to the Department of Printing and Graphic Arts long ago. Early examples are described in Ruth Mortimer's two catalogues, *French 16th Century Books* (Cambridge, 1964) and *Italian 16th Century Books* (Cambridge, 1974); *Sixteenth-Century Architectural Books from Italy and France* (Cambridge, 1971) lists fifty-nine titles, forty-nine of which were given by Philip Hofer. These include two copies of the Como Vitruvius of 1521 and early editions of the works of Serlio, Vignola, Palladio, Philibert de L'Orme and Androuet du Cerceau. Additional architectural books are listed in No. 48 and 49. Notable among numerous emblem books are many early editions of Alciati's *Emblematum libellus* including the first edition (Augsburg, 1531) and the Wechel edition (Paris, 1534), which served as the prototype for subsequent French and German editions. Of special interest are the many manuscript emblem books donated by Hofer. His manuscript copy of Geoffrey Whitney, *A Choice of Emblemes* was presented by Whitney to Robert Dudley, Earl of Leicester in 1585, the year before the first edition of this first English emblem book was published in Leyden. The manuscript of Ottavio Strada, *Simbola Romanorum Imperatorum* (Prague, 1599) is also earlier than the published version, which did not appear until 1602–1603. Other manuscript emblem books include Principio Fabricii, *Allusioni, imprese et emblemi sopra l'arme della Santità di N.S. Gregorio Papa XIII* [Rome, ca. 1588], *Eloquentiae tesserae seu praeceptiones oratoriae amoeniss[im]is* [France, 1662?], Manoel Pinheiro Arnaut, *Templo da Fama* (Lisbon, 1665) and Petrus Buchowski, *Cantica matutina* ([Poland], 1701–1702). The manuscript of a French emblem book, apparently related to Albert Flamen, *Devises et emblesmes d'amour* (Paris, 1653) was included in the bequest, as was a copy of the 1658 edition of the printed book. In *Baroque Book Illustration*, Hofer praised Flamen as a little-known artist whose best work was in a class with Callot's (see No. 30).

N.F.

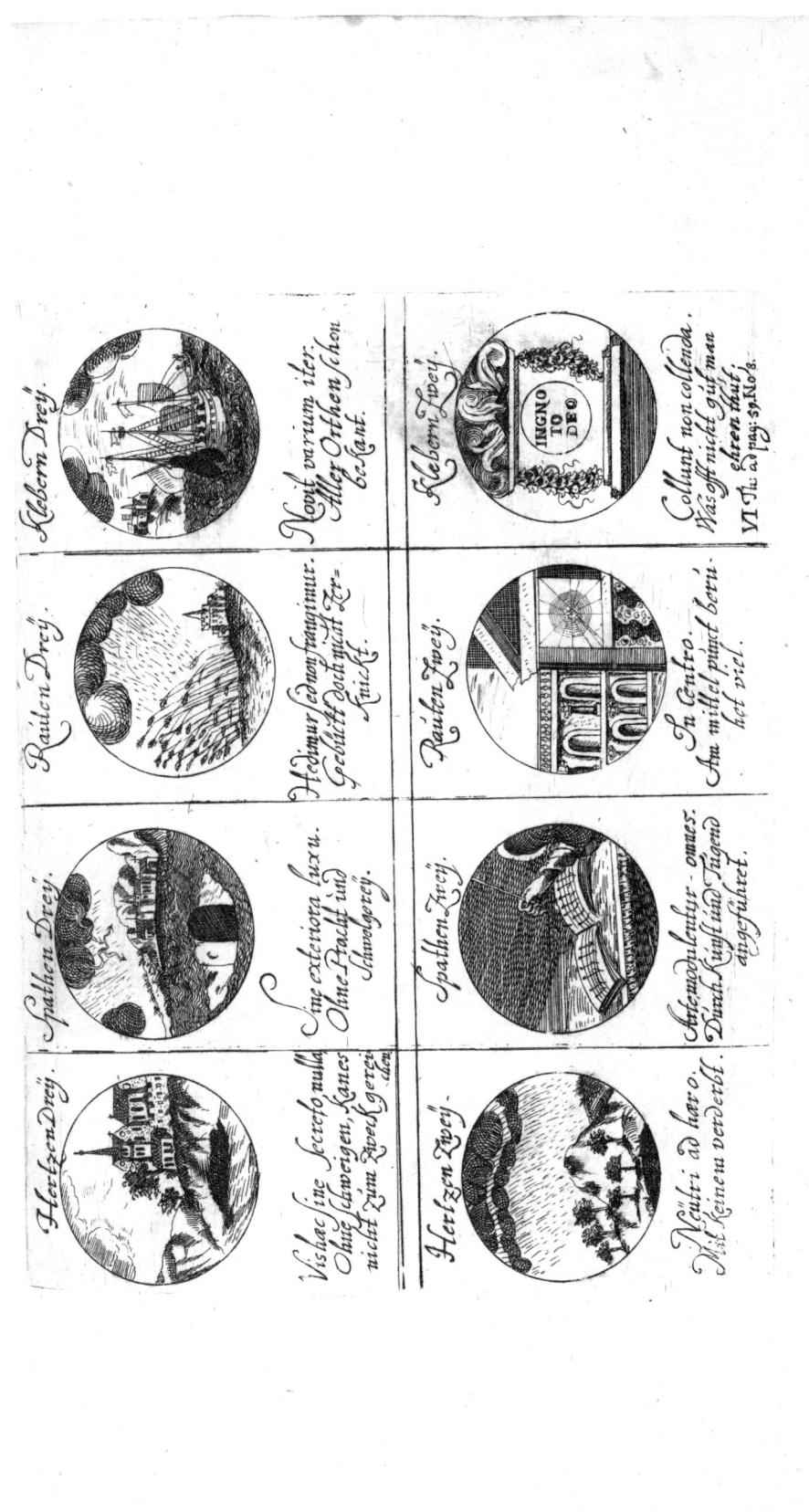

No. 41. Emblems from *Fürstliche Bau-Lust*.

42 ❧ GILLES MARIE OPPENORD, 1672–1742
Drawing Book
Rome? 1698

Drawings by Oppenord in graphite, pen, ink and wash; 86 leaves.

27.1 x 20.4 cm. Vellum wrappers, inscribed on back cover "Recueil de / plusieurs Morceaux / D'architecture des / differents Eglises d'Italie / L'An mdciic / Oppenord fec."; inscribed on spine "n° 117."

THIS REMARKABLE ALBUM of drawings by Gilles-Marie Oppenord is an important document for the study of the origins of French rococo architecture. It dates from the period when Oppenord was pursuing his studies in Italy, and contains a series of details from the works of the greatest Italian baroque architects, including Bernini, Borromini, Ammanati and Palladio. It is clearly not a travel sketchbook, since the drawings are not arranged geographically but instead are roughly grouped by categories: cartouches, consoles, doorways, entablatures, moldings, tombs, vases, etc. Indeed, the album appears to have been very deliberately composed, presumably from preliminary studies, and it has been worked over to achieve a very high and very consistent degree of finish. The latest additions appear to be those in brown ink, which are sometimes even on separate slips of paper, pasted down over parts of the original drawings. It is these additions which most clearly reveal Oppenord's budding rococo tendencies. Creeping vegetation threatens to engulf many baroque monuments; doorways offer unexpected vistas into enchanted gardens which anticipate Watteau.

Oppenord's drawings were avidly collected in his lifetime, by Watteau, among others. Gabriel Huquier, who acquired a vast collection of over 2000, used them as the basis for his *Oeuvres de Gilles-Marie Oppenord*, published in three parts between 1737 and 1751. A copy of the third and largest part, known as *Le Grand Oppenord*, was purchased by the Department of Printing and Graphic Arts in 1985, using Hofer funds. It contains many of Oppenord's own architectural projects, including his designs for the decorations of the Palais Royal. Although the style here is full-blown rococo, the sketchy landscape settings and many specific motifs are directly related to the drawings in the Hofer album. Furthermore, the series as a whole is organized in parts (*Cartouches*, *Fontaines*, *Moulures*, etc.) reminiscent of the categories in the drawing book.

Oppenord, who was chiefly known in his lifetime as an architect, was also active as an illustrator. Headpieces and initial letters by him are included in the 1734 edition of Molière, one of the masterpieces of French rococo book illustration, with full-page plates after François Boucher. The copy in the Department of Printing and Graphic Arts was the gift of James Hazen Hyde; a copy of the second issue of 1737 is in the Hofer bequest. Other important French rococo books include the La Fontaine of 1755–1759 with illustrations after Jean-Baptiste Oudry, represented in the bequest by a set of forty-four proofs before letters and among previous gifts by two superb copies of the book, one on "papier ordinaire" and one on "grand papier, dit impérial." A drawing by Oudry, "La chauve souris, le buisson et le canard," was purchased for the Department of Printing and Graphic Arts with Hofer funds in 1978. The bequest also includes Ovid's *Métamorphoses* (Paris, 1767–1771), according to Gordon Ray "the supreme anthology of French rococo book illustration." Numerous other examples of rococo illustration were previous gifts, and the illustrators, including Charles-Nicolas Cochin, Jean-Michel Moreau and Hubert-François Bourguignon, known as Gravelot, are well-represented in the 1978 Frances L. Hofer bequest of drawings for book illustration.

Another previous Hofer gift was a bound volume of sketches by Giuseppe Galli Bibiena (1696–1757), including drawings for stage sets, festival decorations, and ornamental work. For other books on ornament, see No. 43 and 53. Other architectural books are discussed in No. 41, 48 and 49, French baroque illustrators in No. 33, 38 and 39.

N.F.

REF Guilmard, p. 141–142; Thieme-Becker XXVI, 31–32; Cohen-De Ricci, p. 764–765; *Regency to Empire*, p. 60–62, 352–355; J. Mathey and Carl Nordenfalk, "Watteau and Oppenort," *Burlington Magazine*, XCVII (1955), 132–140.

No. 42. Gilles Marie Oppenord. Architectural drawings.

43   SIMON GRIBELIN, 1661–1733
A New Book of Ornaments Useful to All Artists
[London] Published by the author, 1704

12 engravings by Gribelin, including engraved title; additional engraving bound in; drawing in ink and wash of the Fountaine arms and motto; autograph dedication on verso, inserted before title-page.

20.3 x 25.8 cm. Early 18th-century red morocco, gilt, with the Fountaine elephant stamped in gold on the front cover. Dedication (see above) to Sir Andrew Fountaine with his arms; bookplate of John Charrington Shenley.

HORACE WALPOLE, in *A Catalogue of Engravers* (Strawberry Hill, 1763) asserted that Gribelin had neither "greatness in his manner or capacity. His works have no more merit than finicalness [sic]—and that not in perfection—can give them. His prints are at best neat memorandums." Nevertheless Philip Hofer greatly admired this artist for his extraordinarily detailed workmanship and his consummate talent for graphic design.

Gribelin was born in Blois and worked in Paris before emigrating to London about the year 1680. He was descended from a long line of watchmakers, engravers, goldsmiths and enamelers, and his own publications were primarily directed to practitioners of these trades. Although the designs in *A New Book of Ornaments* recall large-scale architectural decorations of the period of Louis XIV, they were obviously intended as models for objects on a much smaller scale: watches, snuff-boxes, jewelry, gold- and silversmiths' work of every sort. Its modest price—it originally sold for just three shillings—suggests that many copies may have been used in just this way. The Hofer copy, however, belonged to no simple artisan. Inserted before the title-page is an autograph dedication to Sir Andrew Fountaine (1676–1753), a noted collector of china, pictures, coins, books and other objects of art. On the verso is a drawing of the Fountaine coat of arms with the motto "vix ea nostra voco" ("I scarce call these things our own"). The same motto also appears in one of the designs reproduced in plate 9. The pristine condition of this copy is no doubt due to the fact that it remained in the Fountaine family until the sale of their library in 1902.

Also in the bequest is a copy of Colonel William Parsons's translation of André Félibien, *The Tent of Darius Explain'd* (London, 1703). In the preface, Parsons speaks highly of "that Great Artist Mr. Gribelin," who not only engraved the large folding plate after Le Brun's painting of *The Tent of Darius*, but also the small decorative vignettes, which in their miniaturist detail are closely related to the designs in *A New Book of Ornaments*.

Historically, the term "ornament book" has been used in two slightly different ways. On the one hand, it may refer to contemporary pattern books, like Gribelin's suite of engravings. On the other hand, it may also be applied to reproductions of Greek, Roman, Medieval or other decorations, which may serve equally as source books for designers or as references for antiquaries. Examples in the bequest range from a London coffin maker's pattern book of ca. 1790—with actual metal specimens tipped in—through the fantastic designs of Piranesi (No. 49) and Filippo Morghen (*Raccolta delle cose più notabili vedute da Giovanni Wilkins*, Naples? 1764). Giocondo Albertolli is represented by two magnificent volumes: *Alcune decorazioni di nobili sale ed altri ornamenti* ([Milan] 1787) and *Ornamenti diversi* (3 pts. in 1 vol.; Milan [1782–1796]). Some French examples are listed in No. 53. Architectural books from the bequest are discussed in No. 41 and 49.

In 1941, a collotype facsimile of Hofer's copy of *A New Book of Ornaments* was printed at the Meriden Gravure Company and published by the Timothy Press. Hofer provided an introductory essay on Gribelin and his work, and Rudolph Ruzicka contributed technical comments on the collotype process.

N.F.

REF Guilmard, no. 56; Thieme-Becker XV, 19–20; Berlin, Staatliche Museen, *Katalog der Ornamentstichsammlung der Staatlichen Kunstbibliothek* (Berlin and Leipzig, 1939), no. 752; Philip Hofer and Rudolph Ruzicka, *A Book of Ornaments Engraved by Simon Gribelin II* (Meriden, Conn., 1941).

No. 43. Simon Gribelin. Engraved title of *A New Book of Ornaments*.

44 ❧ JAKOB CHRISTOF LE BLON, 1667–1741
Coloritto; Or the Harmony of Colouring in Painting
[London, ca. 1720]

5 mezzotints by Le Blon, 4 of them printed in color. Presentation copy inscribed "from the Author".

28 x 21.5 cm. Contemporary mottled calf, blind-stamped with foliated border.

THE TONAL QUALITY of the mezzotint (No. 34) is reinforced by color in Le Blon's process, which sought to reproduce oil paintings of the old masters. Following the Newtonian principle that all color is composed of a mixture of the three primaries, red, yellow, and blue, Le Blon may be seen as the inventor of the three-color process in printing. As demonstrated here, a female head was printed first in black; then, with the use of separate plates for each color, it was printed successively in blue, yellow, and red, thus modeling the form in color. The fifth plate in this copy depicts a palette with lettered swatches of color; in the accompanying text, the artist instructs the painter in their use to create flesh tones.

This rare little treatise was very influential during the eighteenth century, when demand for color printing led to many experiments (see No. 53). Le Blon took out an English patent for his process, but it was never a commercial success. Its principles of color separation, however, are the basis for modern color printing.

The German-born Le Blon ended his career in Paris, where, in 1756, one of his followers, Antoine Gautier de Montdorge published a second edition of the *Coloritto*, entitled *L'art d'imprimer les tableaux, Traité ... de J.C. Le Blon* (copy in the bequest). The dramatic work of a more controversial follower, Jacques-Fabien Gautier d'Agoty is represented by his *Myologie* of 1748, a previous Hofer gift, as are Jan L'Admiral's color-printed anatomical plates of 1738–1741. The theory of eighteenth-century color printing in the woodcut medium is represented by John Baptist Jackson's *An Essay on the Invention of Engraving and Printing in Chiaro oscuro* of 1754, its practice in his *Titiani Vecelli ... Opera Selectiora* (Venice, 1745).

E.M.G.

REF R.M. Burch, *Colour Printing and Colour Printers* (London, 1910), p. 51f.; Colin and Charlotte Franklin, *A Catalogue of Early Colour Printing* (Oxford, 1977), p. 39–40; Joan M. Friedman, *Color Printing in England, 1486–1870* (New Haven, 1978), p. 9.

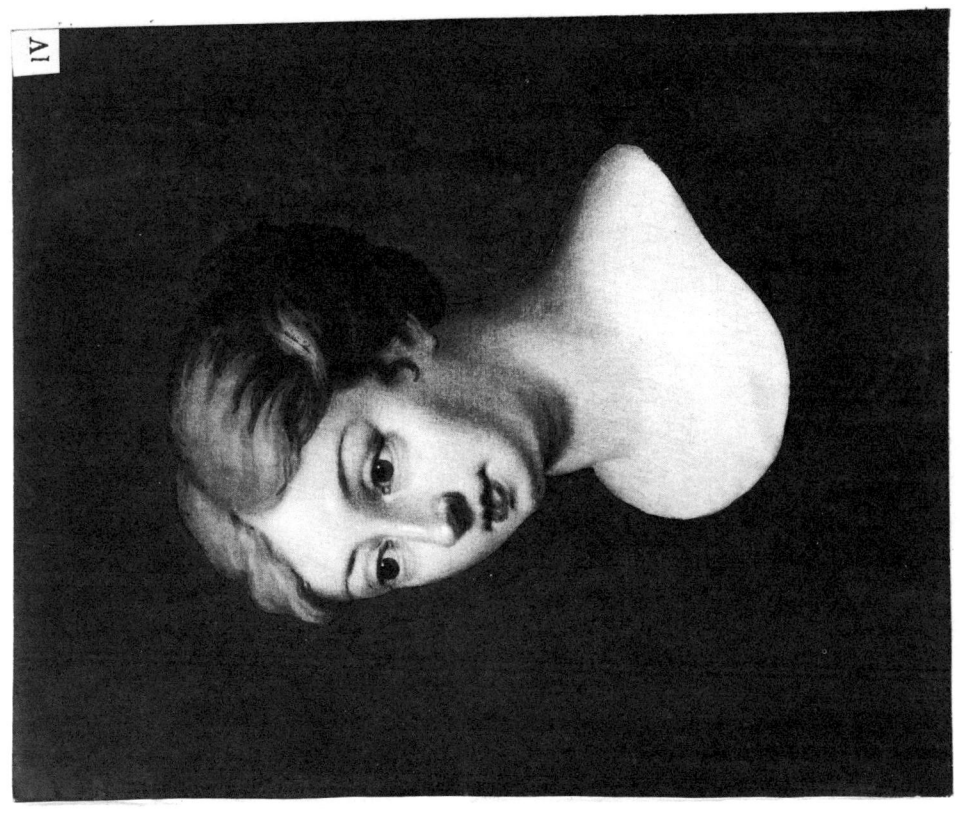

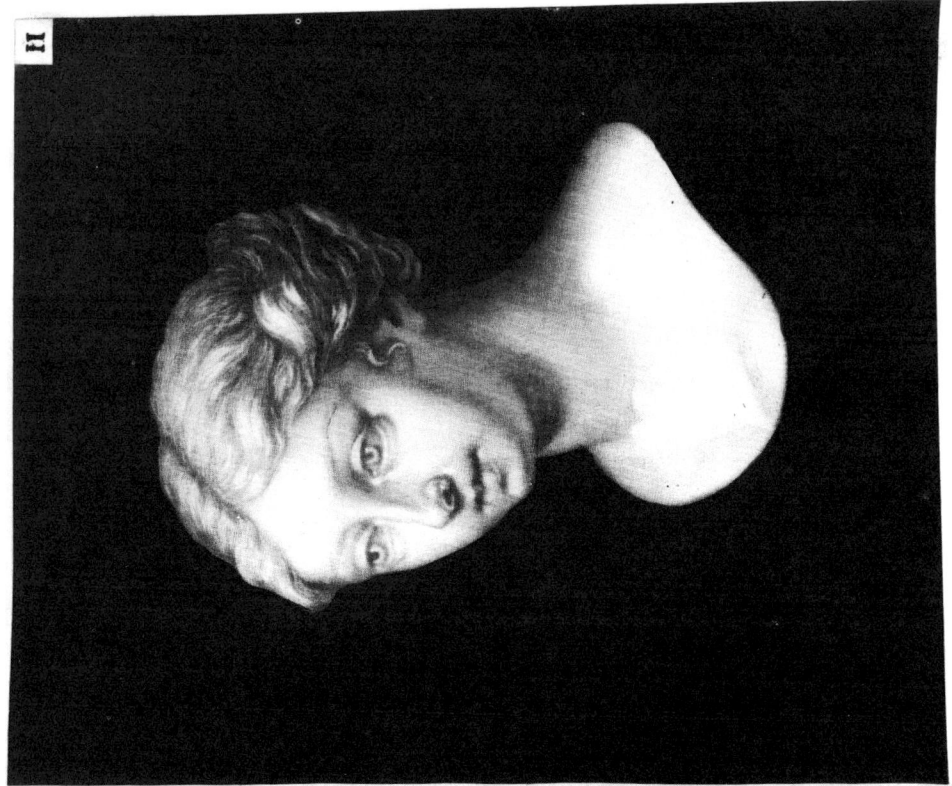

No. 44. Jakob Christof Le Blon. Progressive proofs from *Coloritto*.

45   PHILIBERT HUEBER, 1665–1725
Austria ex Archivis Mellicensibus Illustrata
Leipzig, for Johann Gleditsch, 1722

Engravings and woodcuts by [Johann Gottfried?] Krügner and Ignat[z] Raderer.

37.2 x 24.2 cm. Dark red morocco, gilt.

THE HANDSOME pointillé compartment binding on Philibert Hueber, *Austria ex Archivis Mellicensibus Illustrata*, incorporates the crossed keys of the Benedictine Abbey of Melk. The text is a collection of documents from the Abbey library and many of the plates depict the seals affixed to these manuscripts. Other illustrations include a general view of the Abbey prior to its rebuilding later in the eighteenth century, and an allegorical representation of the library, as well as an allegorical frontispiece. Some of the illustrations are signed "Ignat. Raderer delin." and others "Krügner sculps." thus identifying Raderer as the draughtsman and Krügner as the engraver. It it not unlikely, however, that additional artists were engaged on the project, especially since some of the illustrations are engravings and others are woodcuts. Krügner may probably be identified as Johann Gottfried Krügner, who was active in Leipzig in the mid-eighteenth century.

A manuscript from Melk, the *Modus scribendi* of ca. 1440 (MS Typ 111) was given by Hofer to the Houghton Library in 1983, in honor of James E. Walsh, Keeper of Printed Books (see Philip Hofer, "The Melk *Modus scribendi*, in *Essays in Honor of James Edward Walsh*, Cambridge, 1983, p. 27–28). A transcription and translation of this important early writing manual were published by Stanley Morison in 1940.

Pointillé tooling emerged in France in the third decade of the seventeenth century. Small tools were used to create dotted outlines, which, on richly-tooled bindings, produced sparkling jewel-like effects. The leaf tendrils and the outlines on the Melk binding were created in this way. Other examples of pointillé tooling in the Hofer bequest occur on a sombre binding for Anne of Austria, on *Office de la Semaine Saincte* (Paris, 1655), and on a dos à dos binding in blue and red morocco, on *Heures et Office de la Sainte Vierge* (Paris, 1658). From France, the style spread to other countries such as Austria (exemplified by the Melk binding) and England. A copy of *The Works* of Edward Reynolds (London, 1658), included in the bequest, was bound in dark blue morocco tooled with both solid and pointillé tools by the Queen's Binder A. Howard Nixon has suggested that the Queen's Binder A may be William Nott, who ran one of the largest and most active shops in London during the third quarter of the seventeenth century.

For additional fine bindings, see No. 29 and 39.

N.F.

REF   Walters, *History of Bookbinding*, no. 446; Howard M. Nixon, *Five Centuries of English Bookbinding* (London, 1978), p. 104.

No. 45.   Binding of Philibert Hueber, *Austria ex Archivis Mellicensibus Illustrata*.

46 & CLAUDE LAMESLE, ACTIVE CA. 1737–1769
Epreuves générales des caractères
Paris, 1742

Specimens of type and ornaments, printed on one side of the leaf only.

21.5 x 15 cm. Mottled brown calf. Label of P.J. Eman.

THE TYPES of Claude Lamesle preserve a continuity with the previous century, for in 1737 he purchased the foundry of Jean and Pierre Cot, established in 1670 and containing founts of Jean Jannon, active as early as 1611. The tradition of the old style letter at its best is presented in the *Epreuves générales*, one of the finest French type specimens of the first half of the eighteenth century. In 1758 Lamesle sold his foundry to Nicolas Gando (whose 1745 *Recueil d'ornemens* is in the Hofer collection). Lamesle himself went to Avignon, where in 1769 he issued his *Modèles de caractères*, also in the bequest. Among other eighteenth century French specimens in the bequest may be noted manuals from the firms of Fournier (No. 51), Gillé (Paris, 1773), Luce (Paris, 1740), and Vaussy (Rouen, 1772).

Philip Hofer's interest in letter forms led him to collect type specimens and printers' manuals even before the founding of the Department of Printing and Graphic Arts. They range from the sixteenth to the twentieth century, and the French collection is particularly strong, beginning with Robert Estienne's *Alphabetum Graecum* of 1548. Some two hundred examples in the bequest represent Western Europe and the United States.

E.M.G.

REF   Bigmore and Wyman, I, 419; Birrell & Garnett, no. 35; Audin, no. 27; Updike, I, 269–271.

Gros Canon Maîgre ordinaire,
Numero LVIII.

femmes.   Ce qu'ayant crû elle lui envoya cette Robe par Lycas son serviteur, un jour qu'il sacrifioit sur le Mont Oeta. Mais la chose arriva tout autrement qu'elle ne pensoit, car il n'eut pas sitost pris cet habit, que la malignité du sang de Nessus qui étoit un très-puissant venin, lui entra par tout le corps, & lui causa une ardeur si furieuse, que par

R

No. 46.   Type specimen from Claude Lamesle, *Epreuves générales des caractères*.

47   DANTE ALIGHIERI, 1265–1321
La divina commedia
Venice, Antonio Zatta, 1757–1758

4 vols. 114 full-page engraved plates; 100 engraved canto summaries within pictorial borders; 72 engraved head- and tailpieces. Copy printed in color on large thick paper.

31.5 x 22.5 cm. Contemporary red morocco, double gilt fillets with floral ornaments at inner corners; marbled endpapers. Bookplate of Dogmersfield Library (Sir Henry St. J. Mildmay).

A LARGE COLLECTION of eighteenth-century Italian illustration was built up and given to the Library through the years by Philip Hofer, and the Dante is one of the few still in his personal collection at the time of the bequest. He had already given a regular copy and acquired this color-printed example some years later. Its publisher, Antonio Zatta, was one of the three most important Venetian publishers of the eighteenth century in Venice (Giovanni Battista Albrizzi and Giovanni Battista Pasquali, the other two, are well represented in the collection with all their major books).

Zatta's Dante is an example of the Venetian rococo book at its most colorful and characteristic. It is an elaborate companion to Zatta's 1756 two-volume Petrarch, a previous gift, and is based on Albrizzi's great 1745 folio Tasso (three copies, all variants, in Printing and Graphic Arts). Seventeen different artists shared the tasks of the four Dante volumes, a typical arrangement for a book of this scope. Seven professional engravers prepared the plates after the drawings of ten different draughtsmen; the occasional artist did both. The customary procedure for the plate work was first to etch the copper, then touch it up with engraving. The names of most of the Dante artists—Bartolomeo Crivellari, Francesco Fontebasso, Giuseppe Magnini, Gaetano Zompini, Giuliano Zuliani, for example—appear in the Petrarch and again and again in Venetian illustration. They and many others formed a core of professional book artists working for numerous publishers, and they could turn their skills to allegory, literature, genre, science, or ceremony, all amply represented in the collection.

The Dante is dedicated to the Empress Elizabeth of Russia, an indication of the international character of Venetian publishing at this time. The full-page canto frontispieces are narrative illustrations, while the borders of the canto headings are ornamental designs in cartouche shape, incorporating images suggested by the text. As so often in Dante, the liveliest ones are from the Inferno, where the artist's imagination played with the grotesque, like his medieval predecessors. The basic layout for traditional literature seen in the Dante was carried on by Zatta in his 1772 Ariosto, seen in a large blue paper copy in the Hofer collection. A number of its ornaments come from the Dante, which was the source for much later Venetian book decoration; borrowing, re-working, and copying was an established practice.

Color printing, widely practised in Venice at this time, distinguishes this issue of the Dante. Three single separate colors were used—red, blue, and black—with no overprinting or mixing. Color often contributes to the sumptuous character of Venetian books, and among previous Hofer gifts may be mentioned Giorgio Fossati's 1744 *Raccolta di varie favole* and his *Memorie della vita di San Giuseppe* of 1750 and *Vita del glorioso San Rocco* of 1751. Other examples are Zaccaria Seriman's *Aristippo* of 1744 and his *Viaggio di Enrico Wanton* of 1748. Most striking is the 1761 edition of Antonio Visentini's great book on San Marco, *L'augusta ducale basilica* (see No. 48). Three copies, all variants, are in the collection.

Venice with its lavish productions is but one of the eighteenth-century Italian regions represented in the collection. Numerous shelves are devoted to other towns of the Veneto, to Milan, Florence, Rome, Naples, and many smaller cities, each with its distinctive style, the whole collection numbering well over a thousand volumes.

E.M.G.

REF   Brunet, II, 505; Cornell University Library, *Catalogue of the Dante Collection* (Ithaca, New York, 1921), I, p. 1; G. Morazzoni, *Il libro illustrato del Settecento* (Milan, 1943), p. 225; Maria Lanckorónska, *Die Venezianische Buchgraphik des XVIII Jahrhunderts* (Hamburg, 1950), no. 82; Venice, Biblioteca Nazionale Marciana, *Il libro illustrato nel Settecento a Venezia* (Venice [1955]), no. 5.

No. 47. Giuliano Giampiccoli after Francesco Fontebasso. Illustration from Dante's *Inferno*.

48 ❧ ANTONIO VISENTINI, 1699–1782
Album of Architectural Drawings
Venice, ca. 1760

50 drawings, some double-page, in graphite, pen, ink and wash.

52 x 36.5 cm. Contemporary red morocco, gilt extra. Bookplates of Richard Blackett Beaumont and Sir Alfred Lane Beit. Formerly in the library of the Duke of Newcastle at Clumber. With this are bound 4 sheets of English architectural drawings of a classical temple, executed in graphite, pen, ink and wash; previous owner's note states an attribution to William Chambers.

THE FIFTY DRAWINGS, unsigned and unnumbered, all identified in ink by the same hand, depict in plan and elevation seventeen buildings in Venice and the Veneto. Particular prominence is given to Venetian structures by Palladio (San Giorgio Maggiore, the Carità, the Redentore, and San Francesco della Vigna), reflecting Visentini's devotion to the great Renaissance architect, so revered in the circle of the British Consul Joseph Smith, of which Visentini was part. A record of that association is the final drawing in the album, Smith's palace on the Grand Canal as remodeled by Visentini.

Architect, painter, draughtsman, and printmaker, Visentini spent his life in Venice. Through his long association with Consul Smith, many of the artist's engravings appear in books with the imprint of Giovanni Battista Pasquali (whose mark he designed), the Venetian publisher financed by Smith. The latter's patronage included Antonio Canaletto, for whom Visentini engraved the painter's views in the series *Prospectus Magni Canalis Venetiarum in Aedibus Josephi Smith Angli* of 1735 (second expanded edition of 1742 in the bequest).

The largest concentration of drawings from the Visentini studio is in England (ca. 1000 drawings in the British Museum, the Royal Institute of British Architects, and Windsor Castle). Many of these were in Consul Smith's collection purchased by George III in 1762; others were sold to Englishmen in eighteenth-century Venice as mementos of travel and possible models for country houses at home.

Although Visentini's large production necessitated assistants, they were not associated with this album. These delicate and luminous drawings have been attributed to Visentini's own hand by the late John McAndrew (letter inserted in the album). Only two other drawings were so attributed by McAndrew (in his RIBA catalogue, p. 10).

Architectural books with engravings by Visentini in the Department of Printing and Graphic Arts include:

Visentini, *Raccolta di vari schizi di ornati di celebre autore*. Venice, Francesco Zuccarelli, 1747.

L'augusta ducale basilica dell'evangelista San Marco. Venice, Antonio Zatta, 1761. 3 cops. (Second edition of Visentini's 1726 *Iconografia della ducal basilica*).

Teofilo Gallacini, *Trattato sopra gli errori degli architetti*. Venice, Pasquali, 1767.

Visentini, *Osservazioni che servono di continuazione al trattato di Teofilo Gallacini*. Venice, 1771.

In addition to his engravings after Canaletto's *vedute*, Visentini did a series of architectural initials and headpieces of the islands of the lagoon for Pasquali's 1738 edition of Francesco Guicciardini's *Della istoria d'Italia*.

Another Venetian architectural document in the bequest is Giuseppe Maria Soli's set of drawings for Napoleon's projected royal palace in Piazza San Marco. A large portfolio bound with the arms of Napoleon I as King of Italy, it consists of seven folding double-page drawings in ink and wash, including plans, elevations, a section, and a sheet of cost estimates signed by Soli.

E.M.G.

REF Sotheby & Co., London, *The Clumber Library*, 21 June 1937, pt. 1, no. 203; Anthony Blunt and Edward Croft-Murray, *Venetian Drawings of the XVII & XVIII Centuries at Windsor Castle* (London [1957]), p. 67f.; Royal Institute of British Architects, London, *Catalogue of the Drawings Collection: Antonio Visentini* by John McAndrew [1974]; Frances Vivian, *Il console Smith* [Vicenza, 1971].

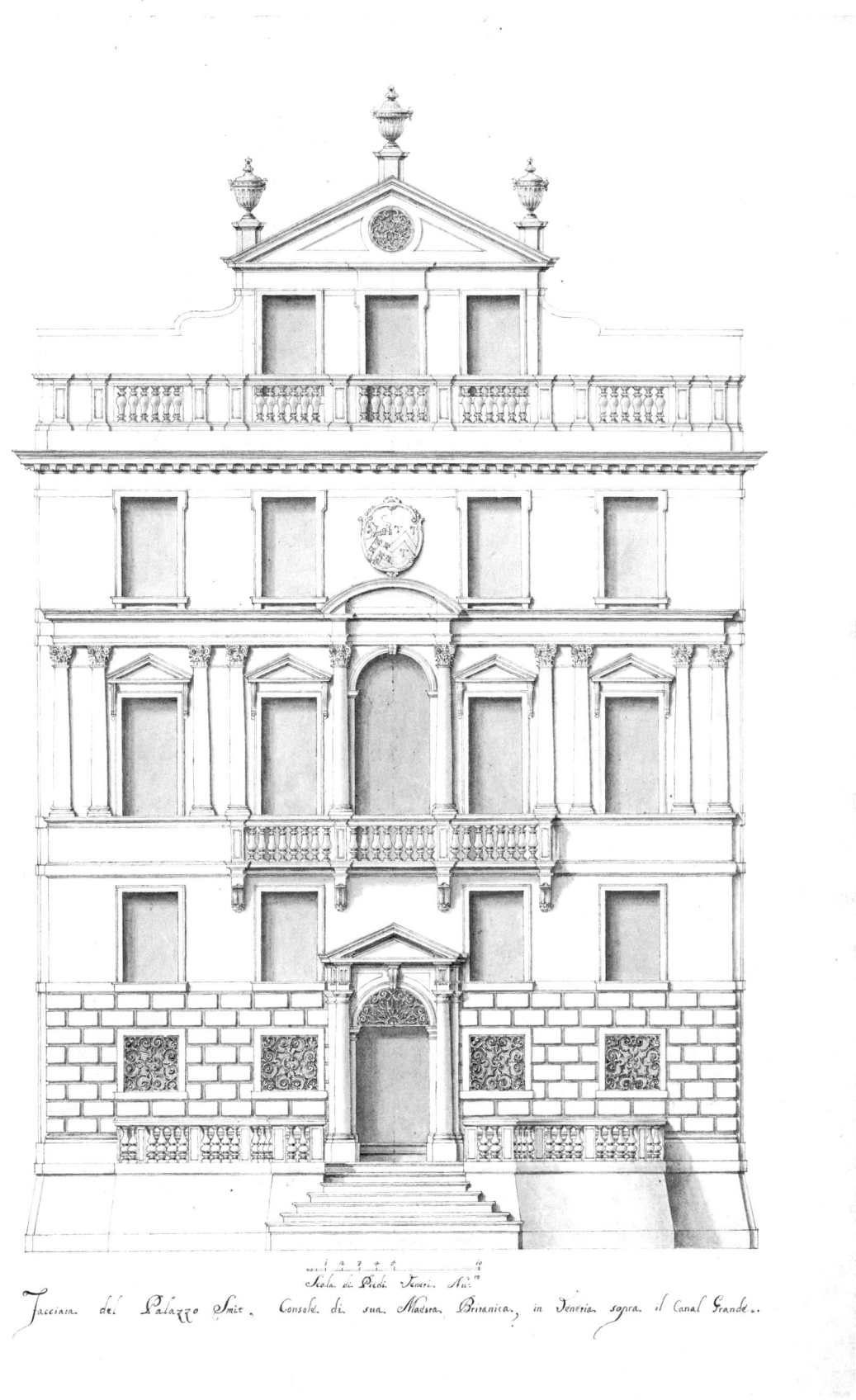

No. 48. Antonio Visentini. Design for the palace of Consul Joseph Smith.

49 ❧ GIOVANNI BATTISTA PIRANESI, 1720–1778
Antichità di Cora
[Rome, G.B. Piranesi, 1764]

Etched title, 10 etched headpiece and full-page illustrations by Piranesi.

54 x 41 cm. Red morocco, gilt extra. Bookplate of Irwin Laughlin. Bound with G.B. Piranesi, *Le rovine del Castello dell'Acqua Giulia* (1761) and Francesco Piranesi, *Il teatro d'Ercolano* (1783).

THE *ANTICHITA DI CORA* is one of five splendid portfolios of the antiquities of Latium, south of Rome, published by Piranesi in the sixth decade of the eighteenth century. In 1761 appeared *Le rovine del Castello dell'Acqua Giulia*; about 1762–1764, the *Descrizione e disegno dell'Emissario del Lago Albano* and *Di due spelonchi ornati dagli antichi alla Riva del Lago Albano*; and in 1764, the *Antichità d'Albano e di Castel Gandolfo*. The artist began his journey south to Cora (Cori on modern maps) after a stay at Castel Gandolfo, the summer residence of Pope Clement XIII, whose family, the Venetian Rezzonico, were patrons of Piranesi, *architetto veneziano*, as he so often styled himself. Author and artist of the *Antichità di Cora*, as well as of the other four books cited above, Piranesi in these volumes combines his skills as architect, antiquarian, and printmaker. He was a partisan of the Italian origin of ancient architecture, and in the Cora volume he concentrates on the the temple of Hercules. His historical account of the ruins and his precise and detailed rendering of plans and elevations are overshadowed by his dramatic compositions and chiaroscuro. So forcefully did Piranesi combine technical mastery of the etched plate with theatrical vision that his view of the Roman world has dominated the European imagination.

Piranesi as a book artist and author is amply represented in the Hofer collection, which contains at least one issue of each of his major publications, some in more than one copy, permitting a study of states and variants in a body of work noted for its complexity. In the bequest is another copy of the *Antichità di Cora*, bound with the *Opere varie* (1750), and four plates of the *Grotteschi* (the Earl of Aylesford's copy). A companion to the first copy of the *Antichità di Cora* discussed here, also bound in red morocco, gilt extra from the collection of Irwin Laughlin, is *Il campo Marzio* of 1762. From the decade of the 1740s is the *Prima parte di architetture* (1743) and the *Varie vedute di Roma* (1748 and 1752 editions). From the 1750s are another copy of the *Opere varie* (1750) and the *Trofei di Ottaviano Augusto* (1753, the sixth Duke of Portland's copy). Another Portland copy is the *Lapides Capitolini* of 1762. Other titles from the sixties are *Della magnificenza ed architettura de' Romani* (1761), bound with *Osservazioni sopra la lettre de M. Mariette* (1765) and *Diverse maniere d'adornare i cammini* (1769). *Vasi, candelabri, cippi* dates from 1778, the year of the artist's death.

Previous Hofer gifts include another copy of the *Antichità d'Albano*, the *Antichità Romane de' tempi della Repubblica* (1748), *Le Antichità Romane* (1756), and the *Lettere di Giustificazione scritte a Milord Charlemont* (1757). Hofer's commitment to Piranesi is further demonstrated in a large drawing in the Frances L. Hofer bequest, executed in pen, ink, wash, and red chalk for *Le Antichità Romane* of 1756 (pl. II in vol. IV; Becker, no. 7).

The Piranesi volumes may be seen as part of the architectural books Philip Hofer collected in great numbers. The sixteenth-century French and Italian examples are recorded in the Mortimer catalogues, and they include the major editions of Androuet du Cerceau and de L'Orme, Alberti, Palladio, Serlio, Vignola, and Vitruvius; from the same century is Vredeman de Vries' *Architectura* of 1581. From a Baroque and modern group too large to enumerate, a few may be mentioned: Leoni's English Palladio of 1716, Salomon Kleiner's *Dilucida Representatio*, his 1737 account of Fischer von Erlach's great Vienna royal library, Ferdinando Galli da Bibiena's *L'architettura civile* of 1711, Humphrey Repton's *Design for the Pavillon at Brighton* of 1806, and Frank Lloyd Wright's *Ausgeführte Bauten* (Berlin, 1910), the book that introduced his work to Europe.

E.M.G.

REF Henri Focillon, *Giovanni Battista Piranesi, essai de catalogue raisonnée* (Paris, 1918), no. 537–550; Focillon, *Giovanni Battista Piranesi* (Paris, 1928), p. 112–113; Arthur M. Hind, *Giovanni Battista Piranesi, A Critical Study* (London, 1922), p. 85; Philip Hofer, "Giovanni Battista Piranesi as a Book Illustrator" [in] Smith College Museum of Art, *Piranesi* (Northampton, Mass., 1961); Andrew Robison, "Giovanni Battista Piranesi: Prolegomena to the Princeton Collection," *The Princeton University Library Chronicle*, XXXI (1970), 187.

No. 49. Giovanni Battista Piranesi. Illustration from *Antichità di Cora*.

50 🙢 LUIGI SUBLEYRAS, 18TH CENTURY
Nella venuta in Roma di Madama Le Comte e dei Signori Watelet e Copette
[Rome] 1764
Intaglio illustrations and borders by ETIENNE DE LAVALLEE-POUSSIN, 1735–1892 and HUBERT ROBERT, 1733–1808

32 etchings, most of them designed by Lavallée-Poussin, engraved by Lavallée-Poussin and other members of the French Academy at Rome, including engraved text within ornamental borders, 2 of these designed and etched by Robert.

22 x 16 cm. Large paper copy. Red morocco, gilt fillet and lettering on covers. Boxed with this copy are 9 proofs before numbers.

A FAVORITE BOOK of Philip Hofer, *Nella venuta in Roma* was published in facsimile by him as Fogg Museum Picture Book Number Five in 1956. Six years later he acquired this copy, on large paper. Set and published in Rome, this little book is a French production steeped in Roman atmosphere. The twelve illustrations allude to the visit of Claude Henri Watelet (1718–1786), an amateur artist and writer, with his pupil and mistress, Marguérite Le Comte, and the Abbé Copette, a member of their household. They visited the Apollo Belvedere, the French ambassador, the Pope, and the waterfall at Tivoli, and they studied ancient art and were received by the Accademia degli Arcadi. Their friends at the French Academy published this account in their honor, and along with the plates illustrating their tour are engraved *sonetti* within ornamental borders. Etienne de Lavallée-Poussin was the artist chiefly concerned, for he designed most of the illustrations and the borders and engraved many of them. Hubert Robert, who had been a pensioner of the Academy for ten years, designed and engraved two of the finest borders, with tiny views of Rome. Other associates of the Academy engraved the remaining plates.

The other copy in the Hofer bequest (18 x 13 cm.) permits a comparison of the two issues and indicates that the large paper copy is the first. Its title contains a line removed from the second issue, and in the latter, the portrait of Madame Le Comte is an etched copy of the first version. There are other bibliographical differences, including a leaf of letterpress with French explanation of the plates in the second issue. Boxed with the first issue are nine proofs before numbers and an earlier, larger state of the portrait. The Frances L. Hofer bequest contains two drawings by Lavallée-Poussin for pl. XII, the first one a preliminary sketch much changed in the final version, which was etched by the artist himself (Becker no. 10).

A recent acquisition of the Department of Printing and Graphic Arts, made possible by Hofer purchase funds, is an extra-illustrated copy of the first edition of Watelet's *L'art de peindre*, Paris, 1760, with fifty added intaglio plates by Watelet, including his etched copy of his own portrait by the younger Cochin.

E.M.G.

REF Brunet, I, 576; Cohen-De Ricci, col. 960–961; [Philip Hofer] *A Visit to Rome in 1764* (Cambridge, Mass., Fogg Museum Picture Book No. 5 [1956]); Philip Hofer, "Venuta in Roma," *Harvard Library Bulletin*, X (1956), 193–200; *Regency to Empire*, no. 55 (entry by D.P.B. with discussion of issues).

No. 50. Hubert Robert. Pictorial border from Luigi Subleyras, *Nella venuta in Roma*.

51   PIERRE SIMON FOURNIER, 1712–1768
Manuel typographique
Paris, Printed for the author, 1764–1766

2 vols. Specimens of type and ornaments, printed on both sides of the leaf; engraved frontispieces by Estienne Fessard after Hubert-François Bourguignon, called Gravelot, and Jacques de Sève; title-page border and other decorations composed of type ornaments; 16 engraved plates.

17 x 11.5 cm. Original printed wrappers, decorated with type ornaments.

FOURNIER LE JEUNE, as he styled himself, was one of the most important figures in eighteenth-century French typography, primarily as a typefounder and as the inventor of the point system which standardized the sizing of type bodies. The second son of Jean-Claude Fournier, a printer of Auxerre and a typefounder who had learned his trade under Cot and Le Bé, Simon-Pierre (as he usually signed himself) was brought up in the country by a female relative but came to Paris in his teens just before his father's death to learn the family trade. His elder brother, "a simple unlettered man," purchased the Le Bé foundry in 1731 and the younger Fournier soon struck out for himself as an engraver of woodblock ornaments and later as a punchcutter of display letters. His first type was a 44-point *gros canon* cut in 1736. In 1737, he published his first table defining the dimensions of type bodies, expressed as multiples of the basic point. This invention was a major development in systematizing type designs for printers. Five years later he issued his first major type catalogue, *Modèles des caractères de l'imprimerie*, which D.B. Updike has praised as "one of the most effective and elegant books of its kind ever issued in France."

The capstone of Fournier's career, however, was the *Manuel typographique*. The Hofer copy is an unusually fine example of that famous treatise, which not only provides a description of the processes of punch cutting and typefounding and a summary of the Fournier point system, but also displays the type specimens and ornaments of his own and other leading foundries of France and Germany. Originally it was conceived as a four-volume work, but the author's illness and subsequent death held its length to only two.

Fournier's view of typography was universal in scope. "After the prime necessities of life," he wrote, "nothing is more precious to us than books. The art of typography, their creator, renders a signal service to society and lends it invaluable support, serving, as it does, to educate the citizen, to widen the field for the progress of sciences and arts, to nourish and cultivate the mind, to elevate the soul, and, generally, taking upon itself to be the messenger and interpreter of wisdom and truth" (Carter, p. 1).

The bequest contains four additional Fournier items: *Modèles des caractères* (1742), *Traité historique et critique* (1765) and two broadsides, a small one of 1751 announcing a mass of thanksgiving for the birth of the Duc de Bourgogne and a large one of 1781, "Caractère gravé pour M. [Benjamin] Franklin."

W.B-S.

REF   Bigmore and Wyman, I, 227–229; Birrell & Garnett, no. 37; Audin, I, 89f.; Updike, I, 248f.; [Paul Beaujon, *i.e.*, Beatrice Warde] "Pierre Simon Fournier and xvIIIth Century French Typography," *The Monotype Recorder*, nos. 212–13 (1926); Harry Carter, *Fournier on Typefounding* (London, 1930).

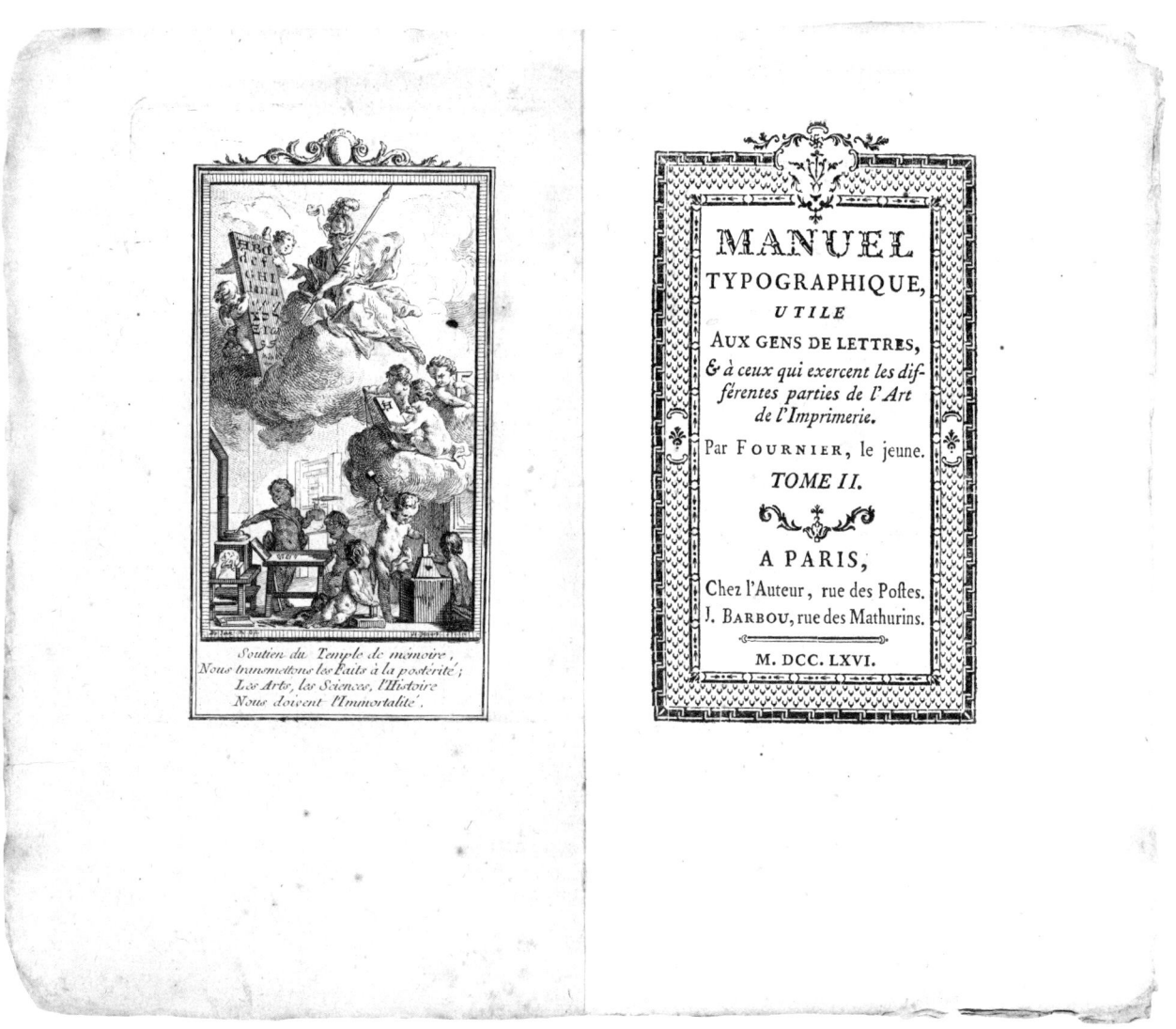

No. 51.   Frontispiece and title-page of Pierre Simon Fournier, *Manuel typographique*.

52 ❧ ENSCHEDÉ FIRM, TYPEFOUNDERS
Epreuves de caractères
Haarlem, J. Enschedé, 1768

Specimens of type and ornaments, printed on one side of the leaf only; 8 engraved plates.

21.5 x 12.5 cm. Black morocco.

IN THIS FRENCH EDITION of the *Proef van Letteren*, also dated 1768 (two copies in the Department of Printing and Graphic Arts, gift of William Bentinck-Smith), the type founder Enschedé published not only a catalogue of available founts, but portraits of its proprietor Johannes Enschedé and its chief punch cutter, the German-born Johann Michael Fleischman, the latter engraved by Cornelis van Noorde. Additional engravings pay homage to Lorenz Coster and his champion Hadrianus Junius, who claimed the Dutch Coster as the founder of printing from movable type. A folding engraving by Cornelis van Noorde depicts the foundry, with punch cutters and casters at work.

Still active today in the printing trade after nearly three hundred years, the Enschedé foundry in the early eighteenth century acquired type from many sources, thus preserving a rare continuity in the history of letters. It possesses a remarkable collection of foundry type, recorded in Charles Enschedé's 1908 *Fonderie de caractères*.

An earlier Enschedé specimen, the *Epreuves de caractères* of 1748, is in the bequest, along with a broadside of 1771. A number of eighteenth-century specimens from the Low Countries are included: from the Netherlands, examples of the firms of Johannes Altheer (Utrecht, 1788), Johann Jacob Bylaert (Amsterdam, 1773), Cornelis Noveman (Haarlem, 1756), Ploos van Amstel, later acquired by Enschedé (Amsterdam, 1784), Voskens and Clerk (Rotterdam, undated specimen). Belgium is represented by J.L. de Boubers (Brussels, 1779) and by J.F. Rosart (Brussels, 1761), the dedication copy to Prince Charles Alexandre, Duke of Lorraine and Bar and governor of the Austrian Netherlands, a copy bound with his coat of arms.

Philip Hofer's frequent trips to Europe and his interest in typography brought him friendship with the late Jan van Krimpen, Enschedé's chief designer for many years. Hofer commissioned from him a manuscript, *A Letter to Philip Hofer on Certain Problems Connected with the Mechanical Cutting of Punches*, 1955, published, with an introduction by John Dreyfus, by the Department of Printing and Graphic Arts in collaboration with David Godine in 1972.

E.M.G.

REF   Bigmore and Wyman, I, 202, Dutch ed.; Birrell & Garnett, no. 71, Dutch ed; Updike, *Printing Types*, II, 35–40; *La maison Enschedé* (Haarlem, 1953), *passim*.

No. 52.   Portrait of J. M. Fleischman from Enschedé, *Epreuves de caractères*.

53 ❧ JEAN PILLEMENT, 1728–1808
Fleurs idealle
Paris, Levier, 1770

Engraved title and 5 additional mezzotints printed in red and black from two plates by Edouard Gautier d'Agoty, 1745–1783, after designs by Pillement.

42.5 x 26.2 cm. Unbound, in box case.

*F*LEURS IDEALLE [sic] is a good example of the kind of rococo confections specialized in by Jean Pillement, interior designer and *peintre de la reine* Marie Antoinette. Pillement's repertory included an almost endless variety of imaginary flowers (*Fleurs persannes, Fleurs de fantaisie, Fleurs de caprice, Fleurs baroques,* etc.) and chinoiseries (*Figures chinoises, Parasols chinois, Balançoires chinoises, Trophées chinoises,* etc.) suitable for either decorative panels or for textile designs. A large number were published by Levier (or Leviez) between 1758 and 1774 in slender *cahiers* of six to eight sheets. A *Nouvelle suitte* [sic] *de cahiers de fleurs idéales* and a *Nouvelle suitte* [sic] *de cahiers chinois*, with color etchings by Anne Allen, were published as late as 1798. According to Thieme-Becker, Allen was Pillement's second wife.

Fleurs idealle was engraved by Edouard Gautier d'Agoty, a member of a prolific family of color printers who continued Le Blon's technique of color mezzotint engraving almost to the end of the eighteenth century. Edouard's father, Jacques-Fabien Gautier d'Agoty, had been Le Blon's assistant, and taught his method to his five sons. Edouard, in turn, passed the method on to Carlo Lasinio (1757–1839), the last printmaker to utilize it, before his early death in Italy. Gautier d'Agoty made only very modest use of the mezzotint rocker in the primarily linear plates of *Fleurs idealle*. Other plates in the series were reproduced as etchings in the chalk manner.

Although François Boucher designed and etched chinoiseries, none are included in the three volumes of furniture and architectural design by him in the bequest. Additional chinoiseries are to be found in George Edwards, *A New Book of Chinese Designs* (London, 1754). For other books on ornament, see No. 42 and 43. Le Blon's color mezzotint technique is discussed in No. 44.

N.F.

REF Guilmard, no. 80; Thieme-Becker XIII, p. 293 and XXVII, pl 42; Berlin, Staatliche Museen, *Katalog der Ornamentstichsammlung der Staatlichen Kunstbibliothek* (Berlin and Leipzig, 1939), no. 449; *Regency to Empire*, no. 115.

No. 53. Jean Pillement. Engraved title of *Fleurs idealle*.

54   [JOHANN WOLFGANG VON GOETHE, 1749–1832]
Das Römische Carneval
Weimar and Gotha, Carl Wilhelm Ettinger, 1789
Printed by Johann Friedrich Unger, Berlin

20 etchings by Georg Melchior Kraus, 1737–1806, after Johann Georg Schütz, 1755–1813, hand-colored.

32.8 x 24.6 cm. Original wrappers. Presented by Goethe to Luise of Saxe-Weimar (inscription on title-page). Stamp of the Bibliothek Schloss Arklitten. Formerly in the collection of Paul Hirsch.

THIS FIRST EDITION of Goethe's *Römische Carneval* is one of the great rarities of German literature. Finely printed in a large format with twenty hand-colored illustrations, the 250 copies of the first edition quickly sold out. After giving his last copy to the Library in Cassel, Goethe himself was unable to find another. The Hofer copy is one originally presented by the author to the Duchess Luise of Saxe-Weimar.

Throughout his life, Goethe was deeply interested in art and maintained many close connections with artists. During his Italian journey (1786–1788) he had numerous contacts with the community of German artists living in Rome, including Angelica Kauffmann and J.H.W. Tischbein, who painted the famous portrait of Goethe in the Roman Campagna (Frankfurt, Städelisches Kunstinstitut). In his *Italienische Reise*, Goethe describes how he requested Georg Schütz, one of his Roman housemates, to make the drawings for *Das Römische Carneval*. Four of these original pen and ink drawings are now in the William A. Speck Collection of Goetheana in the Yale University Library. Georg Melchior Kraus, who etched Schütz's designs, was also a friend of Goethe's, both in his early years and later in Weimar. Kraus's paintings include portraits of Goethe and Luise of Saxe-Weimar.

The Hofer bequest also includes a copy of the first edition of Goethe's *Zur Farbenlehre*, consisting of three volumes plus an atlas of plates. This influential work on color theory was published in Tübingen in 1810. Illustrated editions of *Hermann und Dorothea* (Braunsweig, 1822) and *Faust* (Paris, 1828) are discussed in No. 61 and 64.

N.F.

REF   Thieme-Becker XXI, 449–451 and XXX, 317; Gesamtkatalog der Preussischen Bibliotheken, *Goethe* (Berlin, 1932), no. G.1911; Yale University Library, *Goethe's Work with the Exception of Faust* (New Haven, 1940), no. 2140 and 2148; Watraud Hagen, *Die Drucke von Goethes Werken* (Berlin, 1971), no. 193; [James E. Walsh and Eugene M. Weber], *Goethe: An Exhibition at the Houghton Library* (Cambridge and Boston, 1982), no. 54.

No. 54.   Georg Melchoir Kraus after Johann Georg Schütz. Illustration from Goethe, *Das Römische Carneval*.

55 ✌ WILLIAM BLAKE, 1757–1827
Visions of the Daughters of Albion
[Lambeth] Printed by William Blake, 1793

11 relief etchings printed in green by Blake, hand-colored, possibly by Mrs. Blake.

36.3 x 26.3 cm. Olive green morocco by Douglas Cockerell, 1904. Formerly in the collection of Richard Monckton Milnes, Lord Houghton; sold by his son, the Earl of Crewe, at Sotheby's, 30 March 1903, to Edwards; acquired by Algernon Methuen; sold at Sotheby's 19 February 1936 (through Quaritch) to Philip Hofer.

VISIONS OF THE DAUGHTERS OF ALBION is but one of the Blake items in the Philip Hofer bequest, which join the Houghton Library's already extensive Blake holdings. Designed in 1793, it belongs to the early group of prophetic books written, illuminated and printed by William Blake using his unique relief etching process. This copy was probably printed about 1796–1800, and is one of several copies with simple hand-coloring attributed by Keynes to Mrs. Blake. In 1904, it was elaborately bound in green morocco by Douglas Cockerell.

Formed largely in the 1920s and 1930s, Philip Hofer's Blake collection is remarkable for the number of early states and experimental proofs which it includes, and for the distinguished provenance of several such items. A set of untrimmed proofs for Robert John Thornton's edition of the *Pastorals of Virgil* (Nos. 2–5) once belonged to Samuel Palmer and is accompanied by a letter from that artist. *The Illustrations of the Book of Job*, which include many early states, were formerly in the possession of George Richmond, and the unique experimental proof of plate seven from *Blake's Illustrations of Dante* was acquired from the family of John Linnell. Palmer, Richmond and Linnell formed the nucleus of the small group of artists who recognized Blake's genius and promoted the appreciation of his work during the last decades of his life. Twenty-four proofs for Young's *Night Thoughts* and an experimental state of plate fifty from *Jerusalem* also form part of the bequest, as does a copy of *America, A Prophecy* (Keynes Copy C). *Songs of Innocence and Experience* (posthumous copy b) was an early gift to the Department of Printing and Graphic Arts. A drawing for Thornton's Vergil was part of the Frances L. Hofer bequest. Recently, Hofer funds were used to acquire a second Vergil drawing. These join a third Vergil drawing which was previously acquired with the Caroline Miller Parker fund. Another important gift is an oil portrait of Blake by Thomas Phillips. This is either a study for the painting in the National Portrait Gallery, London, or a copy after it.

For Hofer's publications on Blake, see the references listed below.

N.F.

REF Geoffrey Keynes and Edwin Wolf 3rd, *William Blake's Illuminated Books* (New York, 1953), Copy M, p. 31–32; G.E. Bentley, Jr., *Blake Books* (Oxford, 1977), p. 476; Philip Hofer, "Drawings by William Blake for 'The Book of Job,'" *The Connoisseur* (April 1936), p. 183; *Illustrations of the Book of Job . . . reproduced in facsimile* with a note by Philip Hofer (London and New York), [1937]); Philip Hofer, *An Illustration by William Blake for the "Circle of the Traitors"—Dante's Inferno, Canto XXXII* (Meriden, Conn., n.d.); Philip Hofer and Wilmarth S. Lewis, *"The Beggar's Opera" by Hogarth and Blake* (Cambridge and New Haven, 1965). Exhibitions: National Gallery (1913) no. 92; Philadelphia (1939), no. 58.

No. 55. William Blake. Title-page of *Visions of the Daughters of Albion*.

56 & JOACHIM JOHANN NEPOMUK ANTON SPALOWSKY, 1752–1797
Prodromus in Systema Historicum Testaceorum / Vorschmack einer vollständigen systematischen Geschichte der Schalthiergehäuse
Vienna, Widow of Ignaz Alberti, 1795

Frontispiece engraved by Samuel Czetter after Gandolf Steinhauser. 13 etchings, hand-colored with watercolor, gouache, gold and silver leaf.

51.8 x 35.2 cm. Red morocco with black inlays, gilt; silk doublures.

THE EIGHTEENTH CENTURY, one of the great periods for the advancement of science, was also an age of enlightened amateurs and collectors' cabinets. The wonders of the natural world were portrayed in lavish folios, some of them of real scientific value, others the "coffee table books" of their day. Although the text of Spalowsky's *Prodromus in Systema Historicum Testaceorum* is of little interest, the manner in which the hand-colored plates capture the iridescent quality of the shells has never been surpassed. This was achieved through the use of gold and silver leaf, in some cases heavily overpainted with watercolor, for the shiny inside surfaces of shells, such as the *Haliotis*, or abelone. This coloring is far more sophisticated than that used in an earlier book by Spalowsky, *Abhandlung der Oekonomie und der dazu gehörigen Wissenschaften* (Vienna, 1787), where metallic paints were used for the coins, weights, measures and other numismatic apparatus.

Natural history books in the Hofer bequest range from Konrad von Megenburg's *Buch der Natur* (Augsburg, 1481), one of the first printed books to contain botanical lore, through the exquisitely illustrated *Blumenbuch* of Rudolf Koch (1930; No. 90) and the bestiaries of Marie Angel. Important eighteenth-century books in the bequest include Eleazer Albin, *A Natural History of English Insects* (London, 1720); Antoine Joseph Dezallier d'Argenville, *La Conchyliologie* (Paris, 1757); Franz Michael Regenfuss, *Recueil de coquillages* (Geneva, 1784); and three splendid books by Thomas Martyn, *The Universal Conchologist* (London, 1789); *The English Entomologist* (2 copies; London, 1792); and *Aranei, or a Natural History of Spiders* (London, 1793). John Abbot's *Natural History of the Lepidopterous Insects of Georgia* (London, 1797) was in the bequest; a large group of manuscripts and drawings by Abbot, including watercolors of birds, butterflies and moths, was a previous gift. Another previous gift was Maria Sibylla Merian's *Metamorphosis insectorum surinamensium* (Amsterdam, 1719), perhaps the most magnificent insect book ever produced. Higher forms of life are also well-represented. Two significant examples are George Stubbs' tremendous folio, *The Anatomy of the Horse* (2 copies; London, 1766) from the bequest, and Cornelis Nozeman, *Nederlandsche Vogelen* (Amsterdam, 1770), a previous gift. Botanical books include William Curtis, *Flora Londinensis* (London, 1777–1798) and P. Pallas, *Flora Rossica* (St. Petersburg, 1784), both in the bequest. Two unidentified flower drawings by Pierre-Joseph Redouté and twenty-three drawings by Georg Dionysius Ehret, including two for his *Plantae et papiliones rariores* (London, 1748–1759) and five for C.J. Trew, *Plantae selectae* (Nuremburg, 1750–1770) are in the Frances L. Hofer bequest. An incomplete copy of *Lilacées* by Redouté was a previous gift. Other books on natural science will be found under No. 72 and 74.

N.F.

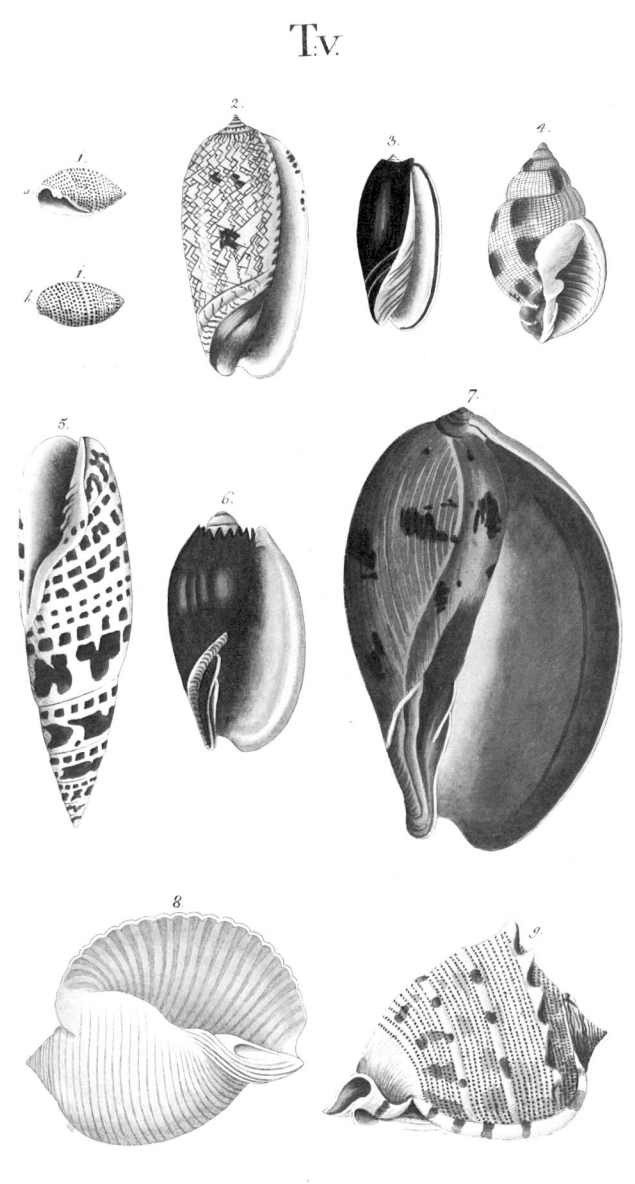

No. 56. Plate V from J.J.N.A. Spalowsky, *Prodromus in Systema Historicum Testaceorum*.

57   JOSE DELGADO Y GALVEZ, 1754–1801
Tauromaquia, o, Arte de torear á caballo y á pie
Madrid, Vega y Compañia, 1804

30 engravings, hand-colored.

18.2 x 11.5 cm. Black morocco.

JOSE DELGADO's little treatise on bullfighting is a good example of a book acquired by Hofer not for its own intrinsic interest but rather for its influence on two of Spain's greatest graphic artists. Although the simple hand-colored engravings in this first illustrated edition are not without their own crude charm, their real importance lies in their possible use by Francisco Goya as source material for his own *Tauromaquia*, published in 1816. Goya's general compositions and a few specific poses suggest an awareness of the earlier book. While the anonymous illustrations are purely descriptive and concentrate on depicting the techniques of bullfighting, Goya in his aquatints creates scenes full of human drama and tragedy. His final plate depicts Delgado, whom he knew as the bullfighter Pepe Illo, being gored to death in the bullring at Madrid. In the twentieth century, Delgado's little book was reinterpreted as a lavish, large scale *livre de peintre*. This edition with twenty-nine aquatints by Pablo Picasso was published in Barcelona in 1959.

Hofer's admiration for Goya led to the formation of a fine collection of prints and drawings. Much of this material is now in the Museum of Fine Arts, Boston. Hofer also considered publishing a major study on the artist, tentatively entitled *A Critical Survey of the Prints and Drawings of Francisco Goya*. Eleanor Sayre, Curator Emeritus of Prints, Drawings and Photographs at the Museum of Fine Arts, collaborated with Hofer on this project in the 1950s.

Hofer's gifts to the Department of Printing and Graphic Arts include a small representative group of nineteenth-century Spanish books. In the bequest, lithography is represented by the *Album Sevillano* (Seville, 1840) and the *Colección de las vistas de los sitios reales* (four parts; Madrid, 1832–33), with lithographs by various artists after paintings by Fernando Brambilla. Books illustrated with wood-engravings include *El Diablo Cojuelo* by Luis Vélez de Guevara (Madrid, 1842) with wood-engravings by Vicente Urrabieta and *Los Españoles pintados par si mismos* (Madrid, 1843; previous gift), a Spanish imitation of *Les Français peints par eux-mêmes* (See No. 70). Another previous gift was the Picasso *Tauromaquia* (Barcelona, 1959) discussed above.

N.F.

REF   Palau, IV, 345; Philip Hofer, Introduction to *La Tauromaquia and The Bulls of Bordeaux* (New York, 1969); Philip Hofer, Introduction to *The Disparates or, the Proverbios* (New York, 1969); Philip Hofer, Introduction to *Los Caprichos* (New York, 1969); Philip Hofer, Introduction to *The Disasters of War* (New York, 1967); Philip Hofer, "Goya's Aquatint Series, 'La Tauromaquia'," *The Print Collector's Quarterly*, XXVII (1940), 337-363.

No. 57. Bullfighting scene from José Delgado y Galvez, *Tauromaquia*.

58 🙵 THOMAS BEWICK, 1753–1828 AND WORKSHOP
History of British Birds
Newcastle, Printed by Edward Walker for T. Bewick, 1805.

237 wood-engravings by Bewick and his workshop.

23.3 x 14.3 cm. Red morocco. Vol. II of a set of 3, including the *Quadrupeds* and *Land Birds*, uniformly bound. Inscribed by Bewick to Dr. Ramsay, 25 November 1815.

Four woodblocks:

"The Night Heron." Woodblock for *British Birds*, vol. II, 1804, p. 43. Drawn and engraved by Bewick. 6.8 x 8 cm.
"The Golden Thrush." Woodblock for *Supplement to British Birds*, Part I, 1820, p. 20. Drawn and engraved by Bewick. 5.4 x 8 cm.
"Hanged Man" (Tailpiece to "The Raven"). Woodblock for *British Birds*, vol. I, 1805, p. 70. Drawn by Bewick and Robert Johnson, 1770–1796; engraved by Luke Clennell, 1781–1840. 5 x 7.8 cm.
"Sow and Piglets" (Tailpiece to the "The Boar and the Ass"). Woodblock for *Fables of Aesop*, 1818, p. 205. Drawn and engraved by Bewick. 3.9 x 7.9 cm.

THOMAS BEWICK is generally credited with the revival of wood-engraving at the turn of the eighteenth century. If he did not actually reinvent the technique, he certainly was largely responsible for its popularity. The cuts in his natural histories and books of fables demonstrate the detail, delicacy and subtlety of effect which the technique could produce in the hands of a master. In addition, wood-engraved blocks could be combined with printing type and printed in an ordinary printing press, an enormous advantage over copperplate engraving, etching, lithography and other techniques commonly used for book illustration. Bewick's apprentices and imitators quickly spread wood-engraving to America and the Continent; it became the most widely used technique for the illustration of books and magazines in the nineteenth century prior to the invention of photomechanical processes.

The importance of Thomas Bewick is reflected in the prominence of his works in the Hofer collection. Included are drawings, woodblocks, and proofs, as well as multiple editions of the major printed books. The bibliography of these books is complex, since the *Quadrupeds*, *British Birds* and *Fables* were all repeatedly reprinted in Bewick's lifetime, with changes to text and illustrations in each new edition. For example, while the "Night Heron" appeared in the first edition of the *Water Birds* (vol. II of *British Birds*) in 1804, the "Hanged Man" tailpiece was not added to the first volume until its third edition, in 1805. The "Golden Thrush" (or Oriole) only made its appearance in 1820 in the *Supplement to British Birds*. Another late design is the "Sow and Piglets" tailpiece for Aesop's *Fables*, first published in 1818. It is interesting to note that preparatory drawings for all four of these woodblocks survive. Those for the "Night Heron" and the "Golden Thrush" are preserved in the Natural History Society of Northumbria in Newcastle upon Tyne. Two drawings for the "Hanged Man" are known: a pencil study by Bewick in the Natural History Society of Northumbria and a transfer drawing by an apprentice, Robert Johnson, in the British Museum. A transfer drawing for the "Sow and Piglets" was part of the Frances L. Hofer bequest and is now in the Department of Printing and Graphic Arts.

Several additional drawings by Bewick and his assistants for Aesop's *Fables* and *British Birds* were also included in the Frances L. Hofer bequest. The Philip Hofer bequest includes a major group of 84 Bewick woodblocks for the *Fables* and a few other blocks for the *Quadrupeds*, *Birds* and *Fables*, most of which are listed above. The blocks for the *Fables* were formerly in the files of the Merrymount Press, Boston. Daniel Berkeley Updike and Rudolph Ruzicka considered using them to illustrate a book on Bewick, but Updike died before the project could be completed. The eighty-four blocks were reprinted by the Gehenna Press in 1969.

Important previous gifts include the manuscript for the *Fables*, given in memory of Hermon D. Smith '21 in 1982, and William Pickering's copy of the collected *Works* (1822). A manuscript relating to *British Birds* (editions of 1797 and 1804) was purchased by the Department of Printing and Graphic Arts in 1957, during Hofer's curatorship. Bewick's followers are also represented in the bequest by books illustrated by

No. 58. Thomas Bewick, "The Night Heron."
Woodblock for *British Birds*.

No. 58. Thomas Bewick, "The Night Heron."
Illustration from *British Birds*.

William Harvey, including a set of proofs for Northcote's *Fables*. For additional books illustrated with wood-engravings, see No. 66 and 70.

N.F.

REF Becker, no. 21; Thomas Hugo, *The Bewick Collector* (London, 1866) and *Supplement* (1868); Rudolph Ruzicka, *Thomas Bewick, Engraver* (Typophile Chap Book no. 8, 1943); S. Roscoe, *Thomas Bewick: A Bibliography Raisonné* (London, 1953); Thomas Bewick, *Select Fables* (Northampton, 1969); Iain Bain, "Thomas Bewick . . . A Checklist of his Correspondence and Other Papers," *The Private Library* (Summer, 1970), p. 16; Iain Bain, *The Watercolours and Drawings of Thomas Bewick and His Workshop Apprentices*, 2 vols. (Cambridge, 1981).

59 ❧ GIOVANNI BATTISTA BODONI, 1740–1813
Cimelio tipografico-pittorico offerto ai conoscitori
Parma, Co'Tipi Bodoniani, 1811

40 engravings, hand-colored; 40 facing poems, each set in a different fount or size, all printed on one side of the leaf only.

31 x 22 cm. Contemporary diced green morocco, gilt anthemion border, with crowned initials of Empress Marie Louise as Duchess of Parma; pink endpapers.

BODONI's *Cimelio tipographico* is intricately related to one of his earlier publications, the *Scherzi Poetici* of 1795, and the numerous Hofer copies of that title present an opportunity to sort out and compare the antecedents of this most refined of type specimens. Giovanni Gherardo de Rossi was the author of the *Scherzi poetici*, which he dedicated to Alessandro di Souza e Holstein, Portuguese envoy to Rome. The modest octavo has a Bodoni colophon and forty engraved plates with the accompanying verses. The little allegorical images of love, 135 x 75 mm., are line engravings in the neo-classic taste. According to the author's dedication, they were drawn and engraved by José Teixeira Barreto, a Portuguese artist resident in Rome, as was de Rossi, director of the Portuguese Academy. One of the compositions, the Eufrosine, is described as based on a painting by Angelica Kauffmann.

Many issues of this title are known, some with borders, some with the plates colored, and several with a new set of plates engraved by Francesco Rosaspina after Teixeira Barreto. Previous Hofer gifts include the edition with the Teixeira Barreto plates, colored in black and yellow, without captions and with the engraved title dated 1794, and three copies of the edition with plates by Rosaspina with captions, two within engraved borders ascribed to Giovanni Mercoli; in one of these copies, the plates are printed in brown within black borders; in the other, both plates and borders are printed in black, the latter Prince Eugène de Beauharnais' copy, with his crowned monogram on the covers. There is also an edition dated 1804.

In 1811 Bodoni himself brought out the *Scherzi poetici e pittorici* as a type specimen entitled *Cimelio tipografico-pittorico offerto agli Augustissimi Genitori del Re di Roma*, consisting of the Rosaspina engravings with the de Rossi verses on facing pages, set in different founts and a number of sizes, each occuping a space no larger than the facing engraving. They have been colored in black and yellow, *all'etrusca*, by Antonio Pasini, according to Bodoni's note to the reader. (The arrangement of titles, plates, and verses in plates 15–18 varies from the 1795 editions.) Typefounders of the rank of Bodoni often combined commemorative volumes with a display of type specimens. The occasion for this issue was the birth of the King of Rome, for, according to the title-page, the *Cimelio* is dedicated to his "august parents," Napoleon I and Marie Louise. In 1818, it was reissued with a new title-page by Bodoni's widow, and the Hofer copy belongs to this second issue. The crowned initials on the cover, of Marie Louise, mother of the King of Rome, may have been added by a later owner. Her own specially illuminated copy of the first issue is in the collection of the Museo Glauco Lombardi in Parma.

Some twenty Bodoni items are part of the bequest, including other such typographic celebrations of royal events as *Pel solenne battesimo di S.A.R. Ludovico Principe primogenito de Parma* of 1774, *Epithalamia exoticis linguis reddita* of 1775 with trial pages, and Ὑπομνημα *Parmense in Adventu Gustavi III Sueciae Regis* of 1784. A previous gift of this genre is Paciaudi's 1769 *Descrizione delle feste celebrate in Parma*, another large portfolio.

No. 59. Frontispiece and title-page of G. B. Bodoni, *Cimelio tipografico-pittorico*.

The bequest also includes a number of early Bodoni specimens, such as the *Essai de caractères russes* of 1782, the *Manuale tipografico* and *Serie de caratteri Greci* both of 1788, as well as correspondence between Bodoni and A.A. Renouard. A previous gift is the 1802 bronze medallion presented to the printer by the city of Parma.

The Bodoni collection in the Department of Printing and Graphic Arts is a large one of some three hundred items. They come not only from the Hofer collection but other sources as well, and particular note should be made of the type specimens, most of them the gift of William Bentinck-Smith, who began his collecting under Hofer's guidance, often choosing items to complement the Hofer holdings, both collections being destined for Harvard. Included are the first Bodoni specimen, the *Fregi e majuscole* of 1771 and the great posthumous *Manuale tipografico* of 1818.

E.M.G.

REF   [Giuseppe De Lama] *Vita del cavaliere Giambattista Bodoni e catalogo cronologico* (Parma, 1816), II, 195; H.C. Brooks, *Compendiosa bibliografia de edizioni Bodoniane* (Florence, 1927), no. 1097; Giampiero Giani, *Catalogo delle autentiche edizioni Bodoniane* (Milan, 1948), no. 196; [Angelo Ciavarella] *Il cimelio tipografico pittorico di Giambattista Bodoni* (Parma, 1983).

60   ALOIS SENEFELDER, 1771–1834
A Complete Course of Lithography
London, R. Ackermann, 1819

24 lithographs by various artists, printed by Ackermann.

28.6 x 22.2 cm. Half calf, marbled boards.

LITHOGRAPHY, the last of the major printmaking processes to be discovered, was invented by Alois Senefelder in 1798. In contrast to other techniques, in which the printing surface is either raised (as in letterpress and wood-engraving) or incised (as in the various kinds of engraving and etching), the first lithographs were printed from an entirely smooth block of Bavarian limestone. The surface, which was coated with gum arabic and then wetted, repelled the printing ink; the drawing, which was made with a special greasy substance, accepted the ink readily. Although artists began experimenting with the process almost immediately, there was no authoritative manual until the publication of Senefelder's treatise. The first German edition was published in 1818, the first French and English editions the following year.

Many important early books on lithography are included in the Hofer bequest. Besides both the French and English first editions of Senefelder's treatise, there is also a bound volume of plates issued to accompany the unillustrated German first edition of 1818. (The German first edition now in the Department of Printing and Graphic Arts was the gift of Paul J. Sachs.) Even rarer is a copy of Senefelder's *Musterbuch über alle lithographischen Kunstmanieren* (Munich, 1808). Since only one volume, a collection of specimens, ever appeared, the projected multivolume *Musterbuch* was to remain a tantalizing fragment until the eventual publication of the treatise. Another early description of the process was Heinrich Rapp, *Das Geheimness des Steindrucks* (Tübingen, 1810). Later manuals include F. Mairet, *Notice sur la lithographie* (2 editions: Dijon, 1818 and Chatillon-sur-Seine, 1824), Charles Hullmandel, *A Manual of Lithography* (London, 1820) and Godefroy Engelmann, *Manuel du dessinateur lithographe* (Paris, 1822).

Books illustrated with lithographs are, of course, an important part of the bequest. Samuel Prout, who contributed two lithographs to the English first edition of Senefelder's treatise, is represented by three items: *Illustrations of the Rhine* (London, [1822–1826]), *Facsimiles of Sketches made in Flanders and Germany* (London, n.d., ca. 1833), and *Sketches in France, Switzerland and Italy* (London, 1839). There are also two books by James Duffield Harding: *Elementary Art: or the Use of the Lead Pencil* (London, 1834), and *Elementary Art: or the Use of Chalk and Lead Pencil* (London, 1846). Because lithography could produce close facsimiles of graphite, chalk and pen drawings, it was often used to illustrate manuals such as these. Other early books illustrated with lithographs will be found listed under No. 64, 65, 68 and 69. Besides

No. 60. Portrait frontispiece of Alois Senefelder, *A Complete Course of Lithography*.

these printed sources, the Hofer bequest also includes a letter written by Senefelder to the British ambassador in Paris.

N.F.

REF Luitpold Dussler, *Die Incunabeln der deutschen Lithographie, 1796–1821* (Berlin, 1925); Michael Twyman, *Lithography 1800–1850* (London, 1970), p. 84–108.

61 🙵 JOHANN WOLFGANG VON GOETHE, 1749–1832
Hermann und Dorothea
Braunschweig, Friedrich Vieweg, 1822

4 engravings by Martin Esslinger after Carl Wilhelm Kolbe, hand-colored.

21.8 x 14.5 cm. 19th-century red morocco. Bookplate with the initials E.H.

ALTHOUGH nineteenth-century French and British book illustration has been much studied and is well known, German illustration of the same period remains relatively unfamiliar. The different illustrated editions of *Hermann und Dorothea*, probably Goethe's most popular work, provide a fascinating overview of shifts in style and technology. They range from the first edition, with an engraved frontispiece by Daniel Chodowiecki (1797) through an edition illustrated with photographs after paintings by Wilhelm Kaulbach and Ludwig von Hofmann (probably 1873). Carl Wilhelm Kolbe (1781–1853), who illustrated the 1822 edition, was a pupil of Chodowiecki and a Romantic painter of some importance. The charm of his genre scenes, which reflect the middle-class values promoted in the work, is further enhanced in this copy by contemporary hand-coloring.

Hofer's gifts to the Department of Printing and Graphic Arts have included two other editions of *Hermann und Dorothea* (1808 and 1820), as well as numerous other nineteenth-century German illustrated books. Moritz von Schwind (1804–1871), Ludwig Richter (1803–1884) and Adolf von Menzel (1815–1905) are especially well-represented. There are also many German children's books, including numerous works by Franz von Pocci and early editions of *Struwwelpeter*. The bequest includes eleven drawings by Moritz Retzsch for Schiller's *Lied von der Glocke* (Tübingen, 1833); the Frances L. Hofer bequest includes drawings by Chodowiecki, Menzel and a fine finished study by Alfred Rethel for *Auch ein Todtentanz aus dem Jahre 1848* (Leipzig, 1849; see Becker, no. 32).

N.F.

REF Nagler, IV, 356–357; Thieme-Becker, XXI, 226–228; Watraud Hagen, *Die Drucke von Goethes Werke* (Berlin, 1971), no. 257.

No. 61. Frontispiece of Goethe, *Hermann und Dorothea*.

62 ❧ GEORGE GORDON BYRON, 1788–1824
The Corsair
Milan, Typographical Society of Italian Classicks, 1826
Illuminations by GIOVANNI BATTISTA GIGOLA, 1769–1841

Copy on vellum. Portrait of Byron, 9 full-page drawings, title-page vignette and 10 head- and tailpieces, in watercolor heightened with gold leaf.

22.4 x 14.8 cm. Black velvet; watered silk doublures gold-tooled with the arms of a count. Contemporary black morocco case.

THIS lavish, hand-illuminated edition of Byron's *Corsair* was produced in Italy less than two years after the poet's death. The artist, Giovanni Battista Gigola, was primarily known for his work as a miniaturist, but also illuminated copies of *Giulietta e Romeo* by Luigi da Porto and *Gli amori pastorali di Dafni e Cloe*. Gigola's illuminations for *The Corsair* reflect his studies in Paris and his awareness of contemporary French art. The rather stocky figures, shallow pictorial space and dramatic lighting of the full-page illustrations can be paralleled in works by Gérard, Prud'hon and Girodet-Trioson. An unexpected vein of fantasy is evident in the head- and tailpieces and in the elaborate borders, which look both backwards to Renaissance and Rococo sources and forward to the Gothic revival of the later nineteenth century. The Società Tipografica dei Classici Italiani specialized in fine editions, known primarily for the quality of their typography. In the 1820s, their list of authors was expanded to include a few non-Italians such as Byron and Sir Walter Scott. Italian printing in the wake of Bodoni is well represented in the Hofer bequest by a total of forty-six nineteenth-century works printed in eighteen different cities.

Hofer acquired his copy of *The Corsair* not only for its illustrations and its typography, but also for its associational value: he believed it to have belonged to Byron's friend Thomas Moore. It is true that the tailpiece to the dedication is inscribed by Gigola "per T. Moore," but the book itself was dedicated by Byron to Moore, and Gigola's inscription seems merely to reflect this fact. Moore was aware of the publication and alludes to it in his journal (February 8–9, 1826). Gigola is said to have illuminated three copies of *The Corsair*, varying the illustrations in every case. One copy is known to be in the Museo Poldi-Pezzoli in Milan and was exhibited there in 1979. Another copy, which belonged in the nineteenth century to the German Count Schoenborn-Wiesentheid, appears to correspond to the Hofer copy. As far as it is possible to judge from published descriptions, the illustrations are identical. In addition, the crowned, seated lion stamped on the doublures of the Hofer copy appears in both the Schoenborn and the Schoenborn-Wiesentheid coats of arms. It therefore appears highly likely that the two copies are one and the same. If this is true, there is no record of the third copy, if indeed it ever existed.

N.F.

REF Anthony Burton and John Murdoch, *Byron: An Exhibition to Commemorate the 150th Anniversary of his Death* (London, Victoria and Albert Museum, 1974), Additions, after S15; Museo Poldi-Pezzoli, *Neoclassico e troubadour nello miniature de Giambattista Gigola* (Milan, 1979), no. 75.

No. 62. Giovanni Battista Gigola. Frontispiece portrait of Byron from *The Corsair*.

63   ELIHU WHITE, 1773–1836
A Specimen of Printing Types
New York, E. White, 1826

Specimens of type and ornaments, printed on one side of the leaf only.

21.4 x 13.9 cm. Tan wrappers. Label of the Typographic Library and Museum of the American Type Founders Company.

ALTHOUGH printing in America got off to an early start with the Cambridge Bay Psalm Book of 1640, typefounding did not become a major business here until after the Revolution. Prior to that time, and indeed long afterwards, most types used by American printers were imported from Europe. It was not until 1796 that the first permanent American type foundry was established in Philadelphia by two Scotsmen, Archibald Binny and James Ronaldson. While earlier ventures had foundered for lack of technical expertise, Binny provided the craftsmanship and Ronaldson the capital necessary for a successful business. The firm prospered for over a decade before issuing its first specimen, a catalog of metal ornaments, in 1809. Their 1812 catalog (previous Hofer gift) is usually described as the first American type specimen, since it was apparently the first such book actually to display type.

Binny and Ronaldson were not without their rivals, however. Two enterprising Connecticut Yankees, Elihu White and William Wing, established a type foundry in Hartford in 1805. Unfortunately, neither White nor Wing knew anything about casting type, and the typecasting machine they designed turned out to be a failure. As the story is usually told, they then resorted to industrial espionage. William Starr, one of their employees, was sent to Philadelphia to learn the secrets of the trade. Starr worked for a short time for Binny and Ronaldson, then returned to Hartford to share his information with White and Wing. From that time on, the business flourished; in 1810, White and Wing transferred their rapidly expanding operations to New York. They issued *their* first specimen in 1812, the same year as Binny and Ronaldson's.

It is interesting to compare White's 1826 specimen with those issued by Binny and Ronaldson and their successors. Previous Hofer gifts include four such specimens, all given in 1971 in honor of William Bentinck-Smith. These are the 1812 Binny and Ronaldson specimen already mentioned, the 1816 and 1822 specimens of James Ronaldson, and the 1839 specimen of Binny's son, John. The prefaces alone make fascinating reading, especially that of 1822, in which James Ronaldson attacks "a foundry in New York" for their "inferences, censures and self-compliments . . . which candor and truth should have kept within moderate limits." Clearly the rivalry was a bitter one and lasted for many years. Something of the character of the two firms is surely reflected in the texts which they used to display their types. The Ronaldson specimen of 1822, the first to use English as well as the usual Latin texts, abounds in pious quotations from the Declaration of Independence and anti-slavery tracts; White's specimen of 1826 contains wittier and racier juxtapositions, for example "BED/$150/HOUR" set in large Pica No. 2. The phrases on other pages suggest that White was also borrowing from contemporary British type specimens.

The Hofer bequest contains a handful of additional early American type specimens, including three from the New England Type Foundry (Boston, 1834, 1844?, and 1855), one each from the Boston Type and Stereotype Company (1845) and Bruce's New York Type-Foundry (1837), and the specimen issued in 1843 by Elihu White's son, John T. White. The vast majority of nineteenth-century American type specimens in the Department of Printing and Graphic Arts, however—like type specimens of all countries and all periods—have been the gift of William Bentinck-Smith.

N.F.

REF   Rollo Silver, *Typefounding in America, 1787–1825* (Charlottesville, 1965), p. 55–63, 66–69; Maurice Annenberg, *Type Foundries of America and their Catalogs* (Baltimore and Washington, 1975), p. 236–238.

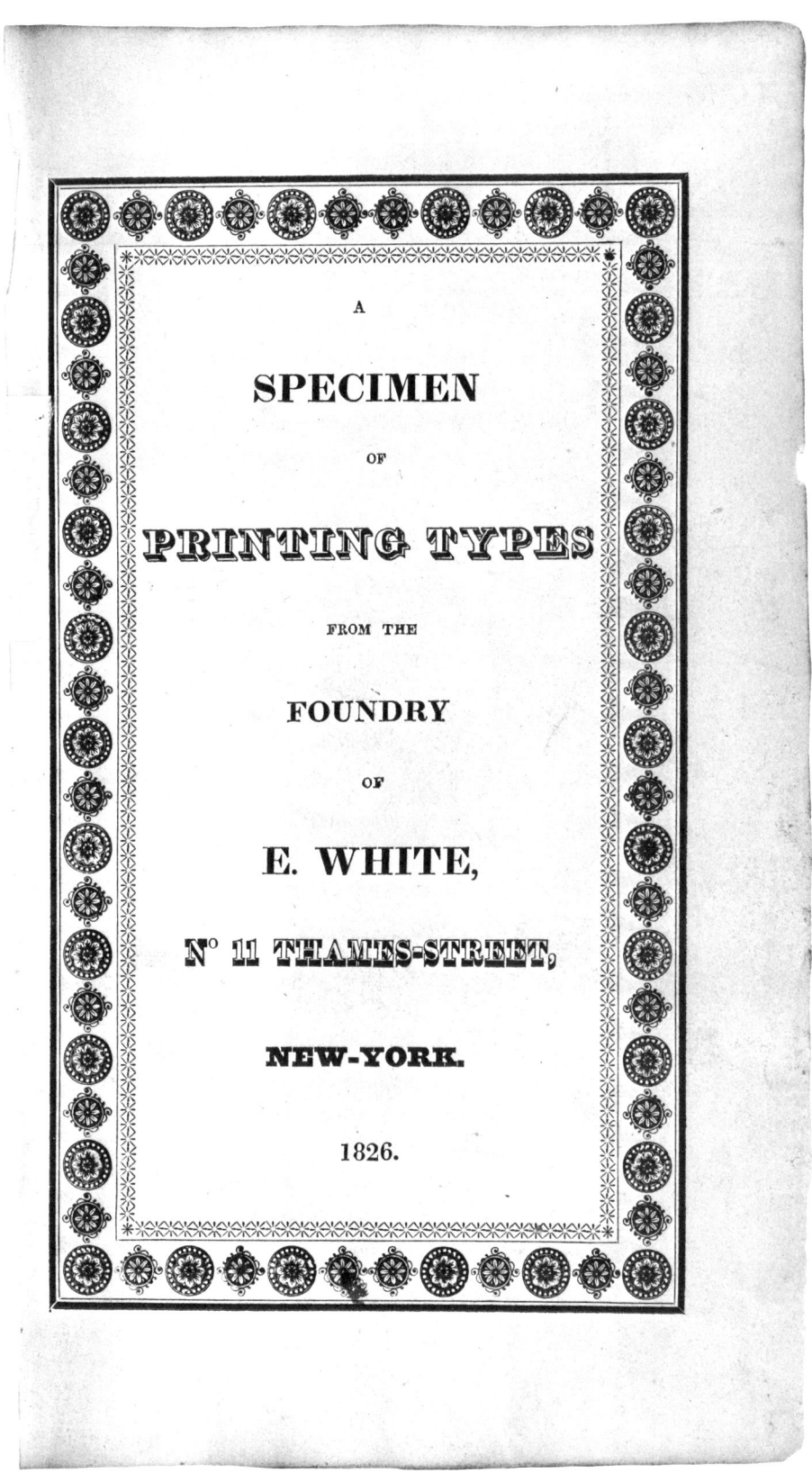

No. 63. Title-page of Elihu White, *A Specimen of Printing Types*.

64 & JOHANN WOLFGANG VON GOETHE, 1749–1832
Faust
Paris, Charles Motte & Sautelet, 1828
Lithographs by EUGENE DELACROIX, 1798–1863

17 lithographs plus portrait by Delacroix on *chine appliqué*, 13 on *chine rose*, 1 on *chine bleu*, 4 on *chine blanc*. Original wrappers by Achille Devéria bound in.

41.2 x 27.8 cm. 19th-century half black morocco. Bookplates of Dr. Lucien-Graux and Dr. P. Blondin.

FEW WORKS have been more influential for the development of modern book illustration than this 1828 edition of Goethe's *Faust*, illustrated with seventeen lithographs by the Romantic painter Eugène Delacroix. Not only did it contribute to the taste for Gothic subject matter which remained in vogue throughout the 1830s and 1840s; in its large format and dramatic use of illustration, it has also been claimed as one of the precursors of the modern *livre de peintre*. Ironically, Delacroix claimed in his correspondence that he was not influenced by Goethe's text at all, but rather by a theatrical performance which he attended in London in 1825. Furthermore, the original plan was to issue the plates separately as an album similar to Goya's *Bulls of Bordeaux*. It was the publisher who insisted on the inclusion of Albert Stapfer's translation of the text, thus turning the production into a true illustrated book rather than an isolated suite of lithographs.

Delacroix's illustrations have become such familiar images that it is difficult to realize just how revolutionary they appeared in their day. These exaggerated and fantastic designs are more akin to caricatures than to the suave and elegant illustrations of the typical neo-classical book. Delacroix, in fact, designed a number of caricatures in the 1810s and 1820s. Achille Devéria's drawings for the front and back wrappers of *Faust* are even more deliberately stylized than Delacroix's illustrations, probably because these wrappers were meant to be eye-catching to potential buyers. Exceptionally, the wrappers have been preserved in the Hofer copy, bound in at the front and back of the book. Printed in black on grayish pink paper which harmonizes with the *chine rose* used for so many of the plates in this particular copy, they provide a suggestion of how garish and almost shocking the book must have appeared to Delacroix's contemporaries when it was first issued. Initially, it enjoyed little critical or financial success.

Besides the copy illustrated here, the Department of Printing and Graphic Arts has another ordinary copy, one proof and seven drawings for *Faust* illustrations, all Hofer gifts. An eighth drawing was the gift of David Becker. Additional material in the collection clearly reflects Delacroix's influence. Perhaps the best example is the series of fifteen etchings illustrating scenes from *Othello*, by Théodore Chassériau (1819–1856), published in 1844. As Baudelaire remarked in his *Salon de 1845*, "dans les illustrations d'Othello, tout le monde avait remarqué la préoccupation d'imiter Delacroix" (*Oeuvres complètes*, Paris, 1961, p. 829). The immediate inspiration probably came, not from the 1828 *Faust*, but from Delacroix's series of lithographs illustrating scenes from *Hamlet*, which appeared in 1843. The Hofer bequest includes a copy of the extremely rare first edition of the Chassériau *Othello*; already in the collection are a drawing for Plate 1, a series of proofs of the plates as published, and five proofs of earlier states. Additional drawings and variant proofs in other collections have been carefully catalogued by Jay M. Fisher in *Théodore Chassériau's Illustrations for Othello*.

N.F.

REF Becker, no. 22, 23 and 30; Ray, I, no. 143; Raymond Escholier, "Le Faust d'Eugène Delacroix," *Gazette des Beaux Arts*, 6ᵉ serie II (1929), 173–184; Jakob Otto Kehrli, *Die Lithographien zu Goethes "Faust" von Eugène Delacroix* (Bern, 1949); Philip Hofer, *Some Drawings and Lithographs for Goethe's Faust by Eugène Delacroix* (Cambridge, 1964); Philip Hofer, *Othello. Fifteen Etchings by Théodore Chassériau* (Cambridge, 1969); Jay M. Fisher, *Théodore Chassériau's Illustrations for Othello* (Baltimore, 1980); Ursula Sinnreich, "E. Delacroix' Faust-illustrationen" [in] Städelschen Kunstinstitut, Frankfurt-am-Main, *Eugène Delacroix: Themen und Variationen: Arbeiten auf Papier* (1987), p. 56–99.

No. 64. Eugène Delacroix, "Faust, Marguerite and Mephistopheles." Illustration from Goethe, *Faust*.

65   HONORE DAUMIER, 1808–1879
Alphabet en bande lithographiée
Paris, Aubert et Cie. [ca. 1835]

24 lithographs by Daumier, hand-colored.

14.8 x 9.3 cm. Original cardboard casing, covered in pink paper with the lithograph for the letter "C" pasted on the front cover.

THIS CHARMING RARITY is one of three children's alphabets known to have been designed by Honoré Daumier. Since it includes a sixty-four page text, it may be considered as the first illustrated book by this artist. Earlier work by Daumier—primarily political and social satires—had appeared in the illustrated journals *La Caricature* and *Le Charivari*, or had been sold as separate prints. Among his later book illustrations are numerous contributions to the studies of social types known as *physiologies*, including the most famous example of this genre, *Les Français peints par eux-mêmes* (8 vols., 1840–1841).

The twenty-four illustrations for Daumier's *Alphabet en bande lithographiée* were printed on two sheets of paper, which were then cut into strips and folded to form an accordian book or *leporello*. In addition to the printed book, the Hofer bequest includes two of these uncut sheets, apparently for a later edition of the same alphabet. It was this later version which, according to Delteil, was deposited for copyright on December 16, 1835. Although extremely rare today, children's books such as this were by no means uncommon in the 1830s. Advertisements for children's alphabets published by Aubert et Cie. appear in *Le Charivari* as early as its first volume (1833). By 1837, Aubert et Cie. were offering a complete line of "Alphabets comiques, grotesques; Alphabets de costumes de divers pays; Alphabets militaires, costumes de théâtre, métiers, scènes diverses, animaux, etc.," by such forgotten artists as Bernard, Bouchot, Bourdet, Challamel, Forest, Lasalle and Traviès, as well as Daumier. Each of these seems to have been issued in the same accordian format, described in the advertisement as "une grande bande de dessins qui se replie sous un joli cartonnage." Uncolored copies sold for 1 franc 50 centimes, hand-colored copies for 3 or 4 francs. Deluxe copies with colored illustrations in silk wrappers, selling for 6 to 10 francs, were also issued. It appears entirely possible that the text which accompanies the Daumier, but does not correspond to it, was originally intended for another of these lost alphabets.

Philip Hofer was a great admirer of Daumier, describing him on one occasion as "the greatest book illustrator since Goya." Besides the *Alphabet en bande lithographiée*, the bequest includes additional works illustrated by Daumier. Examples include: *Alphabet en deux feuilles* (Paris [ca. 1835]); uncut version of *Alphabet en bande lithographiée*); François Fabre, *Némésis médicale* (2 vols.; Paris, 1840); Maurice Alhoy, *Physiologie du voyageur* (Paris [1841]); Louis Huart, *Muséum Parisien* (Paris, 1841); Louis Huart, *Physiologie du flaneur* (Paris, 1841); Félix Deriège, *Physiologie du lion* (Paris [1842]); Honoré Daumier, *Grande Abécédaire en action* (Paris, [1848]) and Louis Huart, *Ulysse ou les porcs vengés* (Paris, 1852). *Les Français peints par eux-mêmes* (8 vols.; Paris, 1840–1841) was a previous gift. Also part of the bequest is a collection of lithographs by Daumier, including many proof impressions on fine paper.

N.F.

REF   *Le Charivari* (17 September 1837); Loys Delteil, *Le peintre-graveur illustré, XX: Honoré Daumier*, II (Paris, 1925), no. 323; Raymond Escholier, *Daumier Peintre et Lithographe* (Paris, 1923), p. 18; Museum of Fine Arts, *Honoré Daumier* (Boston, 1958), no. 186.

No. 65. Honoré Daumier. *Alphabet en bande lithographiée.*

66 🙢 PROSPECTUS DE LIBRAIRIE: PERIODE ROMANTIQUE
[Paris, Various publishers, ca. 1830–1846]

2 vols. 226 prospectuses of books and periodicals; eight examples of publishers' gilt bindings.

33 x 25.3 cm. Specimens mounted on *papier d'Arches*, in modern slipcases.

THIS UNIQUE COLLECTION of prospectuses and book covers documents a critical period in the history of French printing and publishing. The appearance of the French book changed radically in the 1830s and 1840s, first, through the introduction of wood-engraving for illustrations, and second, through the development of the publishers' gilt binding. The period was the heyday of such illustrators as Alfred and Tony Johannot, Auguste Raffet, Célestin Nanteuil, Jean-François Gigoux, and J.J. Grandville (see also No. 70). The works of Ariosto, Tasso and Cervantes, Molière, Racine and La Bruyère, Victor Hugo, Balzac amd Eugène Sue all appeared in handsome illustrated editions. The illustrated journal emerged as a vehicle of popular culture with the appearance of *L'Illustration* (represented both by prospectuses and by a binding specimen), *Le Magasin Pittoresque*, *La Revue des Feuilletons* and *Les Veillées de Famille*. Bourdin, Challamel, Chlendowski, Curmer, Dubochet & Cie., Fournier, Furne & Cie., Gosselin, Hetzel, Kugelmann, Paulin and Warée are just a few of the many contemporary publishers whose books are represented.

Wood-engraving was introduced from England during the first decades of the nineteenth century. Many of the wood-engravers active in Paris were in fact Englishmen. These included Charles Thompson, a pupil of Thomas Bewick (see No. 58), and two of the partners in the prolific firm Andrew, Best and Leloir. These craftsmen engraved the work of the French artists enumerated above. Likewise, the brass binding stamps for many French books were produced in England by J.M. Kronheim; the binding for Molière's *Oeuvres* (Dubochet & Cie., 1843) is signed "Kronheim, London." In the same year, the prospectus for *Un Million de Faits* described that book as "richement cartonné à l'anglaise." Kronheim also signed the binding for Pierre Boitard, *Le Jardin des Plantes* (Dubochet & Cie., 1842); the version of the binding preserved here differs from that reproduced in Malavieille. Two other bindings, for René Le Sage, *Gil Blas* (Warée, 1844) and Töpffer, *Voyages en Zigzag* (Dubochet, 1844) are signed "Haarhaus." A prospectus from Curmer Frères for *Illustrations Encyclopédiques ou Recueil de Vignettes* advertises the firm's new method for producing stereotypes of wood-engravings, and several prospectuses proudly announce the use of such stereotypes for book illustrations. While wood-engravings and stereotypes of wood-engravings remained standard for vignettes in the text, more lavish editions also boasted full-page steel engravings, lithographs, or occasionally etchings.

Several books represented by these prospectuses are in the bequest. These include: René Le Sage, *Histoire de Gil Blas de Santillane* (Paris, 1838) and George Sand *et. al.*, *Le diable à Paris* (2 vols.; Paris, 1845–1846). Many more were previous gifts to the Department of Printing and Graphic Arts, for example: Honoré de Balzac, *La Peau de Chagrin* (Paris, 1838); Jules Janin, *Le Diable boiteux* (Paris, 1842); Pierre Boitard, *Le Jardin des plantes* (Paris, 1842); Silvio Pellico, *Mes Prisons* (Paris, 1843) and Victor Hugo, *Notre Dame de Paris* (Paris, 1844). The binding of the last book is signed "Haarhaus."

N.F.

REF   Ray, II, 247–324; Sophie Malavieille, *Reliures et cartonnages d'éditeur en France au XIXe siècle, 1815–1865* (Editions Promodis, 1985), p. 233–235 and plates 50–52; Edmond Werdet, *De la Librairie Française—Son Passé—Son Présent—Son Avenir* (Paris, 1860), p. 113–288.

No. 66. J. M. Kronheim, Publisher's binding for Molière, *Oeuvres*.

67   LOUIS JACQUES MANDE DAGUERRE, 1787–1841
Historique et description des procédés du Daguerréotype et du Diorama
Paris, Lerebours, Susse Frères, 1839

21 x 13.5 cm. Original printed wrappers. Bookplate of Pierre Lambert.

DAGUERRE'S PROCESS for fixing the image of a camera obscura on a metal plate was made public on August 19, 1839. The first cameras went on sale the same day and immediately sold out. Daguerre's brochure explaining the process and the use of the apparatus also proved extraordinarily popular, with a number of issues appearing within a short period of time. The Hofer bequest includes two different issues of the first edition, both published jointly by the optician Lerebours and the stationer Susse Frères. They differ from the first issue, published by Alphonse Giroux et Cie., chiefly through the inclusion of inserts with advertisements for the instruments constructed by Lerebours and the papers, prints and decorative sculptures sold by Susse Frères. The bequest of these two issues of the Daguerre manual gives Harvard a total of six different issues of the first edition of this incunabulum of photography. All issues are extremely rare and of great interest both to bibliographers and to historians of photography.

The impact of the invention of photography on book illustration was tremendous. The fact that daguerreotypes were printed on metal prevented them from being used as book illustrations. More promising was the calotype process which produced paper prints from paper negatives. A copy of William Henry Fox Talbot's description of his invention, *Some Account of the Art of Photogenic Drawing* (London, 1839), is included in the Hofer bequest, as well as a copy of *Sun Pictures in Scotland* (London, 1845), Talbot's second book illustrated with actual tipped-in photographs. Other photo-illustrated books in the bequest include Virgil's *Carmina Omnia* (Paris, 1858), illustrated with photographs of drawings by Félix Joseph Barrias, and a guidebook by Mrs. Clara Barnes Martin, *Mount Desert on the Coast of Maine*, (Portland, 1877), again with tipped-in photographs. The illustration of books with original mounted prints was expensive, however, and by the 1880s various techniques for reproducing photographs in printer's ink had been developed. These photomechanical processes included carbon printing, collotype and lead-relief printing. Photomechanical methods were also adopted for the transfer of artists' drawings to woodblocks as a preliminary to engraving. Ultimately photo-engraving almost completely replaced hand wood-engraving for the production of decorative elements and small vignettes in the text; Woodburytypes, collotypes and halftones replaced engravings and lithographs as full-page illustrations. By the twentieth century, original prints as book illustrations were almost entirely restricted to deluxe *livres de peintre* and the productions of small private presses.

N.F.

REF   Beaumont Newhall, "A Chronicle of the Birth of Photography," *Harvard Library Bulletin* VII (1953), 208–220; Helmut and Alison Gernsheim, *L.J.M. Daguerre: The History of the Diorama and the Daguerreotype* (London, 1956); Beaumont Newhall, *The History of Photography from 1839 to the Present Day* (New York, 1964).

PRIX : **2** FR.

HISTORIQUE ET DESCRIPTION

DES PROCÉDÉS DU

DAGUERRÉOTYPE

et du Diorama,

PAR DAGUERRE,

Peintre, inventeur du Diorama, officier de la Légion-d'Honneur, membre de plusieurs Académies, etc., etc.

PARIS.
LEREBOURS, OPTICIEN DE L'OBSERVATOIRE,
PLACE DU PONT-NEUF, 13 ;
SUSSE FRÈRES, ÉDITEURS,
PLACE DE LA BOURSE, 31.
1839.

No. 67.   Daguerre, *Historique et description des procédés du Daguerréotype.*

68 ❧ EDWARD LEAR, 1812–1888
Views in Rome and Its Environs
London, Thomas McLean, 1841

Lithographic title-page and 25 lithographs by Lear, printed by Charles Hullmandel, hand-colored and mounted on board. 4-page separate text with list of subscribers.

57 x 46 cm. Publisher's portfolio with morocco spine and moiré cloth sides.

ALTHOUGH long admired for his books of nonsense, Edward Lear is now recognized, as well, as an important landscape artist, travel writer and illustrator, and natural history draughtsman. All these facets of his activity are exceptionally well-represented in the Houghton Library, which, in addition to the Hofer gifts and bequests mentioned here, includes the extensive Lear collection formed by W.B.O. Field, consisting of over 4000 watercolors, manuscripts and printed books.

Lear's first work was as an ornithological draughtsman; his first book, *Illustrations of the Family of the Psittacidae, Or Parrots*, was published before he was twenty years old. He also contributed lithographs to Gould's *Birds of Europe* (1832–1837) and made watercolors of the birds and animals in the private menagerie of Lord Derby, later to be published as *Gleanings from the Menagerie and Aviary at Knowsley Hall* (1846). In 1837 he embarked on his first trip to Italy. Immediately following his arrival in Rome, he began exploring the sites which would be featured in *Views in Rome and Its Environs*. Tivoli, Subiaco, Genazzano and Olevano had all been visited by the spring of 1838, though it appears likely that most, if not all, of the sketches which formed the basis of the lithographs were done in 1840. Related drawings in the Houghton Library bear dates ranging from February 2 through October 18 of that year. Additional related drawings are in the Liverpool City Libraries. Many of the lithographs were apparently executed while Lear was staying with Lord Derby at Knowsley Hall, after his return to England in the spring of 1841. By the spring of 1842, he was back in Italy.

Like many other contemporary travel books, *Views in Rome and Its Environs* was published in two versions, one bound with the plates "plain" and uncolored, the other with hand-colored plates mounted in a portfolio. The Hofer copy is a fine example of the colored version. The four-page letterpress text which accompanies the plates provides a brief description of each site and a list of subscribers. It may be seen as a forerunner of Lear's later, more elaborate travel writings. A copy of the ordinary edition with uncolored plates came to the Houghton Library as part of the W.B.O. Field collection. Philip Hofer's encouragement was a major factor in the formation of Field's collection in the 1920s and 1930s. Field and Hofer were among the first twentieth-century collectors to appreciate Lear as a landscape artist; Hofer's book, *Edward Lear as a Landscape Draughtsman* (Cambridge, 1967), remains one of the best available discussions of Lear's watercolor technique.

In addition to *Views in Rome and its Environs*, the bequest also includes a copy of John Gould's *Birds of Europe* in twenty-two original parts and eleven letters written by Lear to various correspondents (see No. 76). An important previous gift was a group of 160 manuscripts and drawings for nonsense poems, including "Calico Pie," "The Dong with the Luminous Nose," and "The Owl and the Pussy Cat." Another previous gift was Wilkie Collins' copy of *Laughable Lyrics*. The Frances L. Hofer bequest includes forty landscape drawings, many of them made on Lear's trips to Greece and Albania in 1848 and 1849.

N.F.

REF   Becker, no. 33; Abbey, *Travel*, no. 183; Tooley, no. 294; [William B. Osgood Field] *Edward Lear on My Shelves* (Privately Printed, 1933); Philip Hofer, *Edward Lear as a Landscape Draughtsman* (Cambridge, 1967); Vivien Noakes, *Edward Lear, 1812–1888* (London, Royal Academy, 1985), no. 64a.

No. 68. Title-page of Edward Lear, *Views in Rome and Its Environs*.

69 ❧ THOMAS SHOTTER BOYS, 1803–1874
Original Views of London As It Is
London, Thomas Boys, 1842

21 lithographs by Boys, including some progressive proofs, two with graphite additions; printed by Charles Hullmandel. Various sizes, approx. 38 x 56 cm.

THE TOPOGRAPHICAL DRAUGHTSMAN Thomas Shotter Boys was one of the pioneers of color lithography, and his *Picturesque Views in Paris, Ghent, Antwerp, Rouen* (1839) is one of the major landmarks in the development of that technique. Three years later, in *Original Views of London As It Is* (1842), Boys explored the technical possibilities of the tinted lithograph. Tinted lithographs were not uncommon in travel books of the 1830s and 1840s—they had been used by Edward Lear, for example, in *Views in Rome and Its Environs* (No. 68)—but few artists shared Boys's mastery. In tinted lithographs, one stone, usually printed in black, provided all of the linear detail. A second stone, printed in buff or sepia provided the shading, and on occasion a third stone, printed in white, was used for highlights. Boys's skillful handling of these tint stones to produce broad flat tonal areas, analogous to watercolor washes, was probably derived from his experiments with color lithography where he had used similar broad flat areas of color to build up his designs.

Thirteen of the twenty-six published prints are represented in this collection of twenty-one proofs. Most are impressions of the black outlines only. In plate 17, *Piccadilly Looking Towards the City*, two balloons hover eerily in a perfectly blank sky; the dramatic backdrop of light-struck clouds which appears in the finished print was printed entirely from the sepia and white stones. In plate 19, the Duke of York's column is a shadowy presence at the end of Regent Street, lacking the sepia and white highlights which give it definition in the finished print. A series of progressive proofs in the Guildhall Library in London includes separate printings of the tint stones as well. These are lacking from the Hofer set, but two proofs, *London Bridge &c. from Southwark Bridge* and *Blackfriars from Southwark Bridge*, include Boys's own graphite additions. These additions were not included in the published prints and seem to be an attempt to "update" the views by adding smokestacks and modern buildings to the skyline and riverfront.

Boys has received increasing recognition from scholars not only for his achievements in lithography, but also because he was a member of the circle of English artists active in France in the years following the Napoleonic Wars. This group, which also included Richard Parkes Bonington, and Newton and Thales Fielding, was an important cultural link between France and England, and was responsible in part for the rapid transmission of ideas, attitudes, subject matter, motifs and techniques between the two countries during this period.

As a result of Philip Hofer's long standing interest in Thomas Shotter Boys, the Department of Printing and Graphic Arts now possesses a major archive for the study of this artist's work. This includes a group of over two hundred fifty drawings from the Frances L. Hofer bequest, with sketches for most of Boys's major publications. *Original Views of London As It Is*; *Picturesque Architecture in Paris, Ghent, Antwerp, Rouen*; *Sketches on the Moselle, the Rhine, and the Meuse*; and *Picturesque Sketches in Spain* are all represented. A fine hand-colored copy of the plates of *London As It Is* is also in the Frances L. Hofer bequest; a copy of the text is in the Philip Hofer bequest. The Philip Hofer bequest also includes copies of Charles Nodier, *Voyages pittoresques et romantiques dans l'ancienne France* (Paris, 1820–1825) and David Roberts, *Picturesque Sketches in Spain* (London, 1837), both with lithographs by Boys. Especially significant is Boys's own copy of *Picturesque Architecture in Paris, Ghent, Antwerp, Rouen* (London, 1839) with progressive color proofs, notes and newspaper clippings.

N.F.

REF   Becker, no. 26; Abbey, *Scenery*, no. 239; Tooley, no. 105; Michael Twyman, *Lithography 1800–1850* (London, 1970), p. 212–213; James Roundell, *Thomas Shotter Boys* (London, 1974); Marcia Pointon, *The Bonington Circle: English Watercolour and Anglo-French Landscape, 1790–1885* (Brighton, 1985).

No. 69. Thomas Shotter Boys, "Blackfriars from Southwark Bridge." Proof with autograph additions for *London As It Is*.

70   P.J. STAHL (PIERRE-JULES HETZEL, 1814–1886) AND OTHERS
Scènes de la vie privée et publique des animaux
Paris, J. Hetzel et Paulin, 1842
Wood-engravings after J.J. GRANDVILLE, 1803–1847

2 vols. 320 wood-engravings after Grandville.

27 x 19.5 cm. Publisher's gold-stamped green cloth binding.

SCÈNES de la vie privée et publique des animaux was in its day the most popular of the works of Jean-Ignace-Isidore Gérard, known as Grandville. Following the example of the *Fables* of La Fontaine which Grandville had illustrated in 1838, *La vie privée et publique des animaux* consists of a series of tales by well-known contemporary authors in which animals assume the roles of human beings. Social and political satire abound, notably in "Encore une révolution" by P.J. Stahl and "Voyage d'un lion d'Afrique à Paris" by Balzac. The "scènes de la vie privée" and "scènes de la vie publique" of Balzac's *Comédie Humaine* are also openly satirized in the title. In the *Comédie Humaine*, Balzac set out to recount the "natural history" of Parisian society; such comparisons of man and beast, which dominate the literary and popular imagery of the period, find perhaps their most elaborate and witty expression in *La vie privée et publique des animaux*.

Ten drawings for *La vie privée et publique des animaux* came to the Department of Printing and Graphic Arts as part of the Frances L. Hofer bequest in 1978. Reproduced here is a drawing for "Tablettes de la girafe au Jardin des Plantes" by Charles Nodier. Grandville's drawing is essentially the same size as the wood-engraving, of which it is a mirror image. At the bottom of the drawing is a note in Grandville's hand, "A faire mettre sur bois par Français." Louis Français (1814–1897) contributed one of his own designs to *La vie privée et publique des animaux*. To judge from this inscription, he was also employed transferring Grandville's designs to the woodblocks. It is interesting—and presumably a measure of Grandville's prestige as an artist—that he did not carry out this necessary operation himself. Relatively few finished drawings for wood-engravings survive from this period, since it was customary for the artist to make his final drawing directly on the woodblock.

Besides the ten drawings and the two-volume first edition of *Scènes de la vie privée et publique des animaux*, the Hofer bequest includes a single volume in a variant binding and a copy of a later (1867) edition. A copy of the second of Grandville's three lithographed posters advertising the book was an earlier Hofer gift.

The Grandville holdings of the Houghton Library are extremely rich and varied. They include little-known early works, such as *Voyage pour l'Eternité* (1829) as well as familiar late works such as *Un autre monde* (1844). Much of this material has been either the gift or the bequest of Philip Hofer. Included in the bequest are A. Savigny, *Historiettes et images* (1840), Daniel Defoe, *Robinson Crusoe* (1840), Emile Forgues, *Les petites misères de la vie humaine* (1843; with A.L.s. to H. Fournier), Florian, *Fables* (1851), Swift, *Voyage de Gulliver* (1856), and a poster for *Un autre monde*. Ten drawings for *Scènes de la vie privée et publique des animaux* are in the Frances L. Hofer bequest. Notable among previous gifts are the posters for *Fables de Florian*, *Petites misères de la vie humaine*, and *Scènes de la vie privée et publique des animaux*.

Additional Grandville items in the Department of Printing and Graphic Arts have been given by William B. Osgood Field and purchased with income from the William Alexander Evans, Jr. Fund.

N.F.

REF   Becker, no. 19; Ray, II, no. 194; Léon Carteret, *Le trésor du bibliophile romantique et moderne*, III, p. 552–559; Annie Renonciat and Claude Rebeyrat, *La vie et l'oeuvre de J.J. Grandville* (Paris, 1985), p. 202–218 and 289–290.

No. 70. J. J. Grandville, "A Bookworm." Drawing and illustration from *Scènes de la vie privée et publique des animaux*.

71 ❧ JOHN SLIEGH (active 1841–1879)
Scrapbook of Designs for Monograms, Trade Cards,
Title-Pages, Book Covers, etc.
[London, 1849–1879]

2 vols. 494 proofs, tracings and drawings in graphite, ink and watercolor.

37.4 x 28 cm. Half brown morocco, brown pebble-grain cloth sides. Spines stamped in gold: ORNAMENTAL/LETTERS./OWEN JONES/I and ORNAMENTAL LETTERS./OWEN JONES/II.

LITTLE IS KNOWN about the artists who designed the covers of Victorian gift books. One of these elusive figures is John Sliegh (sometimes misspelled Sleigh), who is associated with a small group of books from the 1850s and 1860s. Sliegh's masterpiece is *Odes and Sonnets*, which was published by George Routledge and Company in 1849. Birket Foster provided the illustrations for this book, Sliegh the cover design, ornamental initials and other decorations. Sliegh is credited on the title-page, and the cover is signed with his monogram, making it possible to attribute a few other book covers to him.

The two-volume scrapbook from the Hofer bequest vastly expands our knowledge of Sliegh's career. Many of the items in it may be directly linked with him, either because they are signed, or because they bear his pencilled notations. Two copies of his business card suggest the range of his activities: "Presentation Addresses / Dedications, Memorials, / and every other kind of Document, written & Illuminated / upon Vellum and Paper—or executed in Lithography; by / John Sliegh / 25 Mary Street, / Hampstead Road N.W." Specimens of Sliegh's calligraphy include a "Testimonial to Thomas Bennett Esq." dated February 23, 1869; a certificate for the Society of Painters in Water Colours; a ticket for the Vernon Gallery and a card for A.J. Lewis "At home Saturday Evenings . . . Music at Eight—Oysters at 10.30" as well as a number of trade cards and liquor bottle labels. Sliegh's Gothic script, while highly decorative, is not always very legible. Several sheet music covers, including a watercolor design for *The Juvenile Pianoforte Album* testify to Sliegh's activity in that field. There are few actual book cover designs. Of special interest is a cover for *The Art Union*, "Designed and Executed in Chromo-Lithography by J. Sliegh." The vast majority of the drawings in the two volumes are designs for monograms. Several of these are for members of the Dalziel family, suggesting a connection with that firm of wood-engravers.

The association of the scrapbook with Owen Jones—whose name appears so prominently on the spines— is due to the inclusion of a number of chromolithographs after Jones's designs. Although Sliegh himself was a designer, he was also a lithographer who reproduced the designs of other artists. His work in this capacity for *The Industrial Arts of the Nineteenth Century* (1853) was acknowledged in the preface by Matthew Digby Wyatt. It is likely that he was employed in a similar capacity on *The Book of Common Prayer* (London, 1845) and *A Welcome to Her Royal Highness the Princess of Wales* (1863), two works with illuminations after Jones which are represented in the scrapbook.

Over the years, Hofer gifts have included a large number of Victorian books, many of them richly illustrated with color woodcuts, hand-colored etchings or chromolithographs, and adorned with decorative bindings. Significant examples, drawn chiefly from the 1984 bequest, include the following:

John Lockhart, *Ancient Spanish Ballads*. London, 1842. Borders and ornamental vignettes by Owen Jones. Includes numerous proofs of illustrations and letter from the printer Vizetelly to the publisher John Murray.

Henry Shaw, *Dresses and Decorations of the Middle Ages*. 2 vols. London, 1843.

Henry Shaw, *Alphabet, Numerals and Devices of the Middle Ages*. London, 1843.

Henry Wadsworth Longfellow, *Evangeline*. London, 1856. Cover design by John Sliegh (previous gift).

Odes and Sonnets Illustrated. London, 1859. Cover design and decorations by John Sliegh (previous gift).

N.F.

REF Sybille Pantazzi, "Four Designers of English Publishers' Bindings 1850–1880, and their Signatures," *Papers of the Bibliographic Society of America*, LV (1961), 88–89; Ruari McLean, *Victorian Book Design and Colour Printing* (London, 1972), p. 121, 180, 220; Douglas Ball, *Victorian Publishers' Bindings* (London, 1985), p. 162.

No. 71. John Sliegh. Cover design for *The Juvenile Pianoforte Album*.

72   JOHN FISK ALLEN, 1807–1876
Victoria Regia; or the Great Water Lily of America
Boston, Printed and published for the author by Dutton and Wentworth, 1854
Chromolithographs by WILLIAM SHARP, 1803–1875

6 chromolithographs by Sharp, printed by Sharp & Son, Dorchester, Massachusetts.

71.5 x 55.5 cm. Unbound. 2 copies with variant versions of original paper covers.

WILLIAM SHARP was one of the pioneers of chromolithography in America; *Victoria Regia; or the Great Water Lily of America* is a masterpiece of nineteenth-century American color printing. Trained in England, Sharp was already a competent artist when he emigrated to Boston. There, in 1840 he printed the first American chromolithograph, a portrait of the Reverend F.W.P. Greenwood. Later subjects by Sharp include landscapes, street scenes, floral compositions and sheet music covers. Between 1847 and 1856, Sharp and his son Philip lithographed the ninety-six plates of Charles M. Hovey's *Fruits of America*. Sharp was still working on this project when he was engaged by the amateur botanist John Fisk Allen to illustrate a monograph devoted to the giant waterlily, the Victoria Regia, which Allen had grown at his Salem home from specimens provided by Caleb Cope of Philadelphia and Professor Asa Gray of Harvard.

Bettina Norton has shown that both text and illustrations are closely based on a British publication, *Victoria Regia, or, Illustrations of the Royal Water Lily*, by Walter Fitch, which had appeared in London in 1851. This does not, however, detract from the technical brilliance of Sharp's achievement. The six chromolithographed plates trace the lily through the various stages of blossom and decay. The simple forms appear almost stylized, due to the large scale of the illustrations, and this effect is further heightened by the broad flat areas of printed color. The finest plates, for example the one shown here, compare not unfavorably with the aquatints of R.J. Thornton's *Temple of Flora* (London, 1807), one of the most dramatic botanical books ever printed. The Department of Printing and Graphic Arts has a third copy of *Victoria Regia*, which was presented to the Library of Harvard University by the author in 1854.

The Hofer bequest includes a number of other significant nineteenth-century botanical and ornithological books such as the following:

Robert John Thornton, *New Illustration of the Sexual System of von Linnaeus . . . and The Temple of Flora*. London, 1807.
Robert John Thornton, *Elements of Botany*. 2 vols. London, 1812.
William P.C. Barton, *Vegetable Materia Medica . . . or Medical Botany*. 2 vols. Philadelphia, 1817–1818.
William P.C. Barton, *A Flora of North America*. 3 vols. Philadelphia, 1821–1823.
Jacob George Strutt, *Sylva Britannica. . . .* London, 1822.
Sir James Edward Smith, *A Grammar of Botany*. New York, 1822. Illustrated by Isaac Sprague.
Alexander Wilson, *American Ornithology*. 3 vols. and plates. New York and Philadelphia, 1827–1829.
Manual of the Practical Naturalist . . . Boston, 1831.
Charles M. Hovey, *The Fruits of America*. Boston, 1847–1856. Chromolithographs by William Sharp.
Asa Gray, *The Genera of Plants in the United States*. 2 vols. Boston, 1848.
George Barrell Emerson, *A Report on the Trees and Shrubs of Massachusetts*. 2 vols. Boston, 1875.

Previous gifts include a large group of drawings, proofs and plates of botanical and ornithological subjects by Isaac Sprague. An additional drawing of a zoological specimen is part of the Frances L. Hofer bequest.

N.F.

REF   Nissen, no. 16; Bettina A. Norton, "William Sharp: Accomplished Lithographer," [in] *Art & Commerce: American Prints of the Nineteenth Century* (Charlottesville, Va., 1978), p. 50–75; Peter C. Marzio, *The Democratic Art: Chromolithography 1840–1900* (Boston, 1979), p. 17–18; Gavin D.R. Bridson, Donald E. Wendel and James A. White, *Printmaking in the Service of Botany* (Pittsburgh, 1986), no. 56.

No. 72. William Sharp. Illustration from John Fisk Allen, *Victoria Regia*.

73   FRANCOIS RABELAIS, ca. 1490–1553?
Oeuvres de François Rabelais
Paris, J. Bry aîné, 1854
Wood-engravings after GUSTAVE DORE, 1832–1883

104 wood-engravings after Doré.

30 x 20.5 cm. Original wrappers.

GUSTAVE DORE
Drawing for *Oeuvres de Rabelais*
Paris, Garnier Frères, 1873

Graphite, pen and ink, wash and Chinese white on woodblock.

Approx. 25 x 20 cm. Framed and glazed.

RABELAIS' TALES of the giants Gargantua and Pantagruel ideally suited the Gothic fantasy of Gustave Doré, who illustrated two separate editions of the work, in 1854 and 1873. The 1854 Rabelais was the twenty-one year old artist's first popular success. Although the book was cheaply printed on poor paper, the crude vigor and imaginative power of Doré's illustrations captured the attention of such influential critics as Théophile Gautier. When Doré returned to the theme later in life, his style was more mature and refined. The vastly expanded 1873 edition contains 31 new plates and hundreds of new vignettes, in addition to 98 of the 104 original illustrations. The uncut woodblock in the Hofer bequest was evidently intended for this folio edition. Its size almost exactly corresponds to the size of the new plates, and the delicacy of the drawing, with its fine lines and subtle washes clearly suggests a date in the 1870s. The use of white on black for certain portions of the design is highly characteristic of Doré's late style, appearing not only in illustrations for the 1873 Rabelais, but also in his near contemporary illustrations for Blanchard Jerrold's *London: A Pilgrimage* (1872) and Coleridge's *The Rime of the Ancient Mariner* (1875). The subject, the giant Gargantua dozing during a meal, while his subjects continue to bring cartloads of provisions for his consumption, recalls Daumier's infamous political caricature of 1831. Perhaps it appeared controversial for that reason. The fact that the scene was not chosen for inclusion in the book has ironically preserved it: Doré's drawing would have been destroyed when the block was cut by the wood-engraver. A second uncut woodblock for this edition is in the J. Michel collection, Paris.

In addition to the Rabelais book and block, the Hofer bequest includes copies of *Les differents publics de Paris* (1854), *La légende du juif errant* (1856) and Louis Enault's *Londres* (1876), all illustrated by Doré, as well as six proofs on china paper for La Fontaine, *Fables* (1866). The bequest also includes three illustrated letters by Doré and the manuscript of the *Discours funèbre prononcé sur la tombe de Gustave Doré* by Alexandre Dumas fils. These items join the already extensive Doré holdings of the Department of Printing and Graphic Arts (*Contes drolatiques, Baron Munchhausen, Roland furieux,* etc.) Previous Hofer gifts include two large drawings of subjects from Doré's *London*.

N.F.

REF   Ray, II, no. 242; Henri LeBlanc, *Catalogue de l'oeuvre complet de Gustave Doré* (Paris, 1931), p. 285–293; Louis Dézé, *Gustave Doré: Bibliographie et catalogue complet de l'oeuvre* (Paris, n.d.), p. 72–73; Strasbourg, Musée d'Art Moderne, *Gustave Doré 1832–1883* (Strasbourg, 1983), no. 229–278.

No. 73. Gustave Doré, "Gargantua." Uncut woodblock for *Oeuvres de Rabelais*.

74 ❧ WILLIAM GROSART JOHNSTONE, active ca. 1860
AND ALEXANDER CROALL, 1809–1885
The Nature-Printed British Sea-Weeds
London, Bradbury and Evans, 1859–1860
Nature-printed plates by HENRY BRADBURY, 1829–1860.

4 vols. 24.1 x 15.5 cm. Publisher's gold-stamped green cloth binding.

NATURE PRINTING was introduced to England in the 1850s by Henry Bradbury, who learned the technique at the Imperial Printing Office in Vienna. Like photography, nature printing owed much of its appeal to the fact that its images were produced without the intervention of an artist's hand; impressions of actual specimens were used to create the electrotype plates from which the illustrations were printed. In practice, however, the applications of nature printing were severely limited by the fact that objects could only be reproduced actual scale and in low relief; extremely large objects could not be accommodated, and the squashed-looking impressions of even slightly three-dimensional objects were neither aesthetically appealing nor scientifically useful.

Although the Viennese Alois Auer used nature printing to reproduce such unlikely subjects as fossil fish, snakeskins and a bat's wing, Bradbury concentrated upon the rendering of small and moderate-sized botanical specimens. *The Nature-Printed British Sea-Weeds* was the third of his nature-printed books. Although the text is strictly scientific, the volumes themselves are much more attractive than earlier efforts. Each volume has an engraved title-page designed by John Leighton, incorporating a small nature-printed seaweed appropriate to the content of the book. The striking publisher's binding, blind- and gold-stamped on dark green cloth, was also designed by Leighton; his initials appear at the base of the trident on the spine. Furthermore, the nature prints themselves are especially successful, their low relief and subtle colors suggesting actual mounted specimens of seaweeds. Bradbury died in 1860 at the early age of thirty-one. With his death, nature printing in England virtually ceased.

While other Harvard libraries, such as the Library of the Gray Herbarium and the Arnold Arboretum Libraries, collect nature-printed books for the scientific interest of their contents, the Department of Printing and Graphic Arts collects them as examples of an unusual nineteenth-century printing technique. Philip Hofer's early gifts to the Department include Thomas Moore, *The Ferns of Great Britain and Ireland* (London, 1855), with nature prints by Henry Bradbury. The bequest includes a copy of Alois Auer, *Tafeln zu dem Vortrage der Polygraphische Apparat* (Vienna, 1853). Recently, the Department has used Hofer funds to acquire Auer's *Die Entdeckung des Naturselbstdruckes* (Vienna, 1853) and a portfolio of plates printed by Auer at the Imperial Printing Office in Vienna. A copy of the English edition, *The Discovery of the Natural Printing-Process* (Vienna, 1853), was given to the Library by Charles Eliot Norton. Auer's book contained a violent attack on Bradbury for his adoption (and patent) of the process, which Auer claimed to have invented.

N.F.

REF Georg August Pritzel, *Thesaurus literaturae botanicae* (Milan [1950]), no. 4460; Nissen, no. 1002; Geoffrey Wakeman, "Henry Bradbury's nature printed books," *The Library*, 5th series, XXI (1966), 63–67; Joan M. Friedman, *Color Printing in England 1486–1870* (New Haven, 1978), no. 163–164.

No. 74. Henry Bradbury. Plate LIV from Johnstone and Croall, *The Nature-Printed British Sea-Weeds*.

75 & JAIME FELIPE JOSE BOSCH, 1826–1895
Plainte Moresque
Paris [1866]
Lithograph by EDOUARD MANET, 1832–1883

Sheet music with lithographed cover by Manet, printed by Lemercier.

34.5 x 27 cm.

JAIME BOSCH'S *Plainte Moresque* has one of two sheet music covers known to have been designed by the Impressionist painter Edouard Manet. Both the boldly sketched portrait of the composer-guitarist and the lettering follow Manet's designs. The subject matter and even the guitarist's costume and pose are closely related to Manet's 1861 etching of a *Guitarero*, which in turn was based on a Salon painting of the same year. The recent discovery of a *dépôt légal* copy in the Bibliothèque Nationale, however, has shown that *Plainte Moresque* was not published until 1866. Spanish guitarists and dancers figure prominently in Manet's work of the early 1860s. Both his sheet music covers reflect this interest. The second cover features Lola de Valence, whom Manet also portrayed in a major Salon painting. Bosch, the composer of *Plainte Moresque*, was a personal friend of the artist and dedicated his composition "à son ami E. Manet."

The Hofer bequest includes additional sheet music covers by Henri de Toulouse-Lautrec, Pierre Bonnard and Alfred Jarry, and paperback bookcovers by Toulouse-Lautrec, Bonnard and Pierre Vidal (see No. 77).

Other works by Manet include a copy of *Les Chats* by Champfleury (Paris, 1870) and the 1876 and 1887 editions of Mallarmé's *L'après-midi d'un Faune*. A copy of *Le Fleuve* by Charles Cros (Paris, 1876), with etchings by Manet, was given to the Department of Printing and Graphic Arts by Dr. Myron A. Hofer.

N.F.

REF   Léon Rosenthal, *Manet aquafortiste et lithographe* (Paris, 1925), p. 82–85; Marcel Guérin *L'oeuvre gravé de Manet* (Paris, 1944), no. 70; *The Artist & the Book*, no. 179, note; Metropolitan Museum of Art, *Manet* (New York, 1983), no. 94.

No. 75. Edouard Manet. Cover of Jaime Bosch, *Plainte Moresque*.

76   EDWARD LEAR, 1812–1888
Autograph letter to Mrs. Henry Austin Bruce
England (Ross-on-Wye), 18 October 1868

A.L.S.; 3 pen drawings; manuscript of a nonsense poem, "The Broom, the Shovel, the Poker and the Tongs."

18 x 11.5 cm.

EDWARD LEAR'S nonsense writings are generally more familiar than his landscape drawings (see No. 68) and his natural history illustrations. Philip Hofer's fascination with Lear's nonsense began early and continued throughout his life. He was especially successful in acquiring important nonsense manuscripts, which he often published in order to share them with other Lear enthusiasts. An informal bibliography of "Hofer-Lear books" would list at least ten separate titles, including a 1935 edition of *Nonsense Songs and Laughable Lyrics* with a foreword by Hofer, and facsimiles of the manuscripts of *Calico Pie* (1952), *The Duck and the Kangaroo* (1956) and *Flora Nonsensica* (1963). The letter to Mrs. Bruce with manuscript of "The Broom, the Shovel, the Poker and the Tongs" was one of Hofer's last major Lear acquisitions. It was purchased from Goodspeed's Bookshop in 1967 and published in 1977 with the title *A Lear Song*. One hundred fifty copies were printed by Henry Schniewind at the Four Winds Press, and bound by Gray Parrot using paste paper made by Carol Blinn.

Lear was staying at Perrystone, the home of George and Annsybella Clive, near Ross-on-Wye, when he sent this draft of "The Broom, the Shovel, the Poker and the Tongs" to Mrs. Henry Bruce. "Errifordshire" is Lear's spelling for "Herefordshire." During the same visit, he copied out "The Owl and the Pussycat" on writing paper headed "Perrystone/Ross/Herefordshire"; that manuscript was a previous Hofer gift to the Department of Printing and Graphic Arts. Both "The Owl and Pussycat" and "The Broom, the Shovel, the Poker and the Tongs" were first published in *Nonsense Songs, Stories, Botany and Alphabets* (1871). The manuscript for "The Broom, the Shovel, the Poker and the Tongs" varies very slightly from the poem as published. The most significant difference is that in the published version "Miss Broom" has become "Mrs. Broom."

Artists' letters were a particular interest of Philip Hofer's. The bequest includes several additional letters by Lear, and Beatrix Potter's letters to the Moore children, as well as letters by Joseph Highmore, John Everett Millais, Jean-Dominque Ingres and Gustave Doré (see No. 73). Other letters include correspondence of Giovanni Battista Bodoni, Alois Senefelder, William Pickering, Charles Eliot Norton and Yvette Guilbert. For a record of the Department's complete holdings in this area the manuscript catalogue of the Houghton Library should be consulted.

For additional Lear items given and bequeathed to the Department of Printing and Graphic Arts by Philip Hofer, see No. 68.

N.F.

REF   *A Lear Song: The Broom, the Shovel, the Poker, and the Tongs*, Philip Hofer, ed. (Locust Valley, N.Y., 1977).

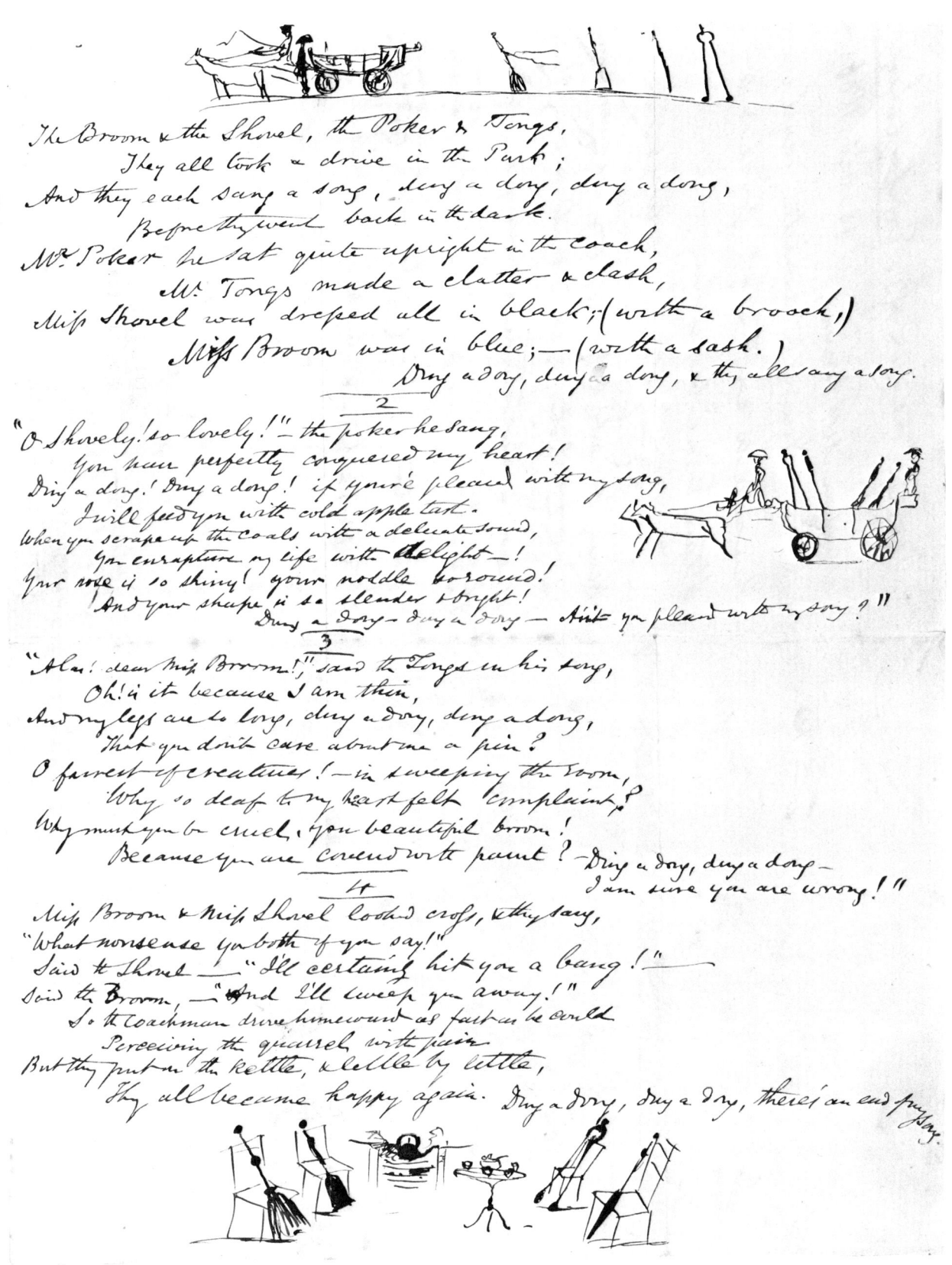

The Broom & the Shovel, the Poker & Tongs,
  They all took a drive in the Park;
And they each sang a song, ding a dong, ding a dong,
  Before they went back in the dark.
Mr. Poker he sat quite upright in the coach,
  Mr. Tongs made a clatter & clash,
Miss Shovel was dressed all in black;—(with a brooch,)
  Miss Broom was in blue;—(with a sash.)
    Ding a dong, ding a dong, & they all sang a song.

2

"O Shovely! so lovely!" the poker he sang,
  You have perfectly conquered my heart!
Ding a dong! Ding a dong! if you're pleased with my song,
  I will feed you with cold apple tart.
When you scrape up the coals with a delicate sound,
  You enrapture my life with delight!
Your nose is so shiny! your noddle so round!
  And your shape is so slender & bright!
    Ding a dong — ding a dong — Ain't you pleased with my song?"

3

"Alas! dear Miss Broom!" said the Tongs in his song,
  Oh! is it because I am thin,
And my legs are so long, ding a dong, ding a dong,
  That you don't care about me a pin?
O fairest of creatures! — in sweeping the room,
  Why so deaf to my heartfelt complaint?
Why must you be cruel, you beautiful broom!
  Because you are covered with paint? — Ding a dong, ding a dong —
    I am sure you are wrong!"

4

Miss Broom & Miss Shovel looked cross, & they say,
  "What nonsense you both of you say!"
Said the Shovel — "I'll certainly hit you a bang!"
Said the Broom, — "And I'll sweep you away!"
So the Coachman drove homeward as fast as he could
  Perceiving the quarrel with pain
But they put on the kettle, & little by little,
  They all became happy again. Ding a dong, ding a dong, there's an end of my song.

No. 76. Edward Lear. Autograph letter to Mrs. Henry Austin Bruce.

77   GUSTAVE GEFFROY, 1856–1926
Yvette Guilbert
[Paris, L'Estampe Originale, 1894]
Lithographs by HENRI DE TOULOUSE-LAUTREC, 1864–1901

16 lithographs, each on letterpress page, all printed in olive green. One of 100 copies. This copy signed Yvette Guilbert.
38.5 x 38.5 cm. Pictorial lithographed boards with title.

AMONG Toulouse-Lautrec's images of Paris in the 1890s, no subject is more vivid than the café singer Yvette Guilbert, whose angular, attenuated silhouette and long black gloves made her a favorite model. With Lautrec's simplification of line and inventiveness of composition, he brought to the book page the same audacity and freshness to be seen in his posters, and the same mastery of lithographic technique.

Less well know than the posters, the books are well represented by gifts during Hofer's lifetime, including copies of Georges Montorgueil's *Le café concert* of 1893, Georges Clemenceau's *Au pied du Sinaï* of 1898 (copy on japan with three extra suites and set of four *planches refusées*) and two copies of Jules Renard's *Histoires naturelles* of 1899, one with ink sketches. For the latter book, there are five preliminary drawings in pencil (Becker, no. 46).

Book covers for popular novels and sheet music were often designed by Lautrec and printed lithographically, so they may be considered among his original graphic work. The bequest contains three of these: Tristan Bernard's *Le fardeau de la liberté* of 1897, Jean de Tinan's *Ninon de Lenclos* of 1898, and Maurice Donnay's undated *Les vieux messieurs*, along with a copy of Victor Joze's *Reine de joie* of 1892, with a frontispiece by Lautrec and covers by Pierre Bonnard. There are four covers for sheet music by Lautrec's cousin Desiré Dihau, with lyrics by Jean Richepin: *Ballade de Noël*, *Berceuse*, *Floréal*, and *Les hirondelles de mer*, and one by Hector Sombre, *Etude de femmes*. There is also an 1895 program cover for the Théâtre de l'Oeuvre. Previous Hofer gifts of novels with Lautrec covers include another copy of Bernard's *Le fardeau de la liberté*, Paul Leclercq's *L'étoile rouge*, and Louis Marsolleau and Arthur Byl's *Hors les lois*, both of 1898, and Leclercq's *Jouets de Paris* of 1901.

E.M.G.

REF   *The Artist & the Book*, no. 301; *From Manet to Hockney*, no. 10; Ray, II, no. 380; Cate and Hitchings, *The Color Revolution, passim*; Adriani Götz and Wolfgang Wittrock, *Toulouse-Lautrec, Das gesamte graphische Werk* (Cologne [1967]), no. 77–93; Riva Castleman and Wolfgang Wittrock, *Henri de Toulouse-Lautrec, Images of the 1890s* (New York, the Museum of Modern Art, 1985), no. 84–92; Harvard College Library, Department of Printing and Graphic Arts, *Toulouse-Lautrec, Book Covers and Brochures* (Cambridge, 1972).

No. 77. Henri de Toulouse-Lautrec. Cover of Gustave Geffroy, *Yvette Guilbert*.

78   JEAN FROISSART, 1338–1410?
The Chronicles of Fraunce, Inglande, and Other Places Adjoynynge
[Hammersmith, Trustees of William Morris at the Kelmscott Press, 1897]
Type and ornaments designed by WILLIAM MORRIS, 1834–1896

2 specimen pages, with ornamental borders, printed in black and red on vellum.

43 x 55 cm. Framed and glazed.

THE KELMSCOTT PRESS, which flourished briefly from 1891 to 1898, was perhaps the most influential private press that ever existed. Not only did its achievements spark the modern private press movement in England and America, its productions also served as inspiration for a whole generation of designers, many of whom eventually went on to work in radically different styles.

William Morris owned a copy of Henry Noel Humphreys's *Illuminated Illustrations of Froissart* (1844–1845) as early as 1857; as early as 1892 he was experimenting with trial pages of a Kelmscott edition. Although Morris designed some borders and initials, and Burne-Jones offered to provide illustrations, the project was repeatedly postponed as work on the Kelmscott Chaucer dragged on. The Kelmscott Froissart would have been on a similar lavish scale: at one time Morris projected two folio volumes, to be bound in white pigskin to designs by Cobden-Sanderson. Morris's death in 1896 put an effective end to these plans, and the project was described as abandoned in the prospectus for the *Shepheardes Calendar*, which is dated November 12, 1896. Thirty-four pages were already in type, however, and in the months that followed, thirty-two copies of sixteen of these pages were printed for Morris's friends; 160 copies of two pages were printed for wider distribution.

This two-page specimen, printed in red and black on vellum, suggests what a handsome book the Froissart might have been. The type is that designed by Morris for the Kelmscott Chaucer in 1892. The borders were cut by W. Spielmeyer and C.E. Keates after Morris's drawings.

Many donors contributed to form the collection of Kelmscott Press books now in the Houghton Library, which was essentially complete even before Hofer became the founding Curator of Printing and Graphic Arts. The collection includes books from the libraries of Walter Crane and Charles Eliot Norton. Hofer added a copy of *Reynard the Fox* (1893), inscribed by Morris to W.H. Hooper, a wood-engraver at the Kelmscott Press. Other Kelmscott books from Hooper's library were the gifts of William B. Osgood Field. In memory of Philip Hofer, Mrs. Bayard L. Kilgour made a recent gift of annotated proofs of the Kelmscott Chaucer.

Books printed at the Doves Press and the Ashendene Press are listed under No. 81 and 93.

N.F.

REF   Sydney C. Cockerell, "An Annotated List of All the Books Printed at the Kelmscott Press in the Order in Which They Were Issued," [in] *A Note By William Morris on His Aims in Founding the Kelmscott Press* (Hammersmith, 1898), no. 46, p. 53–55; William S. Peterson, *A Bibliography of the Kelmscott Press* (Oxford, 1984), p. 126–128; Anthony Bliss and Margaretta M. Lovell, *William Morris, The Sanford and Helen Berger Collection* (Berkeley, 1984), p. 40–42, nos. 173–177; Alice H.R.H. Beckwith, *Victorian Bibliomania: The Illuminated Book in 19th-Century Britain* (Providence, 1987), p. 76.

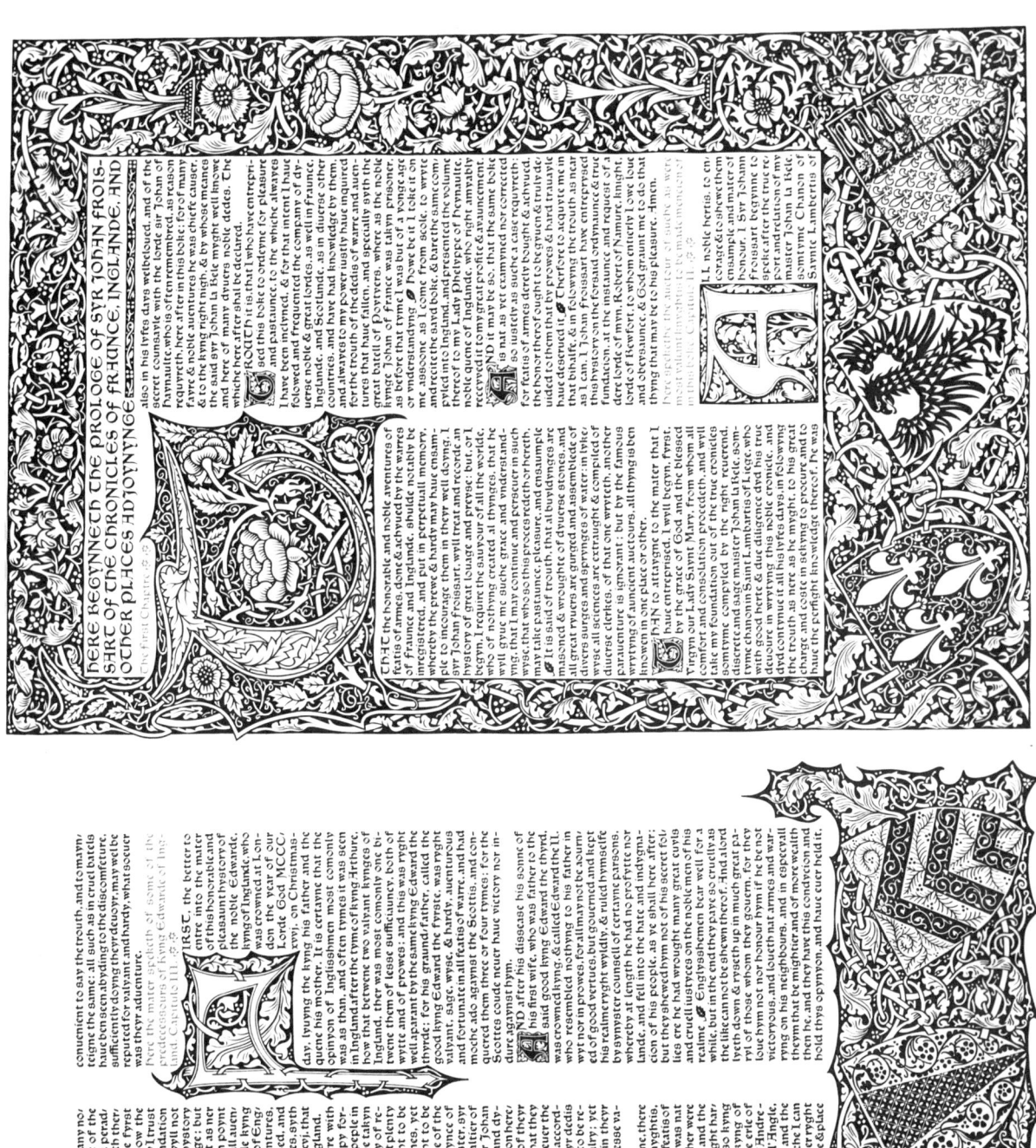

No. 78. William Morris. Specimen pages for Froissart, *Chronicles*.

79 &ed; PAUL VERLAINE, 1844–1896
Parallèlement
Paris, Ambroise Vollard, 1900
Lithographs by PIERRE BONNARD, 1868–1941

108 lithographs by Bonnard, printed in rose-sanguine. One of 30 copies on china. Edition: 200 copies (30 on china, 170 on holland).

30 x 24 cm. Dark blue morocco, gilt fillets, signed David; gray morocco doublures. With this copy is a folder of miscellaneous proofs.

PARALLELEMENT may be seen as the first consciously-crafted modern *livre de peintre*, and it remains one of the greatest, despite its modest size of only 139 pages. With this publication Ambroise Vollard established the twentieth-century French tradition combining text and original illustration by contemporary artists already known as painters or sculptors. He handled many of the Post-Impressionists in his gallery and urged each of these artists to produce print series for books. During the course of his career, Vollard brought out over twenty such books, which left an indelible mark on twentieth-century publishing. After his death in 1939, many of his projects were assumed by others.

Vollard's publications established a new book aesthetic, often combining a classically-structured printed page with a freedom of layout. In the *Parallèlement*, Bonnard's lithographs seem to float over the poetry with rare harmony and tonal delicacy.

The 1889 text had earlier encountered official difficulties, and after Vollard's text was printed, it was recalled, and the title-page with the imprint of the Imprimerie Nationale and the half-title were required to be removed and replaced. This is one of the few copies that remained unchanged and is of added interest in having the second title, half-title, and frontispiece bound in. A folder of proofs includes two signatures as printed, a proof of the frontispiece, and several signatures with proofs before text, including one in a state with an image experimentally placed on a page from which it was removed and placed on another page in the final version.

Other Bonnard items in the bequest include Victor Joze, *Reine de joie* of 1892, with lithographed cover by Bonnard and frontispiece by Toulouse-Lautrec; two sheet music scores for Bonnard's brother-in-law, Claude Terrasse—his *Petites scènes familières* of ca. 1893 with lithographed cover and illustrations for each of the songs, and *Panthéon Courcelles* of 1899 with lyrics by Georges Courteline; Peter Nansen's *Marie* of 1898; André Mellério's *La lithographie originale en couleurs* of the same year (another copy a previous gift); and Roger-Marx's *Simili* of 1930 (one of thirty copies with two extra suites of the engravings). Vollard's second book, the Longus *Daphnis et Chloé* of 1902 with lithographs by Bonnard, was a previous gift. Also included in the bequest is a folder containing prospectuses of Vollard publications and five proof impresssions of the lithographs for *Daphnis et Chloé*.

Vollard publications are well represented in the Department of Printing and Graphic Arts, and previous Hofer gifts include Mirbeau's *Le jardin des supplices* of 1902 with lithographs after August Rodin, Verlaine's *Sagesse* of 1911 with wood-engravings after Maurice Denis, *Les amours de Ronsard* of 1915 with engravings by Emile Bernard, Balzac's *Le chef d'oeuvre inconnu* of 1931 with etchings by Picasso, Flaubert's *La tentation de Saint-Antoine* of 1933 with lithographs by Odilon Redon, and three items illustrated by Georges Rouault: Vollard's *Les réincarnations du Père Ubu* of 1932, *Cirque de l'Etoile Filante* of 1938 and André Suarès' *Passion* of 1939, the latter two with color etchings.

Of Vollard's projected publications, previous Hofer gifts include the four lithographs by Redon of ca. 1900 for Mallarmé's *Un coup de dès* and the Hesiod *Théogonie* with etchings by Georges Braque, published in 1955.

E.M.G.

REF *The Artist & The Book*, no. 27; *From Manet to Hockney*, no. 17; Una E. Johnson, ed., *Ambroise Vollard, Editor* (New York [1977]), *passim*.

*De la grâce externe & légère
Et qui me laiſſait plutôt coi
Font de vous un morceau de roi,
O conſtitutionnel, chère!*

*Toujours eſt-il, regret ou non,
Que je ne sais pourquoi mon âme
Par ces froids penſe à vous, Madame
De qui je ne sais plus le nom.*

No. 79. Pierre Bonnard. Illustration from Verlaine, *Parallèlement*.

80   WASSILY KANDINSKY, 1866–1944
       [*Poems without Words*]
       [Moscow, Ecole Stroganoff, 1903–1904]

15 woodcuts by Kandinsky, including cover, tipped on.

33 x 25 cm. Black wrappers.

THESE SMALL WOODCUTS, printed in black on a white ground, bordered in black and mounted on black paper like a photograph album, reflect Kandinsky's interest in Russian folk art and popular illustration. They also express a lyricism of image without words, an underlying theme in the artist's work, still in a representational mode here. Although Kandinsky studied and worked in Munich from 1896 to 1914, he frequently returned to Russia and participated in exhibitions there.

    The bequest includes another Kandinsky item, the first edition of *Der Blaue Reiter*, edited by Kandinsky and Franz Marc, with illustrations by both these artists and others of the Blaue Reiter group. The second edition of 1914 was a previous Hofer gift, with prospectus and catalogue of the first Blaue Reiter exhibition. Another previous gift was Kandinsky's *Klänge*. Unusual publications by major artists, especially in the early phases of their careers, appealed to Philip Hofer's wide-ranging taste. The young Oskar Kokoschka, for example, is represented in a previous gift, *Theater und Kabarett Fledermaus* (1907), a program for the Viennese cafe.

                                                                                                                E.M.G.

REF   Solomon R. Guggenheim Museum, *Kandinsky in Munich, 1896–1914* (New York [1982]), p. 50–51, no. 210–211; Centre Georges Pompidou, *Kandinsky* ([Paris, 1984]), no. 20; Angelica Zander Rudenstine, ed., *The George Costakis Collection, Russian Avant-Garde Art* (New York, 1981), no. 104; Hans Konrad Röthel, *Kandinsky, Das graphische Werk* (Cologne, 1970), no. 10.

No. 80. Wassily Kandinsky. Cover of *Poems without Words*.

81   THE ENGLISH BIBLE
[London] Hammersmith, The Doves Press, 1903– 1905

5 vols. Proof of the opening chapter of Genesis with heading by Edward Johnston.
33.5 x 23.5 cm. Vellum wrappers.

THE DOVES BIBLE, the finest publication of the Press, has long been a model for twentieth-century letter design and typography. In founding the Press in 1900, Thomas James Cobden-Sanderson (1840–1922), who had established the Doves Bindery in 1893, was following the private press tradition of William Morris and the Kelmscott Press (No. 78). Like his predecessor, Cobden-Sanderson sought the skills of Emery Walker, Morris's technical adviser, who designed the Doves type, based on Nicholas Jenson's Venetian Pliny of 1476.

Set in a single wide column without paragraphs, the stanzas are separated by simple typographic marks. The texture of the page is enlivened by initial letters and headings drawn by Edward Johnston (1872–1944), cut in wood and printed in red, a simple two-color combination favored by the Press. In its reliance on typography alone, without ornamentation, the Doves style is totally different in concept from the Kelmscott.

Cobden-Sanderson's principles of design enunciated in his essay of 1900, "The Ideal Book or Book Beautiful," guided all the Doves publications through the final *catalogue raisonné* of 1916; Walker had left the Press in 1909 in a well-publicised disagreement. Cobden-Sanderson's final, dramatic gesture was to consign the Doves types to oblivion: "To the bed of the River Thames, the River on whose banks I have printed all my printed Books, I . . . bequeath the Doves Press Fount of Type . . . at the time of my death. And may the River, in its tides and flow, pass over them to and from the great sea for ever and ever. . . ."

These proofs, including a rare signature on vellum, join a previous Hofer gift of a group of specimen pages of the Bible, some issued as early as 1901. A number of them are early states annotated for correction by Cobden-Sanderson. Included is a proof of the Genesis page with his pencilled heading and initial letter refined by Johnston.

Additional Doves and Cobden-Sanderson material in the bequest includes a copy in a Doves binding of his *The Ideal Book or Book Beautiful* of 1900, his *Ecce Mundus, Industrial Ideals and the Book Beautiful* of 1902, and a trial issue, dated 1906, of his *Credo*, with his notes and corrections; a copy of the 1909 edition in a Doves binding was a previous gift. Six of the Doves Shakespeares are divided between the bequest and previous gifts, and copies of Emerson's *Essays* of 1906 are found in each category. Previous gifts also include Milton's *Areopagitica* of 1907, St. Francis' *Laudes Creaturarum* of 1910 in a Doves binding, and two copies of *In Principio* of 1911, each in a differently-designed Doves binding; one of them, like one of the Shakespeares, was John Quinn's copy.

E.M.G.

REF   Doves Press, *Catalogue raisonné* (London, 1911), p. 7, 19; Will Ransom, ed., *Kelmscott, Doves and Ashendene* ([Los Angeles] 1952), p. 61f.

IN THE BEGINNING

GOD CREATED THE HEAVEN AND THE EARTH. ¶ AND THE EARTH WAS WITHOUT FORM, AND VOID; AND DARKNESS WAS UPON THE FACE OF THE DEEP, & THE SPIRIT OF GOD MOVED UPON THE FACE OF THE WATERS. ¶ And God said, Let there be light: & there was light. And God saw the light, that it was good: & God divided the light from the darkness. And God called the light Day, and the darkness he called Night. And the evening and the morning were the first day. ¶ And God said, Let there be a firmament in the midst of the waters, & let it divide the waters from the waters. And God made the firmament, and divided the waters which were under the firmament from the waters which were above the firmament: & it was so. And God called the firmament Heaven. And the evening & the morning were the second day. ¶ And God said, Let the waters under the heaven be gathered together unto one place, and let the dry land appear: and it was so. And God called the dry land Earth; and the gathering together of the waters called he Seas: and God saw that it was good. And God said, Let the earth bring forth grass, the herb yielding seed, and the fruit tree yielding fruit after his kind, whose seed is in itself, upon the earth: & it was so. And the earth brought forth grass, & herb yielding seed after his kind, & the tree yielding fruit, whose seed was in itself, after his kind: and God saw that it was good. And the evening & the morning were the third day. ¶ And God said, Let there be lights in the firmament of the heaven to divide the day from the night; and let them be for signs, and for seasons, and for days, & years: and let them be for lights in the firmament of the heaven to give light upon the earth: & it was so. And God made two great lights; the greater light to rule the day, and the lesser light to rule the night: he made the stars also. And God set them in the firmament of the heaven to give light upon the earth, and to rule over the day and over the night, & to divide the light from the darkness: and God saw that it was good. And the evening and the morning were the fourth day. ¶ And God said, Let the waters bring forth abundantly the moving creature that hath life, and fowl that may fly above the earth in the open firmament of heaven. And God created great whales, & every living creature that moveth, which the waters brought forth abundantly, after their kind, & every winged fowl after his kind: & God saw that it was good. And God blessed them, saying, Be fruitful, & multiply, and fill the waters in the seas, and let fowl multiply in the earth. And the evening & the morning were the fifth day. ¶ And God said, Let the earth bring forth the living creature after his kind, cattle, and creeping thing, and beast of the earth after his kind: and it was so. And God made the beast of the earth after his kind, and cattle after their kind, and every thing that creepeth upon the

27

No. 81.   Proof of the opening chapter of Genesis from *The English Bible*. Heading by Edward Johnston.

82 ❧ VOL'GA
[St. Petersburg, P. Golike i A. Vil'borg] 1904
Color lithographs by IVAN YAKOVLEVICH BILIBIN, 1876–1942

37.4 x 31.1 cm. Original printed wrappers. Handwritten label of the Tsarkoe Selo children's library, no. 530. Inscribed in Russian, on title-page, "To darling Alexei, from Papa and Mama, Christmas 1912."

HOFER told how he acquired his copy of Bilibin's *Vol'gá* in an article on "Alexander Benois' Russian Alphabet in Pictures" in the *Harvard Library Bulletin* (Vol. XXVII, No. 1, January 1979). Both *Vol'gá* and the Benois Alphabet were purchased from a "Soviet-sympathizing book-dealer" in New York City in 1932. *Vol'gá* is inscribed in Russian "to darling Alexei"; the Alphabet bears the childish signature "Anastasia" and the date 1905. Hofer was convinced that the books came from the children's library at Tsarkoe Selo and had belonged to the Tsarevich and his sister. He contemplated a second article on the Bilibin book as a sequel to his article on Benois, but never completed it.

Bilibin was a member of the Mir Iskusstva (World of Art) group, headed by Benois and Sergei Diaghilev. Although he is best known for his children's book illustrations, he also contributed drawings to the *World of Art* and other journals, and executed theatrical designs. In all his work, a love for Russian folk art traditions is combined with the influence of Japanese prints and turn-of-the-century Art Nouveau. Recently many of his fairy tale illustrations have been reprinted and are enjoying a renewed popularity. *Vol'gá* remains one of his lesser-known works. It is the story of the folk hero Vol'gá, who possesses marvelous powers: in the illustration shown here, Vol'gá has transformed himself into a pike in order to lead the other fishes from the Black Sea to his overlord at Kiev. The contrast between the dimly lit underwater world of the fishes with the sunlight and open air above water is brilliantly conceived, as is the contrast between the realistic delineation of the fish and the stylized treatment of underwater plants.

In addition to *Vol'gá* and the Benois Alphabet, the Hofer bequest includes nineteen other early twentieth century Russian children's books, dating between 1900 and 1932. Two are reputedly from the Tsarkoe Selo library; three are early editions of books illustrated by Bilibin: *Maria Morevna* (1902), *Vasilisa the Beautiful* (1903) and *The Tsarevich Ivan, the Firebird and the Gray Wolf* (1903). These join a large group of turn-of-the-century Russian children's books which Hofer had already given to the Department of Printing and Graphic Arts. Additional children's books of this period were the gift of Bayard L. Kilgour, Jr.

N.F.

REF   Kilgour, no. 1322; Sergei Golynets, *Ivan Bilibin* (New York and Leningrad, 1981).

No. 82. Ivan Bilibin. Illustration from *Vol'gá*.

83 ❧ PROSPECTUS FOR THE HUMANISTS' LIBRARY
Boston, The Merrymount Press, 1907

Type (and title-page?) designed by Herbert P. Horne; printed in red-orange and black.

20.9 x 12.3 cm.

THE EIGHT VOLUMES of The Humanists' Library (1906–1914) represent Daniel Berkeley Updike's major attempt at limited edition publishing. The early years of Updike's Merrymount Press were largely devoted to trade books for such publishers as R.H. Russell, L.C. Page, Charles Scribner's Sons and Thomas Y. Crowell. Later, institutional and ecclesiastical printing combined with privately printed books accounted for most of the Press's business.

The early work of the Merrymount Press was strongly influenced by William Morris. This influence is especially evident in Updike's own publishing ventures such as *The Altar Book* (1896), but period styles were also employed for trade printing. The Humanists' Library, too, was conceived in a period style: the Italian Renaissance. Herbert Horne's Monteallegro type and decorations were based on fifteenth-century Florentine models, and the books were printed in red-orange and black. To a large extent, however, the style of the Humanists' Library is self-effacing. These are quintessentially readable books, the antithesis of the decorative (but sometimes unreadable) books produced by Morris and his followers. The title-pages of later books in the series were designed by T.M. Cleland and W.A. Dwiggins. Rudolph Ruzicka's long association with the Merrymount Press began in 1907, when he was engaged to engrave one of Dwiggins' title-page designs. It is not clear who designed the title-page of this prospectus. It could almost be the Dwiggins/Ruzicka collaboration, which Ruzicka in *Updike: American Printer* described as lacking all feeling after it was finally engraved.

The prospectus contains a statement of Updike's aims ("to print in a form near akin to the great traditions of the printer's art in its earliest days") and a list of twenty-four projected titles.

The bequest includes six volumes from The Humanists' Library: Leonardo da Vinci, *Thoughts on Art and Life* (No. I, 1906), Pierre de Nolhac, *Petrarch and the Ancient World* (No. III, 1907), Sir Philip Sidney, *The Defence of Poesie* (No. IV, 1908), *The Correspondence of Philip Sidney and Hubert Languet* (No. V, 1912), Pico della Mirandola, *A Platonick Discours upon Love* (No. VII, 1914), and Giovanni della Casa, *A Renaissance Courtesy-Book, Galateo of Manners and Behaviors* (No. VIII, 1914). The remaining volumes, *Erasmus Against War* (No. II, 1907) and Albrecht Dürer, *Records of Journeys to Venice and the Low Countries* (No. VI, 1913) were previous gifts, as was a copy of *The Altar Book* (1896) in sheets. Much additional Updike material was included both in the bequest and among previous gifts.

N.F.

REF American Institute of Graphic Arts, *Updike: American Printer and his Merrymount Press* (New York, 1947); George Parker Winship, *Daniel Berkeley Updike and the Merrymount Press* (Rochester, 1947); Daniel Berkeley Updike, *Notes on the Merrymount Press & its Work* (San Francisco, 1975).

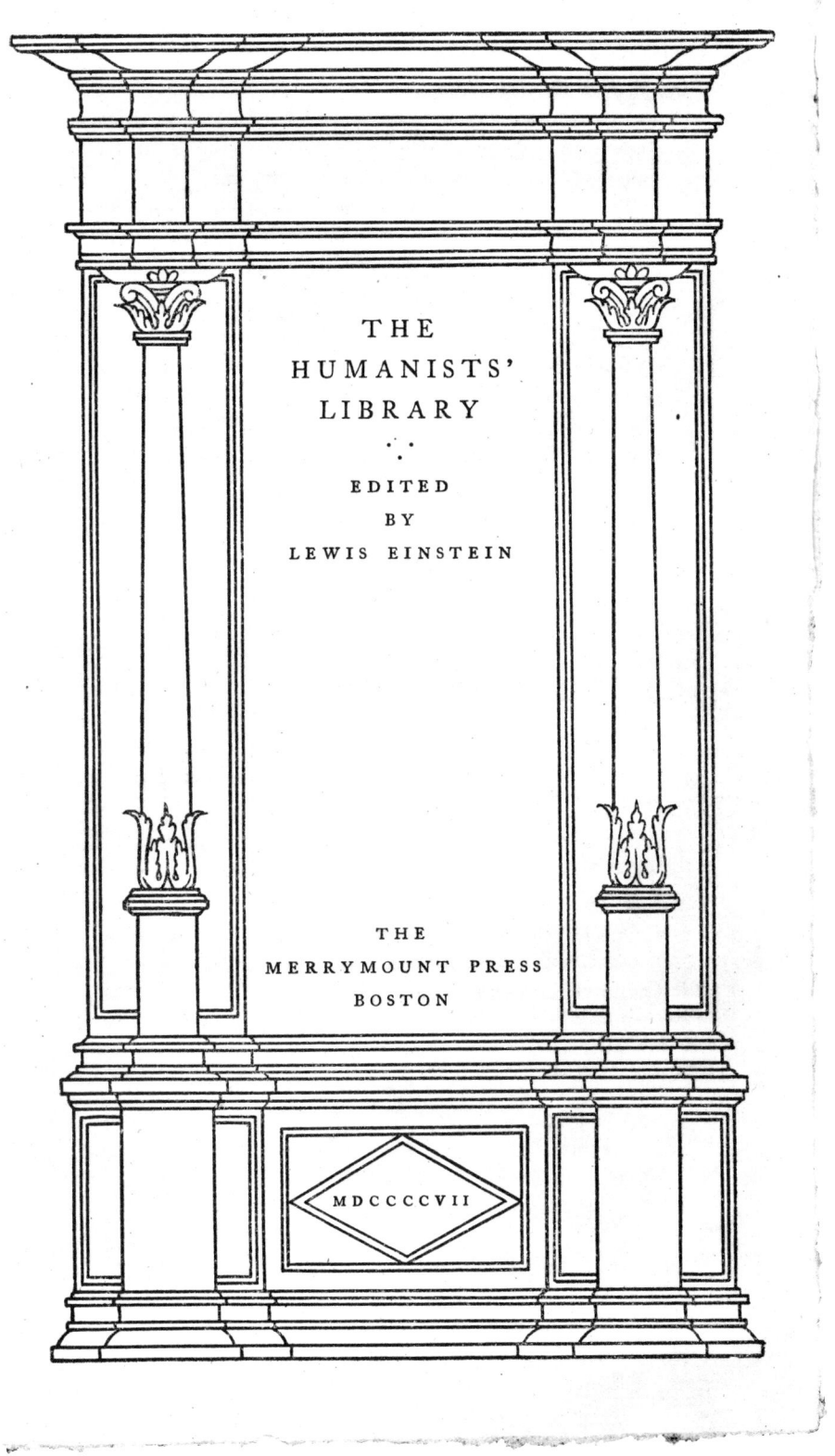

No. 83.   Prospectus for the Humanists' Library.

84   ERIC GILL, 1882–1940
    Drawing Book
    England and France, 1907–1910

Drawings by Gill in graphite and watercolor, 50 leaves.

20.6 x 14 cm. Inserted in publisher's half vellum binding, stamped in silver: "Hofmannsthal / Kleine Dramen"; silver gilt paper sides. Signatures of "A.E.R. Gill (1907)/Hammersmith Terrace, London, w," and Mr. Patching; bookplate of Rodger Glessner.

ERIC GILL in his autobiography compared the thrill he felt the first time he saw Edward Johnston writing—and saw what he wrote—to his feelings when he touched his wife's body for the first time, or first saw the North Transept of Chartres Cathedral. These three themes, lettering, eroticism and architecture, all find expression in the Gill sketchbook in the Hofer bequest. This sketchbook contains an impressive, highly-finished series of drawings of Chartres, which Gill visited in 1907 and 1909 (ff. 3–8; 18–19), some of the very first drawings of the female nude that he ever made (ff. 21–22), and several studies for inscriptional lettering, including the inscription for the monument to Oscar Wilde in Père Lachaise Cemetery, Paris (ff. 36–37). A number of plans of Asheham House, near Lewes, Sussex (ff. 38–41), are evidently related to a project for an open air temple—a sort of modern Stonehenge—which Gill and the sculptor Jacob Epstein (who also collaborated with Gill on the Wilde monument) hoped to establish in the grounds. The price ultimately proved too high, however, and the project was abandoned. In 1912, the house was leased by Virginia and Leonard Woolf, who thus became neighbors and friends of the Gills. Virginia Woolf's essay, *A Haunted House*, was written about Asheham. Although the flyleaf of the Gill sketchbook is inscribed "A.E.R. Gill (1907) / Hammersmith Terrace, London, w," it is clear that most, if not all of the drawings in it were done after Gill and his wife Ethel had left London and moved to the Sussex village of Ditchling. This move took place in October 1907; the Gills remained in Ditchling until 1924, when they moved to Capel-y-ffin in the Welsh Black Mountains.

After serving an apprenticeship in the London architectural office of W.H. Caroë, studying lettering with Edward Johnston at the Central School of Arts and Crafts, and learning masonry and stone-cutting, Gill embarked on a career as a professional stone-cutter in 1903. By 1904, he had received his first commission for book work—consisting of engraved headings and titles—from Count Harry Kessler of the Cranach Press. Other commissions followed, from the Doves Press, Ashendene Press and Insel Verlag. It is above all with two later private presses that Gill is associated, however: St. Dominic's Press, which was established in Ditchling in 1916 by Gill's friend Hilary Pepler, and Robert Gibbings's Golden Cockerel Press at Waltham St. Lawrence. Gill's interest in book design and book illustration led him to learn wood-engraving in the 1910s; his work for St. Dominic's and Golden Cockerel and the work of the group of artists who gathered around him, first in Ditchling and later in Capel-y-ffin, constituted a whole woodcut revival. Encouraged by Gibbings and Stanley Morison, Gill also designed type faces, notably *Perpetua* and *Gill Sans Serif* for the Golden Cockerel Press and Monotype Corporation.

The different phases of Gill's activity are well-documented in the Department of Printing and Graphic Arts. Previous gifts by Hofer and others have resulted in an excellent collection of books containing Gill's designs. The bequest adds important primary source material, including drawings and proofs for three Golden Cockerel books: *Troilus and Criseyede* (1927), *The Canterbury Tales* (1929–1930), and *The Four Gospels* (1931). A special copy of the Vergil published by Count Kessler's Cranach Press, with lettering by Gill and woodcuts by Aristide Maillol, is discussed in No. 89. Of special interest is an alphabet on Hopton-wood stone, with the letters incised and colored. Gill designed a bookplate for Hofer in 1928. Specimens of the types designed by Gill are in the Bentinck-Smith Typographical Collection.

The modern British revival of calligraphy, stemming from Edward Johnston and his pupils, is also well represented in the bequest, which includes examples of the work of Johnston, Alfred Fairbank, Graily Hewitt (see No. 93), Ivy Harper, Heather Child, Marie Angel (No. 100), and Irene Wellington. Besides the alphabet by Gill, the bequest also includes two additional stone alphabets carved by David Kindersley, Gill's last pupil, and three inscriptions cut on wood by Will Carter.

N.F.

No. 84. Eric Gill drawing book: "North Transept of Chartres Cathedral."

REF   Eric Gill, *Autobiography* (New York, 1941); Evan R. Gill, *Bibliography of Eric Gill* (London, 1953); Evan R. Gill, *The Inscriptional Work of Eric Gill* (London, 1964); Roy Brewer, *Eric Gill, The Man Who Loved Letters* (Totowa, New Jersey, 1973); Robert Harling, *The Letter Forms of Eric Gill* (Boston, 1977); Malcolm Yorke, *Eric Gill, Man of Flesh and Spirit* (New York, 1982); Anthony D'Offay, *Eric Gill, 1882–1940* (London [1982]); Philip Hofer, "Inscriptions in the Graphic Arts Department at Harvard," *Notes on Printing and Graphic Arts* 1 (1953), 10–12.

85 · GUILLAUME APOLLINAIRE, 1880–1918
L'Enchanteur pourrissant
Paris, Henry Kahnweiler [1909]
Woodcuts by ANDRE DERAIN, 1880–1954

32 woodcuts by Derain including 13 full-page, head- and tailpieces, initials, and publisher's device. One of 75 copies on Arches. Edition: 106 copies (25 on japan, 75 on Arches, 4 *hors commerce*, 2 with impressions of cancelled blocks). Copy signed by author and artist.

27 x 20 cm. Vellum wrappers.

THIS TRIPLE MONUMENT in the history of the *livre de peintre* brought together three men whose careers were instrumental in shaping twentieth-century European art. *L'Enchanteur pourrissant* is Apollinaire's first book as author, Kahnweiler's first as publisher, and Derain's first as artist. The young German Kahnweiler, rejecting his banking background, had opened his first Paris gallery in 1907, and in the same year he began to handle Derain's work. Two years later, now also a friend of the young Apollinaire, Kahnweiler joined this champion of modern art and letters with the young Fauve artist Derain to produce the first of a long and distinguished line of books. Like Vollard, Kahnweiler saw the book as a medium of expression for the painter and printmaker, as well as for the author, and he published many of his gallery's artists in this form.

L'Enchanteur joins Apollinaire's Celtic protagonist Merlin the enchanter with Derain's stylized forest and figures. The artist brought to the modern woodcut a primitive force and vigor recalling the fifteenth century. He also designed and cut Kahnweiler's device on the title-page, here appearing for the first time: two scallop shells (*coquilles*, the French word for typographical errors) with the initials HK (Henri Kahnweiler) and ad (André Derain), and the tears of the compositor responsible for the typo. In this, his first publication, Kahnweiler established the pattern he was to follow for forty years: a first edition by a contemporary writer, illustrated by a contemporary artist and published in a modest quarto format in an edition of one hundred copies for sale.

Two examples of Derain's later decorative style may be seen in the bequest: woodcuts in André Salmon's *Le calumet* of 1920 and drypoints in Georges Gabory's *Le nez de Cléopatre* of 1922. Previous Hofer gifts of this later Derain manner include Gabory's *La cassette de plomb* of 1920 (engravings), Vincent Muselli's *Les travaux et les jeux* of 1929 (lithographs), the Cartier-Héron de Villefosse *A Tribute to Precious Stones* of 1947 (color lithograph), and *Odes anacréontiques* of 1953 (lithographs; copy with two extra suites, one in black on japan and one in sanguine on china).

Kahnweiler imprints, those under his own name and those under the Galerie Simon and under the Galerie Louise Leiris, figure prominently in the Hofer collection. Max Jacob's *Saint Matorel* trilogy is discussed in No. 87. André Masson's *Carnet de croquis* and *Sur le vif*, both 1950 portfolios of lithographs, are in the bequest. Previous gifts include three Galerie Simon publications of 1921: André Malraux's *Lunes en papier* with woodcuts by Fernand Léger, Raymond Radiguet's *Les Pélican* with etchings by Henri Laurens, and Pierre Reverdy's *Coeur de chêne* with woodcuts by Manolo. Other Galerie Simon books of the twenties are Max Jacob's 1923 *La couronne de Vulcain* with lithographs by Suzanne Roger, Marcel Jouhandeau's 1925 *Brigitte ou la Belle au bois dormant* with lithographs by Marie Laurencin, and Radiguet's 1926 *Denise* with lithographs by Juan Gris. From the Galerie Louise Leiris is Masson's 1952 *Voyage à Venise* with color lithographs.

E.M.G.

No. 85. André Derain. Illustration from Apollinaire, *L'Enchanteur pourrissant*.

REF *The Artist & The Book*, no. 78; *From Manet to Hockney*, no. 26, another edition; Jean Hugues, ed., *50 ans d'édition de D.-H. Kahnweiler* (Paris, 1959), no. 1; Centre Georges Pompidou, *Daniel-Henry Kahnweiler* (Paris, [1984– 1985]), p. 100 and section "Livres de Kahnweiler" by François Chapon, p. 45–76; Apollinaire, *L'Enchanteur pourrissant*, Jean Burgos, ed. (Paris, 1972), ch. 1, p. ix–lxxviii.

86 ❧ GUILLAUME APOLLINAIRE, 1880–1918
Le Bestiaire ou Cortège d'Orphée
Paris, Deplanche, 1911
Woodcuts by RAOUL DUFY, 1877–1953

Special copy in 3 vols.

Copy no. 3 on japan. Edition: 120 copies (29 on japan, 91 on holland). Copy signed by author, artist and publisher, and bound with *Suites et Documents*, consisting of prospectus, subscription form dated 1910, 13 preliminary drawings by Dufy in graphite or graphite and wash, 57 annotated proofs, MS leaves, and preliminary proof of colophon.

Copy no. 0, signed by author and artist, with impressions of cancelled blocks for dépôt legal (1 of 2 such copies).

Supplément: Les Deux Poèmes Refusés, 1921. Copy no. 3 (of 29). Bound with prospectus, 8 preliminary drawings in graphite or graphite and wash, 34 annotated proofs, impressions of cancelled blocks.

35.5 x 10.5 cm. Vellum wrappers.

THE MONUMENTALITY of the twentieth-century *livre de peintre* was established in this publication, and rarely has the genre achieved such harmony between poet and printmaker. In 1906 Apollinaire began these quatrains. Although their genesis has often been ascribed to the influence of Picasso, it is the opinion of Daniel-Henry Kahnweiler, the publisher of Apollinaire, Dufy and Picasso, that "The truth is the contrary. The bestiaire has [sic] been written around 1906, clearly under the influence of Jean Moréas. Picasso had read it and liked it and in 1907, I had the idea with Picasso to publish it with woodcuts by him. He did the two existing woodcuts but nothing else and so, I had to abandon this idea. So, anyhow, the 'quatrains' by Apollinaire were pre-existing" (letter dated 18 February 1964 from Kahnweiler to this writer). In 1908 an early version of the *Bestiaire* entitled "La Marchande des quatre saisons ou le Bestiaire mondain" appeared in *La Phalange* (no. 24, 15 June 1908). By 1910 the poet had revised and expanded the work, and on 29 August of that year he wrote to Dufy (letter pasted in this copy), sending him the remaining poems for the artist to complete his work, their collaboration then being well advanced.

Sharing characteristics with both medieval bestiaries and Renaissance emblem books, Apollinaire's *Bestiaire* consists of thirty quatrains, divided into four sections of animals, insects, fish, and birds. Each is introduced by a poem with the facing figure of Orpheus, while the bestiary verses themselves, in large and well-spaced type, are placed below the images illustrating them.

These are Dufy's first published and most important illustrations. Their boldness and vigor recall his brief association with the *Fauve* style, while their combination of stylized natural form and bold pattern recalls Dufy the decorator, who designed fabrics for Paul Poiret (suggested as a possible subscriber in Apollinaire's MS. list pasted in this copy). These woodcuts take their place, along with André Derain's for Apollinaire's *L'Enchanteur pourrissant* (No. 85) as early examples of the revival of the woodcut in the twentieth century, characterized by compressed compositions and strong blacks and whites, here created by slashing knife lines. They follow the tradition of the fifteenth-century woodcut, deliberately breaking away from the fine line of nineteenth-century wood-engraved illustration.

This special copy documents the development of the publication and the working relation between painter and poet. The latter's letter to Dufy of 29 August 1910, written on graph paper (reproduced in *Vient de Paraître*, 3e année, no. 24, 9 Nov. 1923, issue in memory of Apollinaire, partially reproduced and transcribed in *Oeuvres complètes de Guillaume Apollinaire*, 1966; see ref. paragraph) states that the text is finished, includes the final seven quatrains and a sketch for the printer's mark, and expresses confidence in the collaboration. There follows a list of possible subscribers in Apollinaire's hand.

The development of many of the images, often dramatically changed, may be studied in these supplementary pages, on which are pasted a final proof of each cut and, for eighteen of them, a proof of an earlier

No. 86. Raoul Dufy, "Le Lion." Preliminary drawing for Apollinaire, *Le Bestiaire*.

state. Of particular interest are preliminary drawings for eight different subjects, showing changes in conception, as well as detail. The final image in the bestiary, for example, of "Le boeuf" is represented by five drawings and two proofs. This vigorous, snorting, mythical creature was first drawn and cut as a placid farm animal—the first block Dufy cut for the book, and he pulled but this single proof, according to his penciled note on the sheet. The figure was transformed from a folk-art image to the charging winged figure on the printed page, and the evolution may be traced in the drawings and proofs, along with that of several other figures. As mounted in this copy, four of the first five preliminary drawings are on the rectos of leaves whose versos contain twenty-five of the quatrains, written out in Dufy's hand.

The *Supplément, Les Deux Poèmes Refusés* contains the poems and cuts of "Le condor" and "Le morpion," rejected as *trop libre* for the original edition. This copy contains ten proof states of the title-page vignette, three drawings and ten proof states of "Le morpion," four drawings and six proof states of "Le condor," a drawing and five proof states of the initial, and three proofs of the tailpiece. Impressions of the cancelled blocks are also included.

A later style of Dufy illustration may be seen in unpublished drawings for Vergil's *Bucolics*, a previous Hofer gift. Executed about 1946, the drawings, in pencil and crayon, are preliminary studies for a Société Scripta et Picta edition, finally published in 1953 with illustrations not by Dufy, but by Jacques Villon.

E.M.G.

REF   *The Artist & and Book*, no. 91; Guillaume Apollinaire, *Oeuvres complètes*, Michel Décaudin, ed. (Paris [1966]), IV, 737–738; Philip Hofer, "Four Modern French Illustrated Bestiaries," *Gazette des Beaux-Arts*, XXXIII (1948), 301–316; Anne Hyde Greet, *Apollinaire et le livre de peintre* (Paris, 1977), p. 57–151; Dora Perez-Tibi, "The Illustrated Book" [in] *Raoul Dufy* (London [1983–1984]), p. 117–119. Two recent facsimiles are Apollinaire, *Le Bestiaire*, Lauren Shakely, trans. (New York, 1977), approx. original size; and Apollinaire, *Bestiary*, Pepe Karmel, trans. (Boston, 1980), reduced.

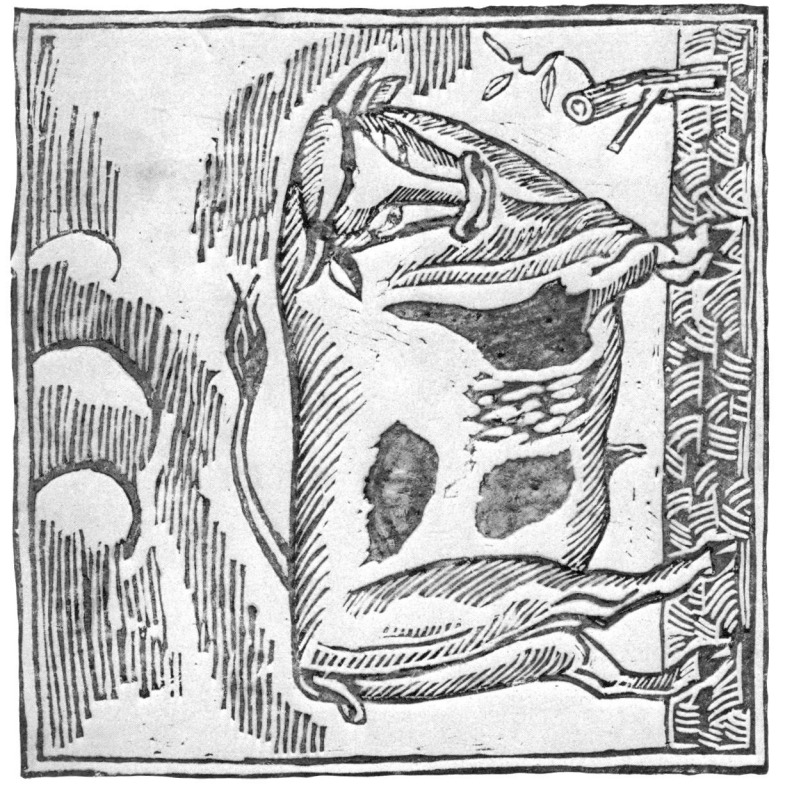

No. 86. Raoul Dufy, "Le Boeuf." Unique trial proof and illustration as published in Apollinaire, *Le Bestiaire*.

175

87   MAX JACOB, 1876–1944
Saint Matorel
Paris, Henry Kahnweiler [1911]
Etchings by PABLO PICASSO, 1881–1973

4 etchings by Picasso. One of 85 copies on holland. Edition: 106 copies (15 on japan, 85 on holland, 4 *hors commerce*, 2 with impression of cancelled blocks). Copy signed by author and artist. Inscribed "Tu a ta marque ici Marcoussis, Au cher Marcoussis son humble admirateur Max Jacob."

27 x 22.5 cm. Vellum wrappers.

KAHNWEILER had intended that this, his second book, which is dedicated to Apollinaire, should be illustrated by André Derain, who had done the first, *L'enchanteur pourrissant* (No. 85). The artist, however, found the text uncongenial, so the publisher turned to the young Picasso, an intimate friend of the author. *Saint Matorel* is the first volume of a trilogy recounting the mystical road traveled by the protagonist, Victor Matorel, employee of the Paris Métro, a journey of conversion and pursuit of the monastic ideal parallel to Jacob's own life. All three volumes were published by Kahnweiler, for whom Derain illustrated the second, *Les oeuvres burlesque et mystiques de Frère Matorel*, while Picasso resumed his role with the third, *Le siège de Jérusalem*. Both the latter titles were Hofer gifts in connection with the 1961 exhibition, *The Artist & the Book*.

Executed during that most important stylistic phase of Picasso's career, his evolution of analytic Cubism, these etchings are significant examples of his relatively rare graphic output at that time. Etched with a light and airy line, such a plate as Mademoiselle Léonie takes its place among the finest examples of this style. Two other major Picasso books are in the bequest: Ovid's *Les Métamorphoses*, 1931, illustrated with etchings, and *Eaux-fortes originales pour textes de Buffon*, 1942, one of five copies on japan *super-nacré* with an extra set of the etchings on china.

Previous Hofer gifts of Picasso material, listed below by date of publication, include:

Honoré de Balzac, *Le chef-d'oeuvre inconnu* (etchings), 1931.
Paul Eluard, *La barre d'appui* (etchings with aquatint), 1936.
Francesco Petrarch, *Cinq sonnets* (etching with aquatint), 1947.
Ramón Reventós, *Dos contes* (engravings), 1947.
Yvon Goll, *Elégie d' Iphétonga* (lithographs), 1949.
Aimé Césaire, *Corps perdu* (etchings and aquatint), 1950.
Tristan Tzara, *De mémoire d'homme* (lithographs; 1 of 20 copies *hors commerce*), 1950.
Roch Grey, *Chevaux de minuit* (engravings), 1956.
Max Jacob, *Cronique des temps héroïques* (lithograph), 1956.
Antoine Artaud, . . . *Autre chose que de l'enfant beau* (color engraving), 1957.
40 dessins en marge de Buffon (linocuts), 1957.
Jaime Sabartès, *Dans l'atelier de Picasso* (lithographs), 1957.
René Char, *L'escalier de Flore* (drypoints; 1 of 4 copies with proof states), 1958.
Lucien Scheler, *Sillage intangible* (drypoint), 1958.
Le frère mendiant (drypoints), 1959.
José (Pepe) Delgado Illo, *La tauromaquia* (aquatints), 1959.
Jacqueline Roque, *Température* (drypoints), 1960.

E.M.G.

REF *The Artist & the Book*, no. 222; Jean Hugues, ed., *50 ans d'édition de D.-H. Kahnweiler* (Paris, 1959), no. 2; Centre Georges Pompidou, *Daniel Henry Kahnweiler* (Paris [1984–1985]), p. 104 and p. 53f; Bernard Geiser, *Picasso peintre-graveur* (Berne, 1933), I, no. 23–28; Sebastian Goeppert, Herma Goeppert-Frank, Patrick Cramer, *Pablo Picasso, The Illustrated Books: catalogue raisonnée* (Geneva, 1983), no. 2; Donna Stein, *Cubist Prints, Cubist Books* (New York, 1983), p. 11, 57f.

No. 87. Pablo Picasso, "Mademoiselle Léonie." Illustration from Max Jacob, *Saint Matorel*.

88 ❧ PETER NEWELL, 1862–1924
Drawings for *The Rocket Book*
New York, Harper and Brothers [1912]

23 drawings by Newell in graphite, watercolor and gouche; alternate and final drawings for cover design, half-title, title-page and 19 of the 22 illustrations.

Various sizes, approx. 28.7 x 22.2 cm.

WHILE PLAYING in the basement, Fritz, the janitor's son, sets off a rocket, which shoots up through the twenty-one stories of the apartment building, causing all kinds of amusing incidents along the way. This is the simple concept behind *The Rocket Book*, written and illustrated by Peter Newell. Previously Newell had represented the humorous havoc created by a gun accidentally fired (*The Hole Book*, 1908) and a runaway baby carriage (*The Slant Book*, 1910). Part of the charm of *The Rocket Book* and *The Hole Book* proceeds from the fact that the pages are actually perforated at the spot the rocket and the bullet are supposed to have passed through. A manuscript from the Hofer bequest shows Newell groping towards the format of *The Slant Book* (a parallelogram): "I think this would be a very novel shape for the book. The pictures and verses would be on the diagonal to conform to the shape of the book . . . Funny situations might be based on the tip of the land—as a baby carriage escaping from the terrified nurse and running down the street, bowling over pedestrians, etc., etc."

Newell's clever formats for children's books have never been surpassed. The use of a single vivid color plus black, which he used for many of his illustrations, was to be adopted by numerous other artists later in the twentieth century. These two factors may help to explain why Newell's books appear so thoroughly modern and undated today, despite the period costumes of the wickedly mischievious little boys and girls.

Philip Hofer enjoyed Peter Newell's books as a child and published an early appreciation of his work in 1934, a mere ten years after the artist's death. Many of the drawings in his collection were acquired from the Newell family or from his publishers, Harper and Brothers. A checklist of the drawings alone suggests what a formidable Newell archive Hofer has left to Harvard:

The Hole Book (1908). 23 drawings, including alternate cover design, title-page and 21 out of 24 illustrations.

The Slant Book (1910). 3 preliminary drawings with the titles *The Bias Book* and *The Tippy Book*. 1 additional preliminary study, 24 final drawings for illustrations, 1 proof of text and caricature signature.

The Burnt Book (unpublished). 4 drawings.

The Rocket Book (1912). See above.

The following drawings were part of the Frances L. Hofer bequest:

Pictures and Rhymes (1899). 4 drawings.

J.K. Bangs, *Mr. Munchausen* (1901). 2 drawings.

[C.L. Dodgson], *Alice's Adventures in Wonderland* (1901). 4 drawings.

[——], *Through the Looking Glass* (1902). 2 drawings.

[——], *The Hunting of the Snark and Other Poems* (1903), 1 drawing.

Harper's Weekly XLVII (1903). 3 drawings.

Favorite Fairy Tales (1907). 1 drawing.

Self-portrait, 5 unidentified subjects.

In addition to these drawings, Hofer's gifts have included multiple copies of most of Newell's published works. One copy of *The Hole Book* is in its original dust jacket.

N.F.

REF   Philip Hofer, "Peter Newell's Pictures and Rhymes," *The Colophon*, Part 19 (1934); Judy L. Larson, *Enchanted Images: American Children's Illustration, 1850–1925* (Santa Barbara Museum of Art, 1980), p. 28–52, 61; Albert Lee, "Book Illustrators, XXIII, Peter Newell," *The Book Buyer*, VIII (1896), p. 348–350.

No. 88. Peter Newell. Drawing for paper cover of *The Rocket Book*.

89 ✤ VERGIL

A. *Eclogae / Eclogen*
German trans. by Rudolf Alexander Schröder
Weimar, Cranach Presse, 1926
Woodcuts by ARISTIDE MAILLOL, 1861–1944
Lettering by ERIC GILL, 1882–1940

B. *Eclogae / The Eclogues*
English trans. by J.H. Mason
[London, Emery Walker Ltd. for the Cranach Press, 1927]
Woodcuts by ARISTIDE MAILLOL
Lettering by ERIC GILL

43 woodcuts designed and cut by Maillol; title-page and initial letters designed and cut by Gill; ornament of these letters designed and cut by Maillol.

A. German edition with text in Latin and German. One of 250 copies on laid rag paper with watermark designed by Maillol. Edition: 294 copies (8 on vellum, 36 on silk rag, 250 on laid rag).

32.5 x 25 cm. White pigskin by Ignaz Wiemeler, with letter dated 14 December 1936 from Wiemeler to Hofer, who commissioned the binding.

B 1. English edition with text in Latin and English. One of 33 copies on imperial Japanese paper. Edition: 264 copies (6 on vellum, 33 on imperial Japanese paper; 225 on hemp and linen paper).

32.5 x 25 cm. Limp vellum, green silk ties. Boxed with this copy is a set of separate prints on yellow Chinese paper for the special edition.

2. English edition. One of 225 copies on hand-made hemp and linen paper.

33 x 25.5 cm. Publisher's wrappers.

Two sets of proofs of the 43 cuts, one on vellum, printed in brown; one on china paper printed in sanguine. In each set, and also in the set on yellow Chinese paper noted in B1, the title-page cut is initialed in pencil by Maillol.

Three sheets of preliminary drawings by Maillol:
  a. Boy and goat, for cut on p. 89. Indelible pencil. 16.4 x 20 cm.
  b. Recto: Goat. Verso: Nude. Indelible pencil. 18.5 x 23.7 cm.
  c. Sheet of five drawings, including studies for pressmark. Graphite. 27 x 21 cm.

THE ENGLISH PRIVATE PRESS TRADITION of fine printing was combined with the French tradition of the *livre de peintre* by Count Harry Kessler, who chose artists skilled in formal graphic statement. The Vergil combines the woodcuts of the French sculptor Aristide Maillol with the lettering of the English sculptor Eric Gill (No. 84). Additional English talents helped to give the book its essential character, for J[ohn] H[enry] Mason was the translator for the English edition, and Emery Walker the publisher. Both these men, in their professional roles as craftsmen, were guides for Kessler in his printing ventures, beginning early in the century when he was associated with the Insel Verlag in Leipzig. He dedicated the Vergil to Walker, William Morris's technical adviser and the connecting link between Kelmscott (No. 78) and the next generation of private presses (see No. 81 and 93).

Begun in 1912, the Vergil has a long and often-told history of delays, many due to the interruption of World War I. Not until 1926 was the German edition published; the French appeared the same year, and the English followed in 1927. The German and English editions are almost identical in layout, with a few minor variations in page design. The English contributions to the Vergil, along with the roman type cut by Edward Prince in the style of Nicolas Jenson, and the italic designed by Edward Johnston, are in complete and classical harmony with Maillol's sculpturesque woodcuts.

Maillol is further represented in the bequest by a suite of the woodcuts for the Longus, *Daphnis and Chloe* of 1937 with a set of proofs, some with background uncut. Previous Hofer gifts of Maillol books

THE WATERING-PLACE, AND, TITYRUS, AS YOU DRIVE THEM DOWN, MIND YOU KEEP OUT OF THE WAY OF THE BUCK, OR HE'LL BUTT YOU WITH HIS HORNS.

MOERIS

Yes and this one too which he sang over to Varus before it was finished.

VARUS, IF OUR MANTUA SURVIVE THESE THREATENING DANGERS, OUR MANTUA TOO NEAR TO THE ILL-FATED CITY OF CREMONA, YOUR MIGHTY NAME SHALL BE BORNE TO THE STARRY SKY BY SINGING SWANS.

89

No. 89.   Aristide Maillol. Illustration from Vergil, *Eclogae*.

include Verhaeren's *Belle chair* of 1931 with lithographs and woodcuts; Vergil's *Georgica / Les Géorgiques* of 1937–1950, originally projected by Kessler, with two suites of the woodcuts, one in black and one in sanguine; and the Horace *Odes* of 1939, with a suite in sanguine.

Three other Kessler-Cranach titles, all of 1931, are included in the bequest: one of the eight vellum copies, and also a regular copy, of the English edition for the Hogarth Press of Rilke's *Duineser Elegien / Elegies from the Castle of Duino*, with initials cut by Gill and gilded; Pierre de Margerie's *Allocution prononcée à l'ouverture de l'exposition "Le Salon des Bibliophiles" à Berlin le xiii October MCMXXIX*, with initial in blue cut by Gill on a block cut by Maillol and gilded, this copy one of fourteen on vellum for Editions de Cluny, Paris, dedicated to Dr. Max Goetz, Kessler's associate; *Das Hohe Lied Salomo* with woodcuts and intials by Gill, one of fifty copies on japan of the German edition with an extra, signed impression of one of the cuts on thick paper. Hofer had made an earlier gift of one of the fifty copies on japan of the Latin edition, *Canticum Canticorum Salomonis*.

Other previous Hofer gifts of the Cranach Press include one of the fifty copies of the 1925 commemorative volume, *In Memoriam Walther Rathenau* by Kessler, Hugo R. Simon, and Georg Bernhard, with title cut by Gill and initial by Maillol, and the English edition of the great *Hamlet* of 1930, illustrated with woodcuts by Edward Gordon Craig, with the imprint of Emery Walker.

E.M.G.

REF *The Artist & the Book*, no. 172; *From Manet to Hockney*, no. 30; Renate Müller-Krumbach, *Harry Graf Kessler und die Cranach Presse in Weimar* (Hamburg, 1969), no. 40, 43; Balston, *Private Press Types*, p. 33f; John Dreyfus, *Italic Quartet* ([Cambridge, 1966]); Marcel Guérin, *Catalogue raisonné de l'oeuvre graphique d'Aristide Maillol* (Geneva, 1965) I, no. 15–59; Anne Hyde Greet, "Conversations in Arcady: Vergil, Maillol and Kessler," *Word & Image*, III (1987), 225–247; Sotheby & Co., London, *The Distinguished Collection of Modern French Illustrated Books of the late M. Nicolas Rauch of Geneva* (24 June, 1963), no. 102.

No. 89. Aristide Maillol. Preliminary drawings and printed pressmark of the Cranach Press.

90 ❧ RUDOLF KOCH, 1876–1934 AND FRITZ KREDEL, 1900–1972
Das Blumenbuch
[Darmstadt, Ernst Ludwig Presse, 1930]

250 woodcuts, hand-colored, drawn by Koch and cut by Kredel. Special edition for the Friends of the Ernst Ludwig Presse. First published by the Insel Verlag, Leipzig, 1929–1930, in an edition of 1000 copies, with cuts hand-colored by Emil Wöllner. One of 10 copies specially printed for Koch. Edition: 145 copies (135 for Friends of the Press; 10 for Koch). Presentation copy; inscribed on title-page from Rudolf Koch to Philip Hofer on his wedding day, 1 November 1930. Copy with hand-lettered inscriptions by Koch added to each cut.

30.5 x 23 cm. White pigskin, blind-tooled with inscriptions and floral designs after Koch.

Set of matted proofs on china paper, hand-colored by Rosel Küchler, each numbered, identified, and signed in pencil with the emblem of the Offenbacher Werkstatt. One of 20 copies, with woodcut title-page cut by Kredel after Berthold Wolpe's calligraphy, dated 1930 and signed on the title-page by Koch, Kredel, and Küchler, and with Wolpe's emblem. Manuscript list of proofs; letters from Koch to Hofer.

Approx. 30 x 23 cm. Mat size 40.5 x 28 cm. 12 folders in 2 brown pigskin boxes, each blind-tooled with a floral design after Koch.

RUDOLF KOCH was proud to be known as *Der Schreiber* in honor of his distinguished work as scribal and typographic letter designer. Trained as a metal craftsman, in 1906 he joined the Rudhard Type Foundry in Offenbach am Main, near Frankfurt, known for the production of founts by such modern designers as Otto Eckmann and Peter Behrens. Purchased by the Klingspor family, the Rudhardsche Giesserei became the Schriftgiesserei Gebrüder Klingspor, and under the leadership of Dr. Karl Klingspor expanded the tradition of contemporary artist-designed type. The most prominent designer was Koch, who produced a number of important twentieth-century types, both black letter and roman. He was an influential teacher at the Technische Lehranstalt and leader of the Offenbacher Werkstatt, the studio where he led and shaped a number of younger colleagues working in many media, but especially in letter design.

Das Blumenbuch began as a simple exercise in flower study, when Koch and his children would collect flowers on Sunday walks. He sketched and colored them, knowing little about the plants, not even their names, but eager to learn. (Hans Heil supplied the names for the final publication.) For six summers Koch collected and drew the flowers, while his friend Fritz Kredel began to cut the blocks. Koch has recorded that the specimens were gathered at random, all from the Offenbach area, and without any particular aim, other than to give "a taste of summer in winter." Divided into four sections of early and late spring, early and late summer, the flat descriptive cuts recall early German herbals.

This special edition differs from the Insel Verlag copies in the use of roman letters for the title-page and titling of the flowers in place of black letter. In this copy, black-letter inscriptions have been added in Koch's hand, thus creating a dramatically different page and changing the character of the book; their simple piety is a reminder of his profound religious faith, frequently expressed in his work.

In the late 1920s, Rudolf Koch and Philip Hofer became acquainted, and their friendship flourished until Koch's untimely death in 1934. (Hofer was fluent in German.) Hofer's large collection of Koch, Kredel, and the circle associated with the Offenbacher Werkstatt and the Klingspor foundry is divided between the bequest and previous gifts, many in duplicate. Graphic and letter design are represented in a number of Klingspor type specimens, a set of Klingspor calendars from 1921 to 1939, Koch's *Neue Schriftvorlagen* of 1925, *Das Schreibbüchlein* of 1930, and *Das ABC Büchlein* of 1934. In addition to many books and series designed by Koch, there is a copy of his blockbook of 1921, *Die Weinachtsgeschichte*, with a set of proofs on japan, and the first edition of the often-reproduced 1918 silhouette book, *Schriftgiesserei im Schattenbild*. A number of items are presentation copies with letters inserted, and there is a box of calligraphy, both manuscript and printed. In the bequest is a group of manuscripts from the Werkstatt representing the work of Willi Harwerth, Fritz Kredel, and Berthold Wolpe: a 1932 *Deutsche Kinder Lieder*, written out by Wolpe and illustrated by Kredel, commissioned by Hofer; a Harwerth *Book of Animals* of 1933, and his little *ABC* of 1933, also commissioned by Hofer and reproduced in facsimile by the Department of Printing and Graphic Arts in 1956. Additional Koch, Kredel, and Harwerth drawings are in the Frances L. Hofer bequest.

E.M.G.

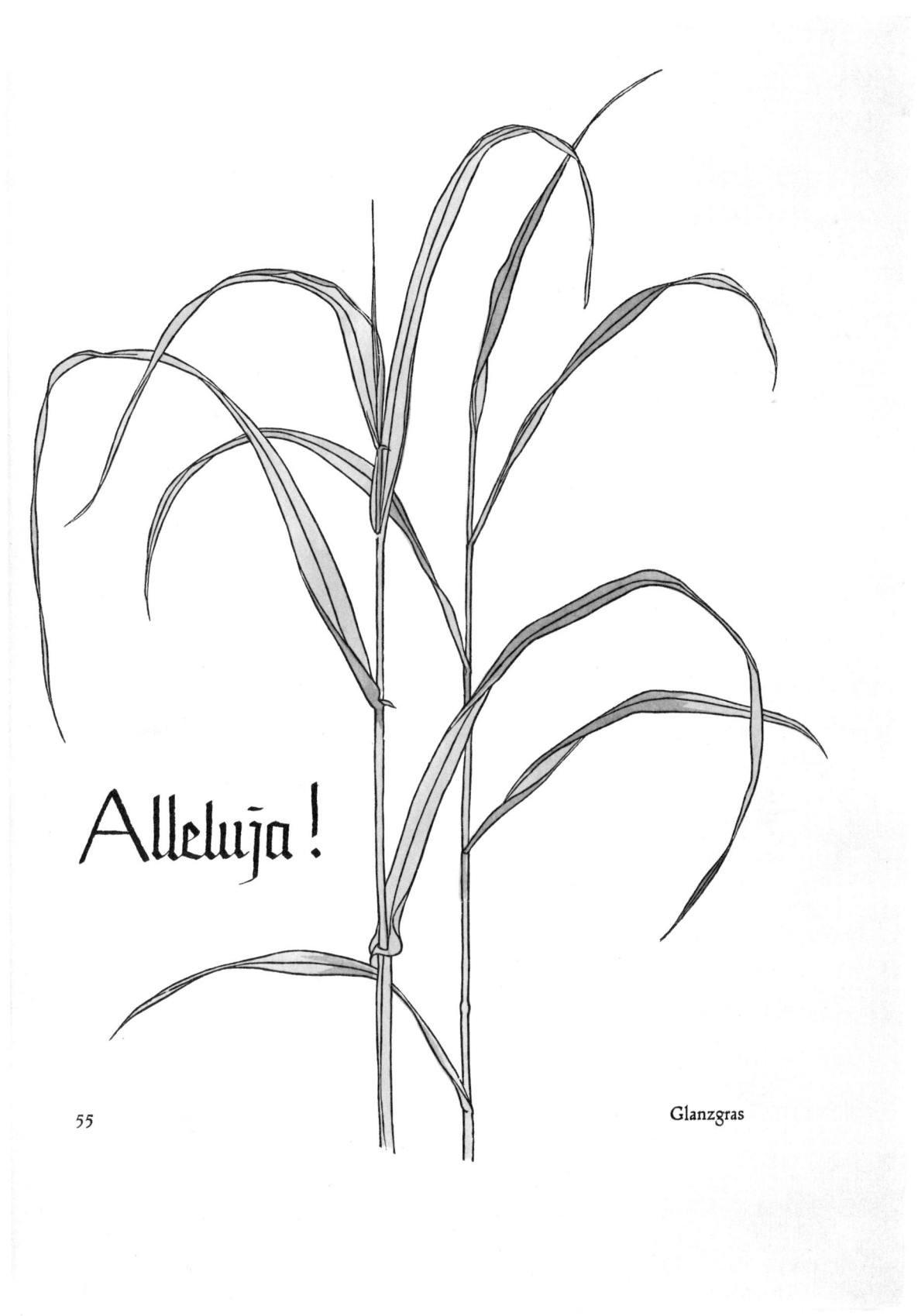

No. 90. Rudolf Koch, "Alleluja." Illustration from *Das Blumenbuch*.

REF   Julius Rodenberg, "The Work of Karl Klingspor," Trans. Anna Simons, *The Fleuron*, V (1926), 1–25; Albert Windisch, "The Work of Rudolf Koch," *The Fleuron*, VI (1928), 1–35; "Rudolf Koch und sein Kreis, *Archiv für Buchgewerbe und Gebrauchsgraphik*, 70 Jahr. Heft 11/12 (1933); Siegfried Guggenheim, "Rudolph Koch, His Work and the Offenbach Workshop," *Print*, V, (1944), 7–42; Rudolf Koch, *The Little ABC Book, A Facsimile of Das ABC Büchlein* with a Memoir by Fritz Kredel and a preface by Warren Chappell (New York [1976]); Rudolf Koch, *An Autobiographical Sketch* (Williamsburg, Mass., 1977).

91 ❧   EUCLID
Elements of Geometry
[London and New York, ca. 1930–1944]
Typography by BRUCE ROGERS, 1870–1957

Proof sheets and paste-up with notes in graphite; drawings in graphite, watercolor and gouache.

Approx. 21.1 × 12.9 cm.

BRUCE ROGERS' English *Euclid*, with an introductory essay by Paul Valéry, was published in 1944 by Random House. The first proof appears to be substantially earlier, however. According to a note by Rogers, it was printed at the Fanfare Press in London, presumably between 1928 and 1932, when Rogers was in England working on the Oxford Lectern Bible. The fact that sixteen pages, including four copies of page 7 and page 8 and two of page 9, are printed in Arrighi type further helps to pinpoint the date. Arrighi, an italic type designed by Frederic Warde to complement Rogers' own Roman Centaur type, was first cut by the English Monotype firm in 1929. Similar reasoning suggests that the remaining eighty pages of proof must be substantially later, and were undoubtedly printed after Rogers' return to America. These eighty pages are printed in Deepdene italic, designed by Frederic W. Goudy and cut by Lanston Monotype in 1933–34. Rogers probably substituted Deepdene for Arrighi following his return to America, since Arrighi was not readily available here.

Both proof stages reflect a similar conception, with colored diagrams at the beginning of each problem and the calligraphic letters "Q.E.D" or "Q.E.F." serving as decorative tailpieces. Within these parameters, the proofs vary considerably, reflecting Rogers' endless tinkering with the layout. Neither set corresponds exactly to the finished book, which, like the later proofs, is printed in Deepdene italic. The use of italic type for the *Euclid* may have been suggested by Rogers' awareness of an early (Venice, 1509) edition, mentioned by Philip Hofer in his introduction to Stanley Morison, *Fra Luca Pacioli* (New York, 1933). Morison's book was designed by Rogers during his English sojourn; corrected proof sheets, with notes by Morison and Rogers, are in the bequest. Another likely influence, which may have inspired the colored diagrams, is Oliver Byrne's *Euclid*, printed by Charles Whittingham for William Pickering in 1847. In an 1939 talk at the Grolier Club, Rogers cited this book as "one of the finest English examples of diagrammatic color printing." A copy was a previous Hofer gift to the Department of Printing and Graphic Arts.

In addition to these items, there is a large amount of Rogers material in the Hofer bequest, ranging from a paste-up of the title page for R.B. Gruelle, *Notes: Critical and Biographical* of 1895, through a copy of *The Camp Steele Alphabet* ("A was an artist in oil/who spent his vacation in toil"), printed at the Marchbanks Press in 1952. Of particular interest are a large scrapbook with Rogers' bookplate, labelled "Specimens of Printing Designed by Bruce Rogers and Done Under his Supervision at the Riverside Press" (1897–1912); Hofer's copy of Geoffroy Tory, *Champfleury* (New York, 1927) with a note that it was "esp[ecially] bound, since his copy of the 1549 Tory *Champfleury* was used by Bruce Rogers in designing *this* Edition"; drawings, proofs and paste-ups for a Book of Common Prayer (1927; never completed; according to Haas the commission was later given to Updike, who finished the book in 1930); and a series of drawings and proofs for *The Divine Comedy* of Dante Alighieri (ca. 1930). Five large cases of ephemera contain many additional drawings, proofs and paste-ups. A significant group of letters includes correspondence with Philip Hofer,

I

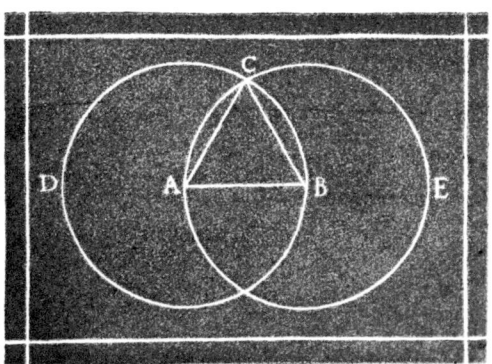

PROBLEM: To *describe an equilateral triangle upon a given finite straight line.*

Let AB *be the given straight line. It is required to describe an equilateral triangle upon* AB.

From the centre A, at the distance AB, describe the circle BCD; from the centre B, at the distance BA, describe the circle ACE; and from C, one of the points in which the circles cut one another, draw the straight lines, CA, CB, to the points A, B. Then ABC shall be an equilateral triangle.

Because the point A is the centre of the circle BCD, therefore AC is equal to AB; and because the point B is the centre of the circle ACE, therefore BC is equal to AB; but it has been proved that AC is equal to AB; therefore AC, BC are each of them equal to AB; but things which are

7

No. 91. Bruce Rogers. First proof of Euclid, *Elements of Geometry.*

Charles Eliot Norton and Daniel Berkeley Updike. This material joins already substantial Rogers holdings, the nucleus of which was a collection of books printed by Bruce Rogers which was given to the Library to commemorate the centenary of Charles Eliot Norton in 1927.

N.F.

REF Bruce Rogers, *Paragraphs on Printing* (New York, 1943); Frederic Warde and Irvin Haas, *Bruce Rogers, Designer of Books; Bruce Rogers: A Bibliography* (Port Washington, N.Y., 1968); Bruce Rogers, *Typographical Partnership: Ten Letters Between Bruce Rogers and Emery Walker* (Cambridge, 1971).

92 STEPHANE MALLARME, 1842–1898
Poésies
Lausanne, Albert Skira & Cie., 1932
Etchings by HENRI MATISSE, 1869–1954

29 etchings by Matisse, including 23 full-page. One of 95 copies on Arches wove. Edition: 145 copies (30 on japan including 5 with original drawing and 2 extra suites and 25 with extra suite, 95 on Arches, 20 *hors commerce*). This copy signed Henri Matisse. Laid into this copy are 3 proofs, each with additional etched *remarques* and the statement, "rayé après tirage du Mallarmé /A. Skira Editeur."

33 x 25 cm. White wrappers loose within half tan morocco boards.

ONE OF THE REAL ACCOMPLISHMENTS of the French *livre de peintre* in its flowering between the two World Wars was the compression of a monumental style onto a printed page. The full freedom, breadth, and fluidity of Matisse's line are preserved in these etchings, placed opposite a text balanced and leaded to a lightness in harmony with the figures and the landscapes. Matisse, more than any of his contemporaries of the School of Paris, was very concerned about the harmony of plates and letterpress, as recorded in an essay "Comment j'ai fait mes livres," for Albert Skira's *Anthologie*. The latter, carrying on in Paris and Lausanne the tradition of Vollard and Kahnweiler, also published Matisse's lithographed *Florilège des amours* by Ronsard in 1948 as well as Picasso's etched Ovid in 1931 (copy in the bequest).

The Ovid was Skira's first publication, and he wished to collaborate with Matisse on the second, a projected edition of La Fontaine, *Amours de Psyché*. The Mallarmé text was chosen instead, and it presented Matisse with the challenge of his first role in a *livre de peintre*. The artist referred to his immense task in deceptively simple words: ". . . voici le travail que j'ai fait après avoir lu Mallarmé avec plaisir" (Duthuit, p. 18). Actually, he worked over a period of two years creating numerous studies and some sixty etchings, from which the final twenty-nine were chosen. They were printed with great care, under the direction of the artist's daughter, at the Parisian atelier of the master printer Roger Lacourière. Correspondence reveals the exacting standards of both artist and printer in their search for fine impressions of the delicate line on the thick paper. A special copy with maquette and planches refusées is in the Cone collection of the Baltimore Museum of Art.

E.M.G.

REF *The Artist & the Book*, no. 196; *From Manet to Hockney*, no. 95; Skira, *Anthologie*, no. 256; Musée Matisse, Nice, *Henri Matisse, L'art du livre* (1986), p. 28f.; Claude Duthuit, *Henri Matisse, catalogue raisonné des ouvrages illustrés* (Paris, 1988), p. 16–34.

No. 92. Henri Matisse. Illustration from Mallarmé, *Poésies*.

93 ❧ THE WISDOM OF JESUS, THE SON OF SIRACH COMMONLY CALLED ECCLESIASTICUS
[London, Ashendene Press, 1932]

Copy on vellum. Initials in gold and color by Graily Hewitt and his assistants, Ida R. Henstock and Helen E. Hinckley.

28.5 x 19 cm. Tan morocco, gilt rules and lettering by W.H. Smith & Sons.

Proofs with corrections by Hewitt and Hornby; correspondence between them, 1931–1932.

AS RECOUNTED in his 1935 foreword to the bibliography of the Ashendene Press, C.H. St. John Hornby (1867–1946) founded it in 1894, having acquired an interest and some experience in printing as a member of the firm of W.H. Smith. He began with an Albion Crown Press in a little garden house at his father's home, Ashendene, in Hertfordshire. After five years and eleven books printed in his spare time in these cramped quarters, he moved to London, to Shelley House in Chelsea.

Like Cobden-Sanderson at the Doves Press (No. 81), Hornby benefited from the skills of Emery Walker, William Morris's technical adviser at the Kelmscott Press (No. 78). Walker designed for Ashendene the Subiaco and Ptolemy types, the former cut by Edward Prince. The punches of these two types are in the collection of the Cambridge University Press, along with material from Kelmscott, Cranach, and Eragny.

Noted by Philip Hofer as "the finest Ashendene Press book I have," the Ecclesiasticus was modestly described by Hornby in the bibliography as "in my humble judgment . . . one of the most satisfactory of the books of the Press." Set in Subiaco type, it was printed in an edition of 328 copies on paper and 25 on vellum. In the latter copies, the larger initials are in gold leaf. The development of the typography and lettering may be studied in these proofs, which consist of galleys and pages for a number of signatures. The galleys contain initials painted in blue by Hewitt, with comments by both Hewitt and Hornby, forming a dialogue on the fine points of form and space; it is clear that each respected and accommodated the other's judgment. In addition, there are letters between the two men concerning the project. Many other letters are in the Ashendene collection at the Bridwell Library, Southern Methodist University, Dallas.

The Hofer bequest contains additional Ashendene books, including St. Francis' *Fioretti* of 1904, second copies of More's *Utopia* of 1906 and of the Boccaccio of 1920 (the first copies both previous gifts), the Lucretius of 1913 in a white pigskin binding by W.H. Smith & Son, and a copy of the 1935 *Descriptive Bibliography*, a presentation copy from Hornby to Hofer, in a binding by W.H. Smith & Son, gold-tooled with the Ashendene pressmark designed by the architect Philip Webb.

Previous Hofer Ashendene gifts include two vellum copies of the 1903 Horace, *Carmina*; the 1909 Plutarch, *Two Consolatory Letters*; the 1909 Dante; the 1913 Malory *Morte D'Arthur*; the 1921 *Vita di Santa Chiara*; and two titles of 1924: the Apuleius *Golden Asse*, and Oscar Wilde's *The Young King*, the latter a presentation copy from Hornby to Hofer. There is also a box of ephemera with Christmas and other keepsakes and a 1930 specimen of the Subiaco and Ptolemy types. Hornby and Hofer shared a personal friendship, carried on to the next Hornby generation, and the bequest contains a number of letters.

The Hofer Ashendenes join another distinguished Harvard collection—Charles Eliot Norton's, which also contains presentation copies from Hornby as early as 1904, thanking Norton for his support, also recorded in the foreword to the bibliography.

Hofer's interest in the revival of lettering and calligraphy in the twentieth century led him to Graily Hewitt, so prominent as scribe and teacher, and in 1949 Hofer purchased three manuscripts from the artist: *The Song of the Three Holy Children* from the book of Daniel of 1929, illuminated by Ida Henstock; the *Epistle of James* of 1933; and the Vergil *Georgics* of 1940–1946. A previous gift is an *Address to Selwyn Image on his Appointment as Slade Professor at Oxford* of 1910, written and illuminated by Louise Powell and gilded by Hewitt.

E.M.G.

REF Ashendene Press, *A Descriptive Bibliography* ([London] 1935), p. 90; Will Ransom, ed., *Kelmscott, Doves and Ashendene* ([Los Angeles] 1952), p. 161f.; Colin Franklin, *The Ashendene Press* (Dallas, 1986), p. 187–197, 242; Balston, *Private Press Types*, p. 23f.

BOR AOMOO
BOR
BOR

BOOK I. And one that was never thought of hath worn a diadem.
Chapter xi. Many mighty men have been greatly disgraced;
v. 5—14 And men of renown have been delivered into other men's
hands.
Blame not before thou hast examined;
Understand first, and then rebuke.
Answer not before thou hast heard;
And interrupt not in the midst of speech.
Strive not in a matter that concerneth thee not;
And where sinners judge, sit not thou with them.

My son, be not busy about many matters:
For if thou meddle much, thou shalt not be unpunished;
And if thou pursue, thou shalt not overtake;
And thou shalt not escape by fleeing.
There is one that laboureth, and taketh pains, and
maketh haste,
And is so much the more behind.
There is one that is sluggish, and hath need of help,
Lacking in strength, and abounding in poverty;
Yet the eyes of the Lord looked upon him for good,
And set him up from his low estate,
And lifted up his head;
And many marvelled at him.

Prosperity and adversity, life and death,
Poverty and riches, are from the Lord.

No. 93. Proof of *Ecclesiasticus* with initials and notations by Graily Hewitt.

94 ❧ WILLIAM ADDISON DWIGGINS, 1880–1956
A Melodrama So Far Without Any Name But Called Cedar Hill
[Hingham, Massachusetts] 1934

Manuscript in pen and ink and graphite; illustrations (some tipped in) in graphite, ink, colored pencil, watercolor and gouache. 19.8 x 13.8 cm. Red paper-covered boards. Bookplate of W.A. Dwiggins.

TO DISCRIMINATING READERS, W.A. Dwiggins is well known as a typographer and designer of books. His types, layouts, title-pages and cover designs were widely used in the books of Alfred A. Knopf and other publishers throughout the first half of the twentieth century. His stylish and witty ornaments and illustrations, often based on the *pochoir* or stencil process, are brilliant examples of art deco book decoration. This was Dwiggins's "work."

"Play" consisted of a private press called "Püterschein-Hingham," a marionette theater which he designed and operated, and science fiction and fantasy stories which he wrote in his spare time. This aspect of Dwiggins' genius was known to relatively few friends; Philip Hofer was especially enthusiastic about these whimsical productions. It was Hofer who urged Dwiggins to publish "The Drums of Kalkapán," the first (though sequentially the last) of the Athalinthia stories, to accompany an article in the 1935 *Dolphin*. Other tales from Athalinthia, "translated" from the imaginary Metralingua Permé were printed by Dwiggins and Dorothy Abbe in 1948 and 1950. The first mention of *Cedar Hill* also occurs in Hofer's 1935 *Dolphin* article. Although the manuscript is dated 1934, the idea originated as early as 1911. It is pure science fiction in the vein of H.G. Wells, whom Dwiggins admired and illustrated: in a futuristic world, humans live in fear of a race of highly-evolved machines. In 1945, the manuscript, now entitled *Millennium I*, was finally published by Alfred Knopf in a slender wartime format. Dwiggins also contemplated a marionette play on the subject and constructed several amazing machine-marionettes, resembling animated versions of his more abstract type ornaments. Stage and marionettes are now in the Boston Public Library.

The Hofer Bequest includes copies of two Athalinthia stories: *The Glistening Hill* (Athalinthia III; 1950) and *The War Against Waake* (Athalinthia V; 1948). Both of these are scarce limited editions, printed at Dwiggins' private press in Hingham. *Millennium I* (New York, 1945), though not so rare, is important because it reflects the final transformation of the *Cedar Hill* manuscript. Two boxes of ephemera include many drawings, proofs and broadsides. Of special interest is a series of drawings for an unidentified type face. A previous gift was a sequence of drawings for Alphonse Daudet, *Tartarin de Tarascon* (Limited Editions, 1942).

Many Dwiggins items in the Bequest are chiefly typographic in their interest. These include:

Paraphs. New York, 1928. Includes A.L.s.

22 Printers' Marks and Seals Designed or Redrawn. New York, 1929.

WAD to RR. A Letter about Designing Type. Cambridge, Massachusetts, 1940. An early publication of the Department of Printing and Graphic Arts. Some designs for this publication are included among the ephemera in the bequest.

The Structure of a Book. Typophiles Monograph XV. [New York] 1945.

MSS. by WAD. New York, 1947.

Additional Dwiggins material in the Department of Printing and Graphic Arts is included in the William Bentinck-Smith Typographical Collection.

N.F.

REF Philip Hofer, "The Work of W.A. Dwiggins," *The Dolphin* no. 2 (1935), 220–256; American Institute of Graphic Arts, *The Work of W.A. Dwiggins* (New York, 1937); Boston Public Library, *Checklist of an Exhibition of the Work of W.A. Dwiggins* (Boston, 1949); Dorothy Abbe, *The Dwiggins Marionettes* (New York [1970]), p. 135–147; Dwight Agner, *The Books of WAD* (Baton Rouge, 1974).

Disintegrating Mechanism

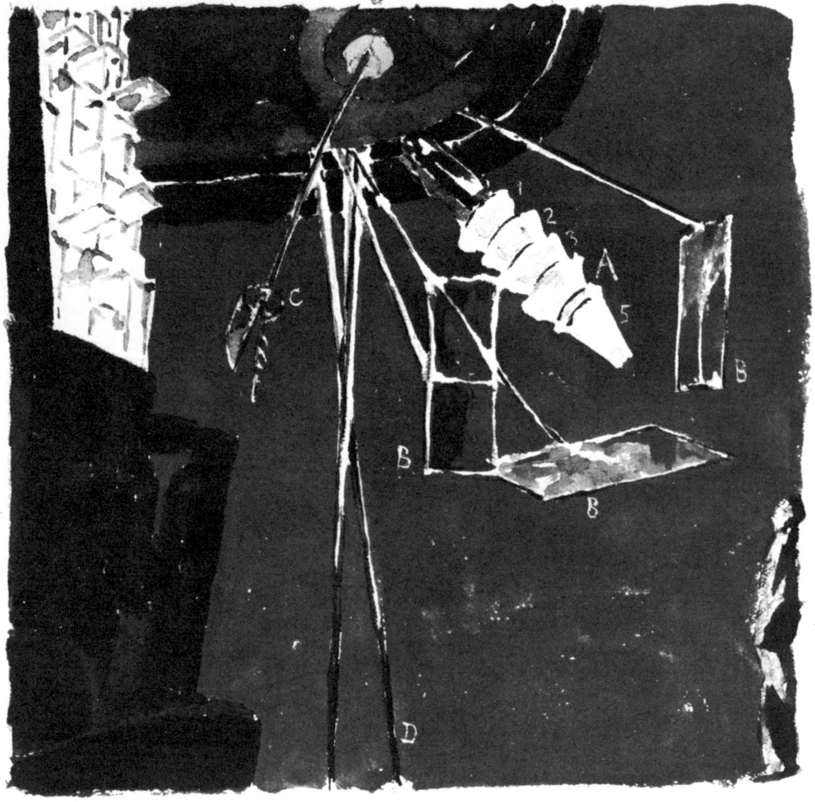

N77

Lights lamps on Ⓐ at 1 second intervals — to vivid green, 1 2 3 4 — dissolves with lamp 5 - violet. When called off lamps go out 4 3 2 1 — various members withdrawn — lamp-arm, legs, shields etc — but the body stays in position, with sensory arm Ⓒ out and active in the 5th episode.

No. 94. W. A. Dwiggins. Manuscript of *Cedar Hill*.

95 ❧ RUDOLPH RUZICKA, 1883–1978
The Houghton Library, Harvard University
[Dobbs Ferry, New York] 1941

Drawing in sepia ink and watercolor.

Approx. 30 x 35 cm. Framed and glazed. Commissioned from the artist.

RUDOLPH RUZICKA's drawing is a study for a print which was issued to coincide with the opening of the Houghton Library in 1942. Early in 1941, Hofer wrote to Ruzicka, proposing that he should do a series of color woodcut views of Harvard buildings, similar to the Boston views which he had designed through the years for Daniel Berkeley Updike's Merrymount Press Christmas cards. By midsummer, it had been decided to limit the projected series of eight views to just two subjects, to be engraved in aquatint by Ruzicka and hand-colored by his daughter Veronica. It was not until October, however, that Ruzicka came to Cambridge to make preliminary sketches of the new rare books library and the Harvard houses seen across the river from the Western Avenue Bridge. The final drawings were completed in Ruzicka's studio in Dobbs Ferry, New York, using these sketches and photographs provided by Hofer. Hofer was delighted with the results and promised to display the two drawings—"alone in the Graphic Arts [study] room on one of the two large tables"—at the opening of the Library. In addition to the hand-colored aquatints, collotype facsimiles of the two views were issued as part of the Printing and Graphic Arts Reproduction Series.

The close friendship between Philip Hofer and Rudolph Ruzicka resulted in numerous commissions and collaborations spanning a period of fifty years. In 1937, Ruzicka executed a bookplate for Hofer, based on a watercolor drawing by Hans Holbein which he had just acquired. The drawing did not come to the Department of Printing and Graphic Arts, but progressive proofs for Ruzicka's seven-color wood-engraving are included in the bequest. The subject is Tantalus reaching for the golden apples which are always just beyond his grasp. For Hofer, the image symbolized the collector in pursuit of books and drawings. *Tantalus* was also the subject of a booklet issued by Hofer's own private press, the Cygnet Press, in 1937.

Other commissions included a paste-paper, "Harvard Towers," designed by Rudolph and executed by Veronica Ruzicka. This paper was later used on the cover of Rosamond B. Loring's *Decorated Book Papers* (Cambridge, 1942), which Hofer edited. Ruzicka also designed two calligraphic broadsides for the Printing and Graphic Arts Reproduction Series: an Alphabet (1950) and Mottoes of Liberty (1972), the latter conceived to protest the Russian invasion of Czechoslovakia in 1968. Hofer was also responsible for Ruzicka's receiving the commission to design new diplomas for Harvard and Radcliffe in 1960.

The Hofer bequest contains a large amount of material documenting Ruzicka's activities through the years. This includes a substantial body of ephemera, as well as correspondence and specimens of Ruzicka's calligraphy and book illustrations. Additional items were previous gifts. It was Hofer's wish that this extensive collection should all go to Harvard "as a memorial to one of the finest men on earth," whom he warmly acknowledged as one of the most vital influences on every aspect of his life. The bequest also contains a broadside and a small amount of ephemera designed by Veronica Ruzicka, whom Hofer also admired. A manuscript alphabet by Veronica Ruzicka was purchased for the Department of Printing and Graphic Arts before Hofer's death.

N.F.

REF   H. Watson Kent, "Rudolph Ruzicka, Master of the Graphic Arts," *PM Journal* I (1935), 8–12; M.A. de Wolfe Howe, "Rudolph Ruzicka, perfectionist," *Boston Public Library Quarterly* III (1951), 3–5; Ray Nash, "The Genius of Rudolph Ruzicka," *American Artist* XXXI (1967), 44–50; Philip Hofer, "Rudolph Ruzicka, Artist and Craftsman," *The Newberry Library Bulletin* VI (1978), 328–338.

No. 95. Rudolph Ruzicka. Drawing of The Houghton Library.

96   JOHN HOWARD BENSON, 1901–1956
        Laus Deo
        [Newport, Rhode Island, 1950]

Inscription on brown slate, illuminated in gold and palladium leaf.

16.9 x 11.8 cm. Commissioned from the artist.

IN 1946, Philip Hofer commissioned John Howard Benson to carve a large alphabet in green Vermont slate to serve as a pendant to an earlier alphabet carved in Hopton-wood stone by the English sculptor Eric Gill (see No. 84). Unlike Gill, Benson had received little formal training in lettering. He studied graphic arts with Joseph Pennell and Allen Lewis in New York, read Edward Johnston's books on calligraphy, and prowled about the graveyards of Newport, Rhode Island, admiring the inscriptions on the old stones. In 1927, he leased the John Stevens Shop, which had been making gravestones in Newport since 1705, and embarked on a career as a professional stone cutter. Twenty years later, Hofer would acclaim him as the greatest American letter cutter of his generation. The green slate alphabet he described as "the most beautiful thing of its kind that I have ever seen." "Your alphabet is like a page from a manuscript," he wrote to Benson in appreciation, and continued "I should like a series of smaller tablets with varying types of lettering most suitable to the inscriptions that they contain, to be placed from time to time in exhibitions of 1.) manuscript illumination; 2.) writing and type specimen books; 3.) fine printing; and 4.) wherever else their appearance and point may not be jarring. For example, why shouldn't an exhibition start with a tablet inscribed 'In principio,' and end with a tablet, 'Laus Deo'?"

    This was the origin of the small "Laus Deo" inscription shown here. Hofer especially admired the calligraphic quality of Benson's carved letters. Other tablets by Benson with inscriptions relating to books and libraries were also forthcoming. These included a quotation from Horace on purple slate, in which the poet bewails his exile and longs for quiet hours among his books, and a silver plaque which explains in French why people do not return the books that they have borrowed: "[parce] qu'il est plus facile de les retenir que ce qui est dedans." Another French quote claims, with a mixture of pessimism and optimism that "les hommes sont méchants, mais leur livres sont bons." A Greek inscription, in silver on purple slate, quotes the words that were once over the door of the library at Alexandria, identifying it as "the healing place of the soul." All these carvings, including the large slate alphabet, are part of the Hofer bequest. Apart from these Hofer commissions, Harvard is, as Hofer described it, "full of" Benson's inscriptional work. One prominent example is the plaque above the door to the Houghton exhibition room.

    Also in the bequest are examples of Benson's calligraphy on paper, including the manuscript for *The First Writing Book: An English Translation and Facsimile Text of Arrighi's Operina* (1954), the second of the Studies in the History of Calligraphy published jointly by Harvard College Library and the Newberry Library in Chicago. For this tour de force, Benson not only translated the text into English, but wrote and rewrote every line so that script and layout closely reflect Arrighi's. The bequest also includes a copy of *Flags of the Old State House* (Newport [1943]), which Benson designed and printed at his Berry Hill Press.

    Other American inscriptions in the Hofer bequest include work by Edward Catich and an alphabet by John E. Benson, John Howard Benson's son and successor at the John Stevens shop. Early American calligraphy is also well represented, both in the bequest and among previous gifts. For modern English calligraphy, see No. 84 and 93. A manuscript attributed to Arrighi is discussed in No. 21.

N.F.

REF Philip Hofer, "The Work of John Howard Benson," *The New Colophon* (1950), p. 208–222; Philip Hofer, "Inscriptions in the Graphic Arts Department at Harvard," *Notes on Printing and Graphic Arts* 1 (1953), 10–12; Philip Hofer, *John Howard Benson and his Work, 1901–1956* (New York, 1957); Department of Printing and Graphic Arts, correspondence.

No. 96. John Howard Benson. Inscription on brown slate.

97   FEDERICO GARCIA LORCA, 1899–1936
    2 Poemas: Romance de la Luna, Luna; Romance de la Guardia Civil Española
    [New York, 1953]
    Woodcuts by ANTONIO FRASCONI, b. 1919

19 woodcuts by Frasconi. Lithographed text in artist's hand. One of about 10 copies.

48.5 x 33.5 cm. White boards, woodcut title in black and red; brown jacket, woodcut title and ornament.

PUBLISHED AND PRINTED by the artist himself in a period when few American publishers were involved with the *livre de peintre*, Frasconi's Lorca was of necessity a very small edition. (The lithographer John Muench printed the text.) The book is an intense and dramatic statement achieved by simple means. The black woodcuts, with an occasional touch of red, are large in scale and silhouetted against ample white space. In like manner, the text, in red in a single wide column, is spaciously arranged, combining with the cuts to form a series of monumental compositions.

    Hofer's interest in the concept of the artist and the book led him to seek out American examples, which were uncommon in the fifties and early sixties, when he had begun to plan *The Artist & the Book* exhibition. He was particularly interested in Leonard Baskin and Ben Shahn, both of whom are represented in the bequest and in previous gifts. He acquired for the Library June Wayne's 1959 *Songs and Sonnets* by John Donne and *21 Etchings and Poems*, published by the Morris Gallery of New York in 1960.

                                                                                                      E.M.G.

REF   *The Artist & the Book*, no. 110.

Los caballos negros son
las herraduras son negras.
Sobre las capas relucen
manchas de tinta y de cera.
Tienen, por eso no lloran,
de plomo las calaveras.
Con el alma de charol
vienen por la carretera.
Jorobados y nocturnos,
por donde animan ordenan
silencios de goma oscura
y miedos de fina arena.
Pasan, si quieren pasar,
y ocultan en la cabeza
una vaga astronomía
de pistolas inconcretas.

No. 97.   Antonio Frasconi. Illustration from Federico García Lorca, *2 Poemas*.

98   HERMANN ZAPF, b. 1918
Shakespeare's Sonnet 2
[Frankfurt am Main] 1957

Calligraphic broadside by Zapf; burnished shell gold on purple Japanese paper.

Approx. 46 x 33 cm. Framed and glazed. Commissioned from the artist.

CALLIGRAPHER, type designer, book designer and author, Hermann Zapf has been one of the dominant figures in typography during the last half of the twentieth century. Hofer first met him in the early 1950s and immediately began commissioning examples of his calligraphy. The idea for the Shakespeare Sonnet originated in 1955, when Hofer learned of a similar specimen which Zapf had created for the Newberry Library in Chicago. It, too, was written in formal italic script in burnished shell gold on purple Japanese paper; the subject was Shakespeare's Sonnet 23 ("As an unperfect actor on the stage..."). Hofer selected Sonnet 3, beginning "When forty winters shall besiege thy brow," for his broadside, and when it arrived in September 1959, pronounced it "even... more beautiful than the Newberry Library one." "I didn't want to make invidious comparisons," he wrote to Zapf. "But I am grateful that you did your best work for Harvard." Other calligraphic broadsides by Zapf in the bequest include an alphabet and quotation from E.A. Lowe, written in formal italic in black and brownish red, and the draft of a second alphabet with quotations from Douglas C. McMurtrie, Jean Cocteau, and Emanuel Geibel. Reproductions of the Shakespeare Sonnet and this second alphabet were later published by the Department of Printing and Graphic Arts.

    Closely related to these broadsides is Zapf's first great book, *Feder und Stichel* (*Pen and Graver*), a collection of alphabets and quotations in a variety of historical scripts, written by Zapf and engraved by August Rosenberger of the Stempel Type Foundry during World War II. The bequest includes two versions of the first edition, which was published in Frankfurt in 1950, one from the private printing of 500 copies, the other one of eighty copies on japan. There is also a copy of the first English translation (New York, 1952). After the war, Zapf was increasingly active as a type designer. In his second major book, the *Manuale Typographicum* (Frankfurt, 1954), the alphabets and quotations (this time relating to typography), were set in twenty-four different Stempel types, seven of them designed by Zapf himself. The *Manuale Typographicum* is represented in the bequest by two sets of specimen pages, one of them inscribed to Paul A. Bennett, and by a copy of the second volume, which appeared in 1968. Zapf also spoke of producing a third volume, a *Manuale Photo-Typographicum*, to demonstrate the creative possibilities of computerized photo-typesetting. Zapf, who had once dreamed of becoming an electrical engineer, was one of the first designers to embrace the new technology with enthusiasm. Since the 1970s, he has devoted his talents to digitized type design.

    A previous Hofer gift was Zapf's *Typographic Variations* (New York, 1964). The Bentinck-Smith Typographical Collection includes many specimens of D. Stempel AG and Mergenthaler Linotype Company, for whom Zapf also did much work. Zapf himself has given the Department of Printing and Graphic Arts a substantial group of books designed by him.

N.F.

REF   Cincinnati Art Museum, *Hermann Zapf, Calligrapher, Type-Designer and Typographer* (Cincinnati, 1960–1961), no. 3; Bibliothèque Albert I, *Calligraphie et Typographie de Hermann Zapf* (Brussels, 1962), no. 3; Darmstadt, Technische Hochschule, *Hermann Zapf* (Hamburg, 1984); Carl Zahn, ed., *Hermann Zapf and his Design Philosophy* (Chicago, 1987).

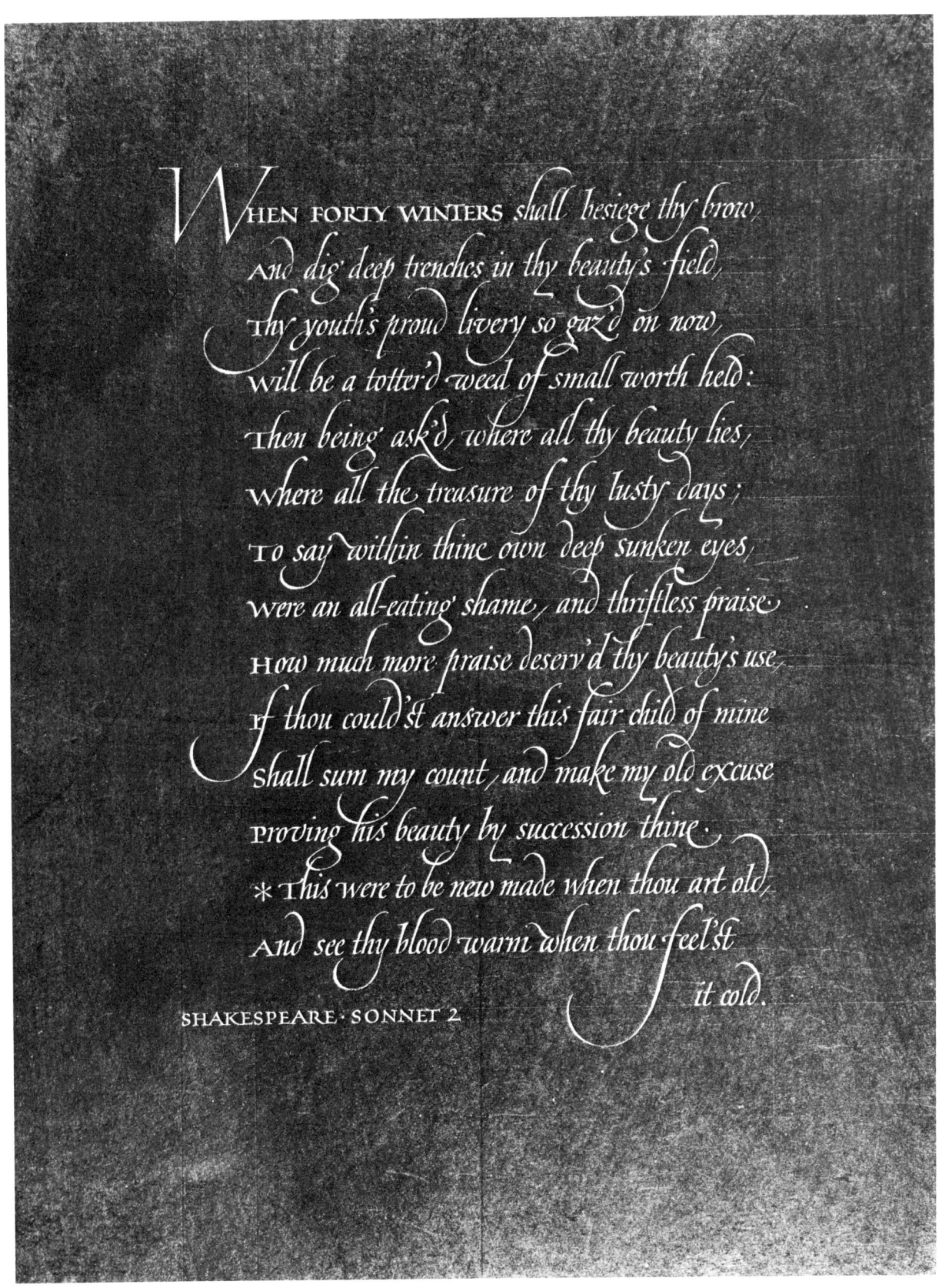

No. 98. Hermann Zapf. Shakespeare *Sonnet* 2. Calligraphic broadside.

99 ❧ FELICE FELICIANO, 1433–1479
Alphabetum Romanum
Giovanni Mardersteig, ed. R.H. Boothroyd, trans.
Verona, Officina Bodoni [1960]

Reproduction, hand-colored by Ameglio Trivella, of Feliciano's manuscript Alphabetum Romanum in the Vatican Library (Codex Vat. Lat. 6852). One of 400 copies of the English edition. There were also editions in German and Italian.

22.5 x 15 cm. Brown morocco, gilt-stamped with the pressmark of the Officina Bodoni.

THE OFFICINA BODONI, the hand press of Giovanni Mardersteig (1892–1977), was first set up in 1922 in Montagnola di Lugano, Switzerland, where he had emigrated for his health from the harsher climate of his native Germany. The press was named for the great Giambattista Bodoni (No. 59), from whose original matrices in the collection of the Museo Bodoniano in Parma, Mardersteig received permission from the Italian government to cast type. In 1927, commissioned to print the national Italian edition of D'Annunzio, the young press moved to Verona, where it exercised a legendary influence on contemporary printing and letter design, carried on in machine-printed books by the founder's son, Martino Mardersteig, at the Stamperia Valdonega.

Giovanni Mardersteig was not only a letter designer and craftsman-printer of the highest quality, but a scholar and editor of rigorous intellectual standards, who closely supervised every step of every title issued by the press, each copy hand-set and hand-printed.

Long a student of Roman lettering, Mardersteig became absorbed in the poet, antiquarian, and calligrapher Felice Feliciano, a fellow-Veronese and one of the first Renaissance humanists to study Roman letters in terms of geometric construction. This *Alphabetum Romanum* reproduces Feliciano's fine capitals from the Vatican manuscript, Codex Vat. Lat. 6852, along with Mardersteig's introduction and analysis. The typeface is Dante, one of three designed by Mardersteig (Griffo and Zeno, the others) and cut by the French punch-cutter Charles Malin; it is the only one of the three made available for machine composition, in a Monotype version.

Giovanni Mardersteig and Philip Hofer shared a special interest in Feliciano, and one of the Hofer manuscripts given to Harvard is a collection of poems and epistles of Feliciano, dated 1471–1472. They also shared a long friendship, and out of this grew a 1970 publication of the Department of Printing and Graphic Arts, a facsimile of the manuscript novella in the collection, *Ippolito e Lionora*, attributed to Leon Battista Alberti and written out in the hand of Feliciano; printed in 200 copies by the Stamperia Valdonega, it contains a preface by Hofer and an essay by Mardersteig.

In the bequest are some thirty books published and printed by Mardersteig at the Officina Bodoni or at the Stamperia Valdonega for other clients. Several are special or presentation copies to Hofer; with the 1952 Boccaccio, *The Nymphs of Fiesole* is boxed a set of proofs of both blocks and text.

E.M.G.

REF "Giovanni Mardersteig and the Officina Bodoni," *The Book Collector*, XXI (Summer 1972), 192; John Barr, *The Officina Bodoni* ([London] The British Library [1978]), no. 60; Giovanni Mardersteig, *The Officina Bodoni*, Hans Schmoller, ed. and trans., (Verona [1980]), no. 121.

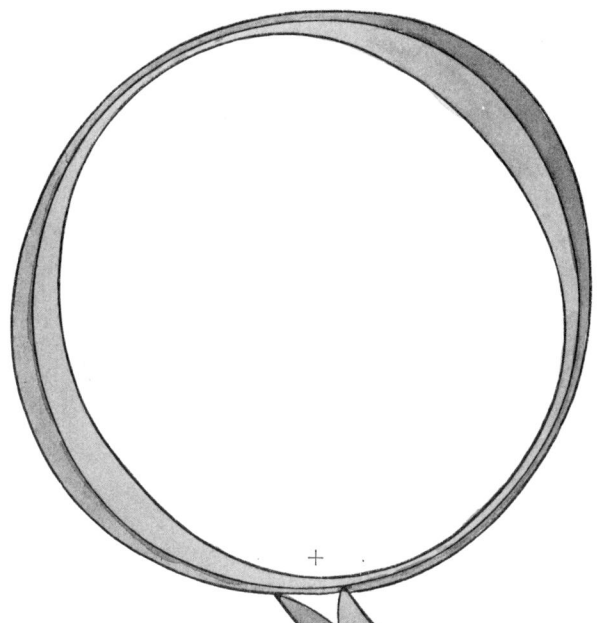

La littera sopradicta si l'ordine del .O., ingrossane e di fuora la Xª. parte come regie secondo do dentro tu uedi. Ma el ti bisogna a questa littera agrandire el quadro $^1/_3$ uerso la parte del .S., et oue la croce è firmata, tira el compasso fina a quel'altra croce del .Q. E per quel modo uiene a formare la coda inferiore, a la quale anche pratica gli vole quanto rasone.

[IX v.]

No. 99. Page from Felice Feliciano, *Alphabetum Romanum*.

100   MARIE ANGEL, b. 1923
A Bestiary
[England, 1958–1960]

Manuscript on vellum; 26 leaves with calligraphic lettering and drawings in watercolor and gouache.

10.1 x 10.1 cm. Unbound. Commissioned from the artist.

An Animated Alphabet
[England, 1967–1970]

Manuscript on vellum; 18 leaves with calligraphic lettering and drawings in watercolor and gouache.

13.1 x 10.1 cm. Unbound. Commissioned from the artist.

HOFER compared Marie Angel's exquisite miniatures to those of another English woman artist, Esther Inglis Kello (1571–1624), whose works he also collected and admired (see No. 27). Angel herself derives her technique from her study of the works of the great Elizabethan miniaturist, Nicholas Hilliard. Her teacher Dorothy Mahoney was the student and later the assistant of Edward Johnston at the Royal College of Art. The traditional roots of Angel's art are thus very strong. She prefers to work in watercolor, gouache and shell gold on vellum, sometimes using skins with interesting colors and markings to deliberately enhance her designs. This may be observed in several drawings in the Hofer bequest.

In 1958, Hofer commissioned Marie Angel to design a pair of monograms for himself and his wife, each animated with an appropriate animal. "My initials are P.H.," he wrote, "and I would like to have a porcupine to symbolize my nature. Curiously, I have always espoused this unattractive beast both out of a sense of humor (I hope) and his decorative qualities as shown in the works done for Louis XII of France, whose emblem he was.... My wife's initials are F.L.H. and though her first name is Frances, absolutely nobody uses it. She is called Bunnie, which suits her and makes my emblem all the more odious by contrast. Could she also have a drawing with her charming emblem, dashing and sitting about the initials?" Angel knew bunnies well—she had had a pet rabbit as a child—but she was unfamiliar with the American porcupine and suggested substituting a hedgehog, a subject more accessible and congenial to an English artist. Her animals are never coyly cute, and although she insisted hedgehogs are charming, the one that she provided as an emblem for Hofer is "snarling in baffled fury because he can't get under the crossbar of the H." The PH and FLH monograms became the first two pieces in a bestiary which was gradually assembled bit by bit between 1958 and 1960.

In a 1958 letter to Hofer, Angel had explained, "Publishers always take one look at my drawings and say—'very nice—but much too expensive to reproduce.'" In 1960, Hofer arranged to have his *Bestiary* reproduced by the Meriden Gravure Company and published by the Department of Printing and Graphic Arts. It was followed by *A New Bestiary* (1964), *Two Poems by Emily Dickinson* (1968), and *An Animated Alphabet* (1971), all commissioned by Hofer and reproduced by Meriden Gravure from the original drawings, the two bestiaries and the alphabet in black and white, the Dickinson in full color. The success of these publications helped to establish Angel's reputation as a book illustrator.

Besides the drawings for *A Bestiary* and *An Animated Alphabet*, the bequest also includes twenty-five drawings for *A New Bestiary* and two early unpublished manuscripts, an *Alphabet* (1956) and a book of *Feathers* (1957). Examples of Angel's calligraphy include her letters to Hofer, many of them illustrated with drawings of plants and animals—especially her beloved cats. The bequest also includes copies of the printed versions of *A Bestiary* and *A New Bestiary* bound in morocco with cork inlays by Kathleen Wick.

Many of Hofer's enthusiasms are reflected in the little body of works which he commissioned and purchased from Marie Angel. By her training, Angel is related to the twentieth-century revival of calligraphy, which Hofer followed with such interest (see No. 84 and 93); technically and aesthetically her designs are related to the illuminated manuscripts which he collected so avidly (see No. 1–12). Alphabets and bestiaries are both areas in which he showed a special interest, acquiring specimens in many different media and from many different periods (see No. 6, 25, 65 and 86). Finally, Hofer's patronage of Marie Angel is an example

No. 100. Marie Angel. Monograms of Philip Hofer and Frances L. Hofer.

of his lifelong commitment, not only to collecting but also to commissioning books (see No. 95 and 96), believing—as St. John Hornby once advised him—that this is the "only way to keep artists and printers of one's own day alive—spiritually, not only physically."

N.F.

REF *Two Thousand Years of Calligraphy*, no. 141 (*A Bestiary*); Marie Angel, *Painting for Calligraphers* (London, 1984); Department of Printing and Graphic Arts, correspondence.

Selected Bibliography

This bibliography is a brief one, citing general and major sources applicable to more than one entry in the catalogue. Other references are placed at the end of each entry.

Abbey, *Scenery*	J. R. Abbey, *Scenery of Great Britain and Ireland in Aquatint and Lithography, 1770–1860*. London, 1952.
Abbey, *Travel*	J. R. Abbey, *Travel in Aquatint and Lithography, 1770–1860*. 2 vols. London, 1956–1957.
Audin	Marius Audin, *Les livrets typographiques des fonderies françaises crées avant 1800*. Paris, 1933.
The Artist & The Book	Museum of Fine Arts and Harvard College Library, *The Artist & The Book 1860–1960*. Boston [1961].
Balston, *Private Press Types*	Thomas Balston, *The Cambridge University Collection of Private Press Types, Kelmscott, Ashendene, Eragny, Cranach*. [Cambridge, Mass.] 1951.
Baroque Book Illustration	Philip Hofer, *Baroque Book Illustration: A Short Survey from the Collection in the Department of Graphic Arts, Harvard College Library*. Cambridge, Mass., 1951.
Bartsch	Adam von Bartsch, *Le peintre graveur*. 21 vols. Leipzig, 1854–1876.
Becker	David P. Becker, *Drawings for Book Illustration. The Hofer Collection*. Cambridge, Mass., Department of Printing and Graphic Arts, The Houghton Library, 1980.
Bigmore and Wyman	E. C. Bigmore and C.W.H. Wyman, *A Bibliography of Printing*. 3 vols. London, 1880–1886.
Birrell & Garnett	Birrell & Garnett, Ltd., *Catalogue of Typefounders' Specimens ... Offered for Sale* [by Graham Pollard]. London, 1928 (Reprint 1972).
British Museum	British Museum, *Short-title Catalogue of Books Printed in Italy and of Italian Books Printed in Other Countries from 1464 to 1600*. London, 1958.
Brunet	Jacques-Charles Brunet, *Manuel du libraire et de l'amateur de livres*. 6 vols. & supplement. Paris, 1860–1870.
Canivet	Diane Canivet, *L'illustration de la poésie et du roman français au XVIIe siècle*. Paris, 1957.
Cate and Hitchings, *The Color Revolution*	Philip Dennis Cate and Sinclair Hamilton Hitchings, *The Color Revolution, Color Lithography in France 1890–1900*. New Brunswick, N.J., Rutgers University Art Gallery, 1978–1979.

Cohen-De Ricci	Henri Cohen, *Guide de l'amateur de livres à gravures du XVIIIe siècle*. Sixième edition augmentée par Seymour De Ricci. Paris, 1912.
De Ricci *Census*	Seymour De Ricci and W. J. Wilson, *Census of Medieval and Renaissance Manuscripts in the United States and Canada*. 2 vols. New York, 1935–1937.
Eichenberg	Fritz Eichenberg, *The Art of the Print*. New York [1976].
Faye and Bond	C. U. Faye and W. H. Bond, *Supplement to the Census of Medieval and Renaissance Manuscripts in the United States and Canada*. New York, 1962.
From Manet to Hockney	Carol Hogben and Rowan Watson, eds., *From Manet to Hockney, Modern Artists' Illustrated Books*. [London] Victoria & Albert Museum [1985].
Goff	Frederick R. Goff, *Incunabula in American Libraries*. New York, 1964.
Guilmard	D. Guilmard, *Les maîtres ornemanistes*. Paris, 1880.
Hind	Arthur M. Hind, *An Introduction to a History of the Woodcut*. 2 vols. London, 1935.
Illuminated and Calligraphic Manuscripts	Harvard College Library, *Illuminated and Calligraphic Manuscripts*. Cambridge, Mass., 1955.
Kilgour	Harvard College Library, *The Kilgour Collection of Russian Literature 1750–1920*. Cambridge, Mass., 1959.
Light	Laura Light, *The Bible in the Twelfth Century*. Cambridge, Mass., 1988.
Mortimer	Mortimer, Ruth, *Harvard College Library, Department of Printing and Graphic Arts, Catalogue of Books and Manuscripts*. Part I: *French 16th Century Books*. 2 vols. Cambridge, Mass., 1964.
Nagler	G. K. Nagler, *Neues allgemeines Künstler-Lexikon*. Vienna, 1924.
Nissen	Claus Nissen, *Die Botanische Buchillustration: ihre Geschichte und Bibliographie*. Stuttgart, 1951.
Palau	Antonio Palau y Dulcet, *Manual del librero hispano-americano*. 28 vols. Barcelona, 1948–1977.
Ray	Gordon N. Ray, *The Art of the French Illustrated Book, 1700–1914*. 2 vols. New York and Ithaca, 1983.
Regency to Empire	The Baltimore Museum of Art and the Minneapolis Institute of Arts, *Regency to Empire, French Printmaking 1715–1814*. [Minneapolis] 1985.
Sander	Max Sander, *Le livre à figures italien depuis 1467 jusqu'à 1530*. 6 vols. New York, 1941.
Skira	Albert Skira, *Anthologie du livre illustré par les peintres et sculpteurs de l'école de Paris*. Geneva [1946].
Thieme-Becker	Ulrich Thieme and Felix Becker, *Allgemeines Lexikon der bildenden Künstler von der Antike bis zur Gegenwart*. 37 vols. Leipzig, 1907–1950.
Tooley	R. V. Tooley, *English Books with Coloured Plates, 1790 to 1860*. London, 1954.

Two Thousand Years of Calligraphy	Baltimore Museum of Art, Peabody Institute Library and Walters Art Gallery, *Two Thousand Years of Calligraphy*. Baltimore, 1965.
Updike	Daniel Berkeley Updike, *Printing Types, Their History, Forms, and Use*. 2 vols. Cambridge, Mass., 1937.
Vinet	Ernest Vinet, *Bibliographie méthodique et raisonnée des beaux-arts*. Paris, 1874.
Walters, *History of Bookbinding*	Walters Art Gallery, *The History of Bookbinding 525–1950 A.D.* Baltimore, 1957.
Walters, *Manuscripts*	Walters Art Gallery, *Illuminated Books of the Middle Ages and Renaissance*. Baltimore, 1949.

Different phases of the Hofer collection are discussed in the five entries below. The sixth is a checklist of Philip Hofer's own publications to 1978.

William A. Jackson, "Contemporary Collectors XXIV: Philip Hofer," *The Book Collector*, IX (1960), 151–164, 292–300.

James E. Walsh, "Notes on the Philip Hofer Reference Collection," *The Book Collector*, XVII (1969).

John M. Rosenfield, Fumiko E. Cranston, Edwin Cranston, *The Courtly Tradition in Japanese Art and Literature*. Cambridge, Mass., Fogg Art Museum, 1973.

Konrad Oberhuber and William W. Robinson, eds., *Master Drawings and Watercolors. The Hofer Collection*. Cambridge, Mass., Fogg Art Museum, 1984.

William Bentinck-Smith, "Prince of the Eye: Philip Hofer and the Harvard Library," *Harvard Library Bulletin*, XXXII (1984), 317–347.

Philip Hofer as Author and Publisher. Harvard College Library, Department of Printing and Graphic Arts 1968, and *Philip Hofer as Author and Publisher, A Supplement*, 1978.

Authors

References are to entry numbers. Principal authors and principal references are given in **bold face** type.

Aedo y Gallart, Diego de 29
Aegidius Assisiensis 17
Aelian 26
Aesop 13, **15**, **18**, **35**, **38**, **58**
Agricola, Georg 25
Aguilon, François d' 29
Alberti, Leon Battista 49, 99
Albin, Eleazer 56
Alciati, Andrea 41
Alhoy, Maurice 65
Allen, John Fisk 72
Altoviti, Giovanni 30
Amico, Bernardino 30
Anacreon 85
Androuet du Cerceau, Jacques 41, 49
Anthony of Florence, St. 17
Apollinaire, Guillaume 85, **86**
Apuleius 93
Ariosto, Lodovico 66
Arrighi, *see* Ludovico degli Arrighi
Aristotle 8
Artaud, Antonin 87
Auer, Alois 74
Augustine, Saint 11
Avice, Henri d' 33

Balzac, Honoré de 66, 70, 79, 87
Bangs, John Kendrick 88
Barberini, Maffeo 29
Bardi, Ferdinando 31
Bardin, Philippe 38
Barton, William P. C. 72
Beauchesne, Jean de 27
Beaugrand, Jean I de 27
Bede 1
Behn, Aphra 35
Benlowes, Edward 35
Benserade, Isaac de 38
Berchorius, Petrus 13
Bergomensis, Jacopo Foresti de 17
Bernard, Tristan 77
Bernhard, Georg 89
Bettini, Antonio 17
Bewick, Thomas 58
Bible 3, 4, 7, 9, 16, 17, **18**, 25, 26, 39, 55, **81**, 93

Bidloo, Govert 24
Biehl, Charlotte Dorothea 36
Blake, William 55
Boccaccio, Giovanni 13, **93**, 99
Bodoni, Giovanni Battista 59
Boitard, Pierre 66
Bonarelli, Prospero 30
Bonaventura, St. 17
Book of Hours, *see* Horae B.M.V.
Bosch, Jaime Felipe José 75
Bosse, Abraham 32
Bracciolini, Poggio 20
Brandano, Alessandro 39
Breviary 29
Buchowski, Petrus 41
Buffon, Georges Louis Leclerc de 87
Buommattei, Benedetto 31
Byrne, Oliver 91
Byron, George Gordon 62

Calendar 10
Carducci, Alessandro 31
Carryl, Guy Wetmore 15
Casa, Giovanni della 83
Casserio, Giulio 24, **31**
Cavalca, Domenico 17
Cavalcante, Andrea 31
Certamen equestre 36
Cervantes Saavedra, Miguel de 36, 66
Césaire, Aimé 87
Cessolis, Jacobus de 17
Champfleury 75
Chapelain, Jean 32
Chappuis, Jean 11
Char, René 87
Christianae juventutis crepundia 25
Cicero 26
Clemenceau, Georges 77
Cobden-Sanderson, T. J. 81
Colonna, Egidio 14
Contrasto di carnesciale et la quaresima 17
Coppola, Gian Carlo 31
Courteline, Georges 79
Croall, Alexander 74
Cros, Charles 75

Curtis, William 56
Cyrillus de Quidenon 13, 15

Daguerre, Louis Jacques Mandé 67
Dahlberg, Eric 36
Dante Alighieri 47, 55, 91, 93
Defoe, Daniel 70
Delgado y Galvez, José 57, **87**
Delord, Taxile 70
Denny, William 35
Deriège, Félix 65
Desargues, Gérard 32
Desmarets de Saint Sorlin, Jean 32
Dezallier d'Argenville, Antoine Joseph 56
Dickinson, Emily 100
Dihau, Desiré 77
Dionysius Areopagita 29
Dodart, Denys 38
Dodgson, Charles Lutwidge 88
Donnay, Maurice 77
Dürer, Albrecht 18, 83
Dwiggins, William Addison 94

Edwards, George 53
Eluard, Paul 87
Emerson, George Barrell 72
Emerson, Ralph Waldo 81
Enault, Louis 73
Engelmann, Godefroy 60
Epistole et Evangelii 17
Erasmus, Desiderius 22, **25**, **83**
Euclid 91
Eusebius 26
Evelyn, John 34

Fabre, François 65
Fabricii, Principio 41
Faerno, Gabriello 15
Félibien, André 43
Feliciano, Felice 99
Fischer von Erlach, J. E. 49
Flaubert, Gustave 79
Fleury, Jules, see Champfleury
Florian, Jean Pierre Claris de 70
Forgues, Emile 70

Fossati, Giorgio 47
Francis of Assisi, St. 81, 93
Froissart, Jean 78
Frontinus 12
Fuchs, Gottfried 36
Fuchs, Leonhard 25
Fürstliche Bau-Lust 41

Gabory, Georges 85
Gallacini, Teofilo 48
Galli da Bibiena, Ferdinando 49
Gamelin, Jacques 24
García Lorca, Federico 97
Gautier d'Agoty, Jacques 44
Gautier de Montdorge, Antoine 44
Gay, John 15
Geffroy, Gustave 77
Geminus 24
Gevaerts, Jan Casper 29, 30
Girolamo di S. Stefano 20
Goethe, Johann Wolfgang von 15, **54**, **61**, **64**
Goll, Yvon 87
Gould, John 68
Gray, Asa 72
Grey, Roch (Hélène baronne d'Oettingen) 87
Gruelle, R. B. 91
Grynaeus, Simon 28
Guicciardini, Francesco 48

Hagen, Giuseppe 39
Herckmans, Elias 37
Herodotus 17
Héron de Villefosse, René 85
Hesiod 79
Hetzel, Pierre-Jules, see Stahl, P. J.
Holberg, Ludvig 36
Horace 39, 89, 93
Horae B.M.V. 7, **16**, **19**
Hovey, Charles M. 72
Howells, James 32
Huart, Louis 65, 70
Hueber, Philibert 45
Hugo da Folieto 6
Hugo, Herman 29
Hugo, Victor 66
Hullmandel, Charles 60
Humbert, Henri 30

Iliazd (Ilya Zdanevich) 87
Illo, José, see Delgado y Galvez, José
Illo, Pepe, see Delgado y Galvez, José

Jackson, John Baptist 44
Jacob, Max 85, **87**
Jacobaeus, Holger 36
Jacopone da Todi 17
Janin, Jules 66

Jerome, St. 17
John Chrysostom, St. 6
Johnstone, William Grosart 74
Jouhandeau, Marcel 85
Joze, Victor 77, 79
Juvenal 39

Kessler, Harry 89
Kleiner, Salomon 49
Konrad von Megenburg 13, 56
Krylov, Ivan 15

L'Admiral, Jan 24, 44
L'Orme, Philibert de 41, 49
La Bruyère, Jean de 66
La Fontaine, Jean de 15, 70, 73
La Motte, Antione Houdar de 15
Lapide, Cornelius Cornelii à 29
Le Blon, Jakob Christof 44
Le Sage, Alain-René 66
Lear, Edward 68, **76**
Leclerc, Sébastien 38, **39**
Leclercq, Paul 77
Lectionary 2
Leonardo da Vinci 83
Livy 17
Lockhart, John 71
Longfellow, Henry Wadsworth 71
Longus 79, 89
Loring, Rosamund B. 95
Lucretius 93
Ludovico degli Arrighi 21, 23, 96

Magini, Giovanni Antonio 39
Mallarmé, Stéphane 75, **79**, **92**
Malory, Sir Thomas 93
Malraux, André 85
Manesseh ben Israel 37
Margerie, Pierre de 89
Marolles, Michel de 39
Marselaer, Frederik van 29
Marsolleau, Louis 77
Martin, Mrs. Clara Barnes 67
Martyn, Thomas 56
Mascardi, Agostino 29
Melanchthon, Philipp 22
Mellério, André 79
Mercator, Gerardus 28
Meun, Jean de 11
Milton, John 34, **40**, 81
Mirbeau, Octave 79
Missal 4, 16
Modus scribendi 45
Molière, Jean-Baptiste Poquelin 66
Mollet, André 36
Montorgueil, Georges 77
Moore, Thomas 74
More, Sir Thomas 93
Morison, Stanley 91

Münster, Sebastian 25
Muselli, Vincent 85

Nahman, Moses ben 15
Nansen, Peter 79
Newell, Peter 88
Nodier, Charles 69, 70
Nolhac, Pierre de 83
Northcote, James 58
Nozeman, Cornelis 56

Ogilby, John 35
Onosander 12
Ortelius, Abraham 28
Ovid 33, 38, 87

Palladio, Andrea 41, 49
Pallas, P. 56
Parsons, William 43
Pellico, Silvio 66
Peri, Giovanni Domenico 30
Perrault, Charles 38
Petrarch, Francesco 17, 87
Phaedrus 15
Phile, Manuel 26
Pico della Mirandola, Giovanni 83
Pietrasanta, Silvestro 29
Pinheiro Arnaut, Manoel 41
Pipino, Francesco 20
Piranesi, Giovanni Battista 49
Plutarch 14, 93
Pocci, Franz von 61
Polo, Marco 20
Processional 5
Psalter 3, **9**
Ptolemy 13
Pulci, Luigi 17

Rabelais, François 73
Racine, Jean 66
Radiguet, Raymond 85
Rapp, Heinrich 60
Regenfuss, Franz Michael 56
Regiomontanus 17
Renard, Jules 15, 77
Repton, Humphrey 49
Reventós, Ramon 87
Reverdy, Pierre 85
Reynolds, Edward 45
Richepin, Jean 77
Rilke, Rainer Maria 89
Roberts, David 69
Roger-Marx, Claude 79
Rogers, Bruce 91
Ronsard, Pierre de 79
Roque, Jacqueline 87
Rossi, Giovanni Gherardo de 59
Rubens, Philip 29
Rudbeck, Olof 36

Sabartès, Jaime 87
Sacro Bosco, Johannes de 17
Salmon, André 85
Salvadori, Andrea 30
Sand, George 66
Sandrart, Joachim 36
Sarbievski, Maciej Kazimierz 29
Savigny, A. 70
Savonarola, Girolamo 17
Saxton, Christopher 28
Schabaelje, Jan Philipsz 37
Scheler, Lucien 87
Scheurl, Christoph 13
Schiller, Johann Christoph Friedrich von 61
Scudéry, Georges de 33
Seneca 29
Sencfelder, Alois 60
Seriman, Zaccaria 47
Serlio, Sebastiano 41, 49
Shakespeare, William 64, 81, **89**, 98
Shaw, Henry 71
Sidney, Sir Philip 83
Simon, Hugo F. 89
Six, Jan 37
Smart, Christopher 15
Smith, James Edward 72

Spalowsky, Joachim Johann Nepomuk Anton 56
Stahl, P. J. 70
Stapfer, Albert 64
Strada, Ottavio 41
Strutt, Jacob George 72
Stumpf, Hans 25
Suarès, André 79
Subleyras, Luigi 50
Sue, Eugène 66
Swift, Jonathan 70

Talbot, William Henry Fox 67
Täntzer, Johann 36
Tasso, Torquato 66
Terence 39
Terrasse, Claude 79
Thornton, Robert John 55, 72
Tinan, Jean de 77
Töpffer, Rodolphe 66
Tory, Geoffroy 91
Trew, C. J. 56
Tzara, Tristan 87

Uberto & Philomena 17
Urban VIII, *see* Barberini, Maffeo

Valéry, Paul 91
Valturio, Roberto 17
Vberto & Philomena 17
Vélez de Guevara, Luis 57
Vergil 39, 55, 67, **89**, 93
Verhaeren, Emile 89
Verlaine, Paul 79
Vesalius, Andreas 24, 25
Vignola, Giacomo Barozzio, called 41
Villena, Enrique de 14
Vitruvius 41
Vol'gá 82
Voyage de S.M. Louis-Philippe 30
Vredeman de Vries, Jan 49

Watelet, Claude Henri 50
Wells, H. G. 94
Whitney, Geoffrey 41
Wilde, Oscar 93
Wilson, Alexander 72
Worm, Ole 36
Wright, Frank Lloyd 49
Wyatt, Matthew Digby 71

Young, Edward 55

Artists, Engravers and Scribes

References are to entry numbers. Principal artists and principal references are given in **bold face** type.

Abbot, John 56
Albertolli, Giocondo 43
Aldrich, Henry 40
Allen, Anne 53
Ammanati, Bartolomeo 42
Amphiareo, Vespasiano 23
Andrew, Best and Leloir 66
Angel, Marie 6, 54, 56, 84, 100
Arrighi, *see* Ludovico degli Arrighi

Baldung Grien, Hans 18
Barlow, Francis 35
Barrias, Félix Joseph 67
Baskin, Leonard 15, 97
Beauchesne, Jean de 27
Beaugrand, Jean II de 27
Beham, Hans Sebald 18
Bella, Stefano della 31
Benois, Alexander 82
Benson, John E. 96
Benson, John Howard 96
Bernard, Emile 79
Bernini, Giovanni Lorenzo 42

Bewick, Thomas 58, 66
Bilibin, Ivan Yakovlevich 82
Blake, William 55
Blinn, Carol 76
Blondel, Jacques-François 36
Bonington, Richard Parkes 69
Bonnard, Pierre 15, 75, 77, **79**
Boutet de Monvel, Louis Maurice 15
Borromini, Francesco 42
Bosse, Abraham 32, 38
Bosse, Willem 37
Bouche, Peter Paul 40
Boucher, François 42, 53
Boys, Thomas Shotter 69
Bradbury, Henry 74
Brambilla, Fernando 57
Braque, Georges 79
Burghers, Michael 40
Burgkmair, Hans 18
Burne-Jones, Edward 78

Calcar, Jan Stephan van 24
Calder, Alexander 15

Callot, Jacques 30
Canaletto, Antonio 48
Caroë, W. H. 84
Carpi, Ugo da 21
Carter, Will 84
Cataneo, Bernardo 23
Catich, Edward M. 96
Chambers, William 48
Chassériau, Théodore 64
Chauveau, François 15, 32, 33
Chevalier, Guillaume Sulpice, *see* Gavarni
Child, Heather 84
Chodowiecki, Daniel 61
Cleland, Thomas Maitland 83
Clennell, Luke 58
Cleyn, Franz 35
Cochin, Charles-Nicolas 15, 33, 42, 50
Colombe, Jean 4
Conretto da Monte Regalo 23
Coppenol, Lieven Willemsz van 37
Cortona, Pietro da 36
Coypel, Charles Antoine 15

Craig, Edward Gordon 89
Cranach, Lucas 18
Cresci, Giovanni Francesco 23
Crivellari, Bartolomeo 47
Curione, Lodovico 23
Czetter, Samuel 56
Daguerre, Louis Jacques Mandé 67
Daumier, Honoré 65, 73
Delacroix, Eugène 64
Denis, Maurice 79
Derain, André 85, 87
Devéria, Achille 64
Diaghilev, Sergei 82
Doré, Gustave 73, 76
Dudley, Thomas 35
Dufy, Raoul 6, 86
Dürer, Albrecht 13, 18
Dwiggins, William Addison 83, 94

Ehret, Georg Dionysius 56
Eimmart, Georg Christoph 36
Epstein, Jacob 84
Esslinger, Martin 61
Evelyn, John 34

Fairbank, Alfred 84
Faithorne, William 40
Fanti, Sigismondo 23
Feliciano, Felice 99
Fessard, Etienne 51
Fielding, Newton 69
Fielding, Thales 69
Flamen, Albert 41
Fontebasso, Francesco 47
Fossati, Giorgio 15, 47
Foster, Birket 71
Français, Louis 70
Frasconi, Antonio 97
Fugger, Wolfgang 23

Galle, Theodore 29
Galli Bibiena, Giuseppe 42
Garamont, Claude 26
Gautier d'Agoty, Edouard 53
Gautier d'Agoty, Jacques 44
Gautier d'Agoty, Jacques-Fabien 24, 53
Gautier de Montdorge, Antoine 44
Gavarni 65, 66
Geeraerts, Marcus 15, 35
Gérard, Jean-Ignace-Isidore, see Grandville
Gigola, Giovanni Battista 62
Gigoux, Jean-François 66
Gill, Eric 84, 89, 96
Gillot, Claude 15
Goudy, Frederic W. 91
Goya y Lucientes, Francisco 57, 64
Graf, Urs 25

Grandville, J. J. 66, 70
Granjon, Robert 23
Gravelot, Hubert-François Bourguignon, called 42, 51
Gribelin, Simon 43
Gris, Juan 85

Hamon, Pierre 27
Harding, James Duffield 60
Harper, Ivy 84
Harvey, William 58
Henstock, Ida R. 93
Hercolani, Giuliantonio 23
Hertochs, A. 34
Hewitt, Graily 84, 93
Highmore, Joseph 76
Hilliard, Nicholas 100
Hinckley, Helen E. 93
Hofmann, Ludwig von 61
Holbein, Hans 22, 25, 28, 95
Hollar, Wenceslaus 35
Hondius, Jodocus 23
Hooghe, Romeyn de 15, 36
Horne, Herbert P. 83
Humphreys, Henry Noel 78
Huquier, Gabriel 42

Ingres, Jean Dominique 76
Initials and monograms, AH 34
Initials and monograms, CV 22
Ivanov, Ivan 15

Jackson, John Baptist 44
Jarry, Alfred 75
Johannot, Alfred 66
Johannot, Tony 66
Johnson, Robert 58
Johnston, Edward 81, 84, 89, 96, 100
Jones, Owen 71

Kandinsky, Wassily 80
Kauffmann, Angelica 54, 59
Kaulbach, Wilhelm von 15, 61
Keates, C. E. 78
Kello, Esther (Inglis) 27, 100
Kindersley, David 84
Klöcker, David 36
Koch, Rudolf 56, 90
Kolbe, Carl Wilhelm 61
Kraus, Georg Melchior 54
Kredel, Fritz 90
Krügner, Johann Gottfried 45
Küchler, Rosel 90

Lasinio, Carlo 53
Laurencin, Marie 85
Laurens, Henri 85
Lavallée-Poussin, Etienne de 50
Le Blon, Jakob Christof 44, 53

Le Brun, Charles 36, 38, 43
Le Gagneur, Guillaume 23
Le Pautre, Jean 33, 36
Lear, Edward 68, 76
Leclerc, Sébastien 38, 39
Léger, Fernand 85
Lens, Bernard, the elder 40
Leone, Laurenziano 23
Lewis, Allen 96
Liagno, Teodoro Filippo di 31
Linnell, John 55
Lucas, Francisco 23
Ludovico degli Arrighi, Vicentino 21, 96
Lurçat, Jean 15

Madariaga, Pedro de 23
Magnini, Giuseppe 47
Mahoney, Dorothy 100
Maillol, Aristide 84, 89
Manet, Edouard 75
Manolo (Manuel Martinez Hugué) 85
Marc, Franz 80
Marcks, Gerhard 15
Marot, Jean 33
Martin, John 34, 40
Masson, André 85
Master of Morgan 453 7
Matisse, Henri 92
Medina, John Baptist 40
Mellan, Claude 32, 33
Menzel, Adolf von 61
Mercoli, Giovanni 59
Merian, Maria Sibylla 56
Millais, John Everett 76
Monnet, Charles 33
Monnier, Henry 65
Moreau, Jean-Michel 33, 42
Morghen, Filippo 43
Morris, William 78

Nanteuil, Célestin 66
Nanteuil, Robert 33
Newell, Peter 88
Noorde, Cornelis van 52

Oppenord, Gilles-Marie 42
Oudry, Jean-Baptiste 15, 42

Palatino, Giovanni Battista 23
Palladio, Andrea 42
Palmer, Samuel 55
Parigi, Alfonso 31
Parigi, Giulio 30
Pasini, Antonio 59
Passe, Crispin de 41
Pennell, Joseph 96
Perret, Clément 23
Phillips, Thomas 55

ARTISTS, ENGRAVERS AND SCRIBES 213

Picasso, Pablo 15, 57, 86, 87
Pillement, Jean 53
Piranesi, Giovanni Battista 43, 49
Pocci, Franz von 61
Potter, Beatrix 76
Powell, Louise 93
Prout, Samuel 60

Rackham, Arthur 15
Raderer, Ignatz 45
Raffet, Auguste 66
Raimondi, Vincenzo 21
Redouté, Pierre Joseph 56
Redon, Odilon 79
Rembrandt Hermanszoon van Rijn 37
Rethel, Alfred 61
Retzsch, Moritz 61
Ribera, Jusepe de 34
Richmond, George 55
Richter, Ludwig 61
Robert, Hubert 50
Roberts, David 69
Rodin, Auguste 79
Roger, Suzanne 85
Rogers, Bruce 91
Rosaspina, Francesco 59
Rossi, Marco Antonio de 23
Rouault, Georges 79
Ruano, Ferdinando 21, 23
Rubens, Peter Paul 29, 30
Rupert, Prince 34
Ruzicka, Rudolph 22, 58, 83, 95
Ruzicka, Veronica 95

Ryther, Augustine 28

Sadeler, Aegidius 15
Salomon, Bernard 15
San Vito, Bartolomeo 23
Sandrart, Joachim 36
Saxton, Christopher 28
Schäufelein, Hans 18
Schütz, Johann Georg 54
Schuster, Johann 41
Schwind, Moritz von 61
Sève, Jacques de 51
Shahn, Ben 15, 97
Sharp, William 72
Shaw, Henry 71
Silvestre, Israel 33
Sliegh, John 71
Soli, Giuseppe Maria 48
Solis, Vergil 15
Spielmeyer, W. 78
Spina, Bernardino 23
Stanfield, Clarkson 69
Stein, Walter 15
Steinhauser, Gandolf 56
Stubbs, George 56

Taglienti, Giovanni Antonio 23
Talbot, William Henry Fox 67
Teixeira Barreto, José 59
Thompson, Charles 66
Tischbein, Johann Heinrich Wilhelm 54
Titian (Tiziano Vecelli) 15, 24
Toulouse-Lautrec, Henri de 15, 75, 77

Traut, Wolf 18
Trivella, Armeglio 99
Tulden, Theodor van 30

Urrabieta, Vicente 57

Valverde, Juan de 24
Vergezio, Angelo 26
Verovio, Simone 23
Vicentino, see Ludovico degli Arrighi (Vicentino)
Vidal, Pierre 75
Vignon, Claude 32
Villard de Honnecourt 4, 6
Visentini, Antonio 48
Vogtherr, Heinrich 25

Warde, Frederic 91
Watelet, Claude Henri 50
Watteau, Antoine 42
Wayne, June 97
Webb, Philip 93
Weiditz, Hans 18
Wellington, Irene 84
White, Robert 40
Wöllner, Emil 90
Wolgemut, Michael 18
Wolpe, Berthold 90
Wyss, Urbanus 23

Yciar, Juan de 23

Zapf, Hermann 98
Zompini, Gaetano 47
Zuliani, Giuliano 47

Printers, Publishers and Typefounders

References are to entry numbers. Principal printers and principal references are given in **bold face** type.

Abbe, Dorothy 94
Ackermann, Rudolph 60
Alberti, Ignaz, Widow of 56
Altheer, Johannes 52
Arndes, Steffen 16
Ashendene Press 84, 93
Aubert et Cie. 65
Auer, Alois 74
Austria, K.K. Hof- und Staatsdruckerei 74

Bämler, Johann 13
Beedle, G. 34
Berry Hill Press 96
Binny & Ronaldson 63
Binny, Archibald 63

Binny, John 63
Blake, William 55
Bodoni, Giovanni Battista 59
Bodoni, Officina 99
Bonhomini, João Pedro 20
Boston Type and Stereotype Company 63
Boubers, J. L. de 52
Bourdin, Ernest 66
Boys, Thomas 69
Bradbury and Evans 74
Bradbury, Henry 74
Bruce, George & Co. 63
Bry, J. aîné 73
Bylaert, Johann Jacob 52

Cambridge University Press 93
Centenera, Antonio de 14
Challamel 66
Chlendowski 66
Cobden-Sanderson, T. J. 81
Collins, J. 34
Cot, Jean and Pierre 46, 51
Cranach Press 84, 89, 93
Crowell, Thomas Y. 83
Curmer, Henri-Léon 66
Cygnet Press 95

Dalziel Brothers 71
Department of Printing and Graphic Arts 95, 98, 100
Deplanche 86

Doves Press 81, 84
Dubochet, J.J. et Compagnie 66
Dürer, Albrecht 18
Dutton and Wentworth 72
Dwiggins, William Addison 94

Eberdt, Johann Georg 36
Engelmann, Godefroy 60
Enschedé Type Foundry 52
Eragny Press 93
Ernst Ludwig Presse 90
Estampe originale 77
Estienne, Robert 25, 26, 46
Ettinger, Carl Wilhelm 54
Eustache, Guillaume 19

Fanfare Press 91
Fernandes, Valentim 20
Fleischman, Johann Michael 52
Flesher, Miles 40
Four Winds Press 76
Fournier, Henri 66
Fournier, Jean-Claude 51
Fournier, Pierre-Simon 51
France, Imprimerie Royale 38
Froben, Johann 22, 25
Froschauer, Christoph 25
Furne, Charles et Compagnie 66

Gando, Nicolas 46
Garnier Frères 73
Gehenna Press 58
Gibbings, Robert 84
Giroux, Alphonse et Cie. 67
Gleditsch, Johann 45
Godbid, William 35
Golden Cockerell 84
Golike, P. i A. Vil'borg 82
Gosselin, Charles 66
Gribelin, Simon 43

Harper and Brothers 88
Harrison of Paris 15
Harvard College Library 96
Hetzel, J. et Paulin 70
Hetzel, Jules 66
Hogarth Press 89
Holle, Lienhart 13
Hornby, C. H. St. John 93, 100
Hullmandel, Charles 60, 68, 69
Huquier, Gabriel 42

Imperial Printing Office, *see* Austria, K.K. Hof- und Staatsdruckerei
Imprimerie Royal, *see* France, Imprimerie Royale
Insel Verlag 84, 89, 90
Isengrin, Michael 25

Janet, Denis 15
Jombert, Charles-Antoine 32
Juan de Burgos 14

Kahnweiler, Daniel-Henry 85, 86, 87, 92
Kelmscott Press 78, 81, 89, 93
Kerver, Thielman 16, 19
Kessler, Count Harry 84, 89
Klingspor Type Foundry 90
Knopf, Alfred A. 94
Koberger, Anton 16, 18
Koch, Simon 16
Kress, Christopher 13
Krimpen, Jan van 52
Kugelmann 66

Lamesle, Claude 46
Landini, Giovanni Battista 31
Langlois, N. 39
Lanston Monotype Corporation 91
Le Bé Type Foundry 51
Leeu, Gerard 15
Leiris, Louise (Galerie) 85
Lemercier 75
Lerebours 67
Lescailje, Jacob 37
Levier 53
Leviez, *see* Levier
Longman and Rees 58
Ludovico degli Arrighi 21

Manuzio, Aldo 18
Marchbanks Press 91
Mardersteig, Giovanni 99
Martin, Edmé 33
Mason, J. H. 89
McLean, Thomas 68
Mergenthaler Linotype Company 98
Meriden Gravure Company 43, 100
Merrymount Press 58, 83, 95
Meursius, Johannes 29
Monotype Corporation 84
Moretus, Balthasar 29
Moretus, Jan 29
Morgiani, Lorenzo 17
Morris Gallery 97
Motte & Sautelet 64
Murray, John 71

New England Type Foundry 63
Newberry Library 96
Noveman, Cornelis 52
Nutius, Martin 29

Offenbacher Werkstatt 90
Officina Bodoni, see Bodoni, Officina
Oporin, Johann 25
Oppermann, Georg Heinrich 41

Page, L. C. 83
Paulin, Jean-Baptiste-Alexandre 66
Pepler, Hilary 84
Petri, Adam 25
Petri, Heinrich 25
Petri, Johannes 17
Philippe, Sebastien 30
Pickering, William 58, 76, 91
Pigouchet, Philippe 16
Piranesi, G. B. 49
Plantin, Christopher 29
Ploos van Amstel 52
Polono, Stanislao 14
Prince, Edward 89, 93
Püterschein-Hingham 94

Random House 91
Ronaldson, James 63
Rosart, J. F. 52
Routledge, George and Co. 71
Rudhard Type Foundry 90
Russell, R. H. 83

Saint Dominic's Press 84
Schniewind, Henry 76
Scribner's, Charles, Sons 83
Senefelder, Alois 76
Sharp & Son 72
Simon, Galerie 85
Skira, Albert & Cie. 92
Smith, W. H. 93
Società Tipografica dei Classici Italiani 62
Sorg, Anton 13, 15
Spindeler, Nicolás 14
Stempel Type Foundry 98
Stroganoff, Ecole 80
Susse Frères 67

Timothy Press 43
Tonson, Jacob 40
Tournes, Jean de 15
Tuppo, Francesco del 15
Typographical Society of Italian Classicks 62

Unger, Johann Friedrich 54
Ungut, Meinardo 14
Updike, Daniel Berkeley 58, 83, 91, 95

Valdonega, Stamperia 99
Vautroullier, Thomas 27
Vega y Compañia 57
Vieweg, Friedrich 61
Vizetelly Brothers and Co. 71
Vollard, Ambroise 79, 92
Voskens and Clerk 52

Walker, Edward 58
Walker, Emery 81, 89, 93
Warée, Charles 66
Wechel, Christian 41

White, Elihu 63
White, John T. 63
Whittingham, Charles 91
Wing, William 63

Zainer, Günther 13
Zainer, Johann 13
Zatta, Antonio 47

Binders

References are to entry numbers. References to unsigned bindings of special interest will be found in the General Index under *Bindings*.

Bedford, Francis 20

Cobden-Sanderson, Thomas James 78
Cockerell, Douglas 55

Doves Bindery 81

Haring, C. 17
Haarhaus, Robert 66

Kronheim, J. M. 66

Leighton, John 74
McLeish, C. & C. 14
Nott, William 45
Parrot, Gray 76
Queen's Binder A 45

Ridge, S., of Grantham 8
Sliegh, John 71
Smith, W. H. & Sons 93
Trautz-Bauzonnet 11
Wick, Kathleen 100
Wiemeler, Ignaz 89

Provenance

References are to entry numbers

Amelot, Antoine Jacques 33
American Type Founders Company 63
Anne of Austria, Queen of France 33, 39
Arklitten, Schloss 54
Aylesford, Earl of 49

Beatty, A. Chester 1, 26
Beauharnais, Eugène de 39, 59
Beaumont, Richard Blackett 48
Beckford, William 39
Beit, Sir Alfred Lane 48
Bentinck-Smith, William 18, 26, 63, 94, 98
Blondin, P. 64
Blumka Galleries 10
Borghese, Scipione 29
Bourbon, Charles Louis de, Duke of Parma 16
Brooke, John Arthur 20
Bruce, Mrs. Henry Austin 76
Bunbury, Henry Edward 35
Butler, Charles 8

Catherine II, Empress of Russia 39
Christina, Queen of Sweden 39

Cockerell, Sydney C. 11
Colbert de Seignelay, Jean-Baptiste 39
Collins, Wilkie 68
Crane, Walter 78
Crewe, Earl of 55

Dudley, Robert 41

Edwards, Bookseller 55
Egerton, Sir Thomas 27

Fairfax, Thomas 11
Field, William B. Osgood 78
Fountaine, Sir Andrew 43

Gennadius, John 8
Gladbach, Monastery of St. Vitus 1
Glessner, Rodger 84
Goldschmidt, E. P. 27
Goodspeed's Bookshop 76

Hanmer, Sir Thomas 35
Harmsworth, Sir Leicester 20
Harper and Brothers 88
Heber, Richard 11, 17
Hirsch, Paul 54

Hirst, John 8
Hoe, Robert 28, 32
Hoepli, Ulrico 2
Hollis, Thomas 32
Hooper, William Harcourt 78
Houghton, Richard Monckton Milnes, Lord 55
Hoym, Charles-Henri, Comte d' 39
Huntington Library 28
Huth, Alfred H. 20
Hyde, James Hazen 42

Isabella Clara Eugenia, Vice Regent of the Netherlands 29

Joan of Navarre, Queen of England 11

Kraus, H. P. 3, 5, 9
Kress, Anton 13
Kress, Christopher 13

Lambert, Pierre 67
Laughlin, Irwin 49
Linnell, John 55
Louis XIII 27, 39
Louis XIV 39

Lucien-Graux 64
Luise, Grandduchess of Saxe-Weimar 54
Lyell, James P. R. 14

Marie Louise, Empress of France 59
Maria Thérèse, Queen of France 39
Martini, Giuseppe 2, 8
Mathon, Simon 9
Methuen, Algernon 55
Mildmay, Sir Henry St. John 47
Montferrand, André de 13
Moore, Thomas 62
Morimondo, Abbey of St. Mary 2
Morris, William 11

Newcastle, Duke of 48
Norton, Charles Eliot 74, 78, 93

Palmer, Samuel 55

Panton, John 28
Patching 84
Paul, John Jay 35
Perrins, C. W. Dyson 15
Phillipps, Sir Thomas 1, 12, 33
Pickering, William 58
Pirckheimer, Willibald 18
Portland, Duke of 49

Quinn, John 81

Ramsay, Dr. 58
Richmond, George 55
Robiano, Comte de 24
Robinson, William H., Ltd. 12
Rosenthal, Nathan 5
Rushmore, Arthur 88

St. Riquier, Abbey of 9
Sert, Professor and Mrs. José Luis 15

Shenley, John Charrington 43
Sporey, P. E. 18
Stroganoff, Count Gregoire 4
Sumner, Charles 27

Thompson, Henry Yates 11
Thorold, Sir John 8
Thorpe, Thomas 11
Thou, Jacques-Auguste de 39
Tsarkoe Selo 82
Tyrell, Walter R. 28

Updike, Daniel Berkeley 58

Wartenberg, Franz von 29
Weaver, Harold Baillie 8
Williams, John Camp 28

Yarnold, Charles 1

General

References are to entry numbers.

Alphabets 25, 65, 95, 96, 100
Anatomical books 24
Aquatint 57, 72, 95
Architecture 19, 32, 41, 42, 48, 49
Arnold Arboretum 74

Baudelaire, Charles 64
Bennett, Thomas 71
Berry, Jean, duc de 11
Bestiaries 6, 15, 26, 100
Bestiaries, *see also* Fables and bestiaries
Bindings 1, 5, 6, 10, 16, 29, 39, 45, 59, 89, 100
Book covers 75, 77
Book covers, *see also* Publishers' bindings
Book design 81, 91, 93
Botanical books 56, 72, 74, 90
Bowyer, William 27
Bruce, Mrs. Henry Austin 76

Calligraphy 23, 27, 37, 71, 84, 90, 93, 95, 96, 98, 99, 100
Caricature 65
Charles XI, King of Sweden 36
Children's books 25, 61, 65, 82, 88
Chinoiserie 53
Christina, Queen of Sweden 39
Chromolithography 71, 72

Clive, Annsybella 76
Clive, George 76
Colbert, Jacques-Nicolas 39
Colbert, Jean-Baptiste 39
Colbert, Jules-Armand 39
Collotype 43
Color printing 44, 47, 53
Colored copies 13, 18, 19, 28, 55, 56, 61, 65, 68, 90

Daguerreotype 67
Drawing books 39, 42, 48, 84
Drawings 3, 8, 24, 29, 33, 42, 48, 55, 58, 61, 70, 71, 73, 76, 84, 88, 89, 91, 94, 95, 100

Emblem books 41
Engraving 32, 33, 36, 43, 47
Etching 32, 33, 35, 36, 37, 38, 39, 41, 49, 55, 56, 66, 87, 92

Fables and bestiaries 13, 15, 35, 38, 58, 70, 73, 86, 100
Festival books 30, 31, 33, 36, 41, 54
Field, William B. Osgood 68
Fireworks 36
Flamel, Nicolas 11
François I 26

Gardens 38, 41
Gautier, Théophile 73
Goetz, Max 89
Gray Herbarium 74
Gritti, Andrea 21
Guilbert, Yvette 76

Heinrich, Duke of Saxony 41
Hofmannsthal, Hugo von 84

Letters 60, 70, 71, 73, 76, 91, 100
Lewis, A. J. 71
Libraries 45
Lithography 57, 60, 64, 65, 66, 68, 69, 70, 72, 75, 77, 79, 82
Louis XIV, King of France 33, 36, 39

Manuals, Artists' 32, 34, 38, 39, 44, 60, 67
Maps 13, 28
Mazarin, Jules 33
Melk, Abbey of 45
Mezzotint 32, 34, 44, 53
Monograms 71, 100
Morison, Stanley 27, 45
Morris, William 13, 83
Music 5, 9, 14
Music, *see also* Sheet music

Natural history 26, 56, 58, 72
Nature printing 74
Norton, Charles Eliot 76, 91
Numismatics 56

Ornament 42, 43, 53
Ornithological books 56, 58, 68, 72

Paste-papers 95
Photography 61, 67
Physiologies 65
Pochoir 94
Posters 70, 75
Private presses 78, 81, 93
Prospectuses 66, 83
Publishers' bindings 66, 70, 71, 74

Ruzicka, Rudolph 43, 58, 83

Science fiction 94
Sheet music 75, 77
Sketchbooks, *see* Drawing books
Smith, Consul Joseph 48
Steel-engraving 66
Steinhöwel, Heinrich 13
Stereotype 66
Stone-cutting 84, 96
Suleiman the Magnificent 21

Theatre 37, 42, 82, 94
Theatre, *see also* Festival books
Travel 20, 50, 68, 69
Type design 26, 78, 83, 84, 90, 91, 94, 93, 98, 99

Type specimens 46, 52, 59, 63, 98

Updike, Daniel Berkeley 51, 91

Vasari, Giorgio 24

Walpole, Horace 43
Wilde, Oscar 84
William III, King of England 36
Woolf, Virginia 84
Wood-engraving 57, 58, 66, 67, 70, 71, 73, 84, 95
Woodcuts 13, 16, 18, 25, 45, 80, 85, 86, 89, 90, 97
Writing books 23, 27

Zoological books, *see* Natural history

VIGNETTES

p. x Rudolph Ruzicka. Bookplate of Philip Hofer, based on a watercolor by Hans Holbein.

p. xiv Eric Gill. Bookplate of Philip Hofer.

p. 206 W.A. Dwiggins. Drawing for colophon in *WAD to RR. A Letter about Designing Type.*

p. 218 W.A. Dwiggins. Pressmark of the Cygnet Press, with the initials of Philip Hofer and George Parker Winship.

The photograph of Philip Hofer's office on p. xiii is by John Nordell.